# A Primer on American Courts

# A Primer on American Courts

**William S. Miller**

*Marymount University*

PEARSON

Longman

New York  San Francisco  Boston
London  Toronto  Sydney  Tokyo  Singapore  Madrid
Mexico City  Munich  Paris  Cape Town  Hong Kong  Montreal

Executive Editor: Eric Stano
Senior Marketing Manager: Elizabeth Fogarty
Production Manager: Charles Annis
Project Coordination, Text Design and Electronic Page Makeup: WestWords, Inc.
Cover Designer: Kay Petronio
Cover Design Manager: John Callahan
Cover Image: Brand X Pictures
Senior Manufacturing Buyer: Dennis J. Para
Printer and Binder: Phoenix Color Corp.
Cover Printer: Phoenix Color Corp.

Library of Congress Cataloging-in-Publication Data

MIller, William S.
   A primer on American Courts / William Miller.—1st ed.
     p.  cm.
   Includes bibliographical references and index.
   ISBN 0-321-10615-6 (pbk. : alk. paper)
1. Courts—United States.   2. Procedure (Law)—United States.   I. Title.
KF8720.M55 2004
347.73'1—dc22

                                             2004026405

Please visit our website at http://www.ablongman.com

ISBN 0-321-10615-6

3 4 5 6 7 8 9 10—PBT—08 07 06 05

For KC

# Contents

# Preface

This book began some years ago as a series of fact sheets for my undergraduate students in American Constitutional Law. The fact sheets had two purposes: (1) to address questions that had come up time and time again in both the law school and undergraduate law classes that I had taught, and (2) to provide information about the law and the courts that the students should know. This latter information reflected, of course, my own interests and perspectives—what *I* thought was important and intriguing. It also included information that I believed, at least from my personal recollection, would have removed some of the obstacles to my own early study of the law. Sometimes the smallest thing—not only an unfamiliar term, but also a particular use of an otherwise familiar term or a lack of awareness of the larger substantive or procedural contexts in which different terms or concepts are related—constitutes a stubborn barrier to a new student's growth in legal learning. The lawyer or legal writer often forgets that so trivial a matter can prove so frustrating a barrier to the uninitiated.

The student, in turn, should know that the law is a technical subject and a highly developed one at that. The law is not simply reducible to political or sociological or historical categories and concepts: its substantive and procedural rules and principles must be addressed and learned on their own ground. To do that, the legal vocabulary—the terms of the art—must be mastered.

The questions that students perennially asked reinforced this belief. In students' first law classes, they did not ask about courts as institutions of conflict resolution or about the role of the judiciary in establishing constitutionalism in the United States. They were struggling mightily to understand the words on the page of the casebook that they were reading, and they were trying to grasp the essential arguments in the court opinions that were assigned. Burdening them further with the reminder that each case also reflects a particular procedural setting that conditions the legal arguments seemed almost to make me guilty of "piling on."

Although the students' difficulty in understanding the cases and discussing them in class was frustrating at first to me as a new teacher, I now do not see how it could have been, or how it can ever be, any different. Students embarking on the study of law, whether in order to acquire a law degree or a passing grade in an undergraduate law course, require a basic understanding of procedural as well as substantive legal concepts in order to get the enterprise off the ground. To this must be added some basic historical information as well. The law and legal institutions are preeminently human institutions. We can only understand what they are if we have some understanding of how and why they came to be what they are.

This little book is an attempt to provide some of this necessary information and to supplement the material that appears in many casebooks for law courses. It is written from the perspective of a lawyer, not of a political scientist, and while I suspect that any practicing lawyer could have written the book or something similar to it, the billable hours that it would take to do so are probably prohibitive for most. I not only have tried to cover what is absolutely necessary to the subject, but have also included discussions about facts and issues that pique my interest, and I have provided references that will enable students to pursue these subjects further. Still, this is intended to be a primer, not a desk encyclopedia, on American courts.

Preparing this book for publication presented two great difficulties: the battle with footnotes and the danger of oversimplification. Legal writers will tell you that nothing is so characteristic of legal literature as the large number of footnotes and references. Even the commonest fact is often referenced. Some law reviews take pride in the height of the footnote level on each page; the ideal seems to be the page with a single line of text running across the top and the rest of the page devoted to footnotes and detailed references. Conventional wisdom among college textbook writers, on the other hand, is that footnotes should be avoided because undergraduates simply will not read them.

I have tried to steer a responsible middle course, minimizing footnotes but still using quite a few. For those readers who just "don't do" footnotes, legal studies are probably not for you. The law, said Justice Joseph Story, "is a jealous mistress, and requires a long and constant courtship. It is not to be won by trifling favours, but by lavish homage." For those readers who wish to hold me to a higher standard of accountability, I reply that statements based on material that I found in more than one source generally are not footnoted; statements based on particular cases, statutes, or other sources generally are.

The book is also intended to expose students as much as possible to the primary sources of law, particularly statutes. In political science and other undergraduate courses, most of the information about laws comes from secondary sources—from an author telling students *about* a law. Better that students of the law examine the primary materials themselves than take someone else's word for it. Accordingly, this book includes many statutes and quotations in the text, in sidebars, and in footnotes.

Passages from court opinions posed a particular problem not only because the courts' words should generally be quoted and not paraphrased, but also because any quoted passage from an opinion has been removed from a larger context that is sure to influence its meaning. (Even lawyers would like to ignore that fact when writing their briefs and arguments. Finding that single sentence or short paragraph in an opinion to nail down a point of law strengthens the prose, but the literary value of legal writing is always trumped by the scholarly value when opposing counsel or the court restores the larger context that weakens or even repudiates the point in the brief.) The *Primer's* limitation of space discouraged longer quotes. Therefore, I have cited any and all cases to which I have referred in the text so that readers may examine the original contexts.

Rivaling the challenge of the footnotes was the challenge of avoiding misleading oversimplification. In the discussion of law, as in the discussion of other complicated subjects, almost every generality that glitters is false. Legal rules and principles are loaded with significant exceptions, yet the *initial* discussion of law must be simple enough for the untrained to grasp without immediately having to fight through the smothering, but eventually unavoidable, provisos and qualifications to each assertion. In particular, as I wrote the chapters on legal history, jurisdiction, and litigation, I was haunted by the realization that there were exceptions, qualifications, and conditions to just about everything I said. The book is thus largely a collection of half-truths, but perhaps useful half-truths. When students reach the point at which they can recognize these limitations and can begin to supply the missing halves of the statements in the book, the *Primer* will have done its job.

## NOTE TO STUDENTS

It may be a good idea to read Appendix A, "Finding and Citing Legal Sources," before reading Chapters 2 through 5. The references in the latter four chapters assume familiarity with the formalities of legal notation described in the appendix.

If cases are assigned contemporaneously with the assignments from the *Primer,* it may also be helpful to read Appendix B, "Analyzing Opinions and Briefing Cases." Learning to discern and articulate the essential arguments in judicial opinions is a skill—I think it is more a knack—that I found difficult to learn and even more difficult to teach. It does not seem to depend on either hard work or IQ. At some point in the semester or the first year of study, the spark of illumination just seems to appear, and from that point on it is difficult to imagine the time when the knack was not present. The appendix is my best effort at helping to turn on the mental light bulb.

I have cited Internet addresses for sources whenever they are available in order to encourage you to look up the sources at home. All Supreme Court citations, for example, contain a reference to their Findlaw.com URL, which is explained in more detail in the "Finding and Citing Legal Sources" appendix. Other free online services, such as lexisOne.com, can be used as well. In the chapter on courts, I have listed web sites of the courts or of professional associations where the courts do not have web sites. Most of these sites contain a wealth of pertinent information. There is still a degree of risk involved with citing Internet sources. Web addresses change and some sources disappear at the most inconvenient times, but the Internet materials cited in the *Primer* have been around for several years now, and I am pretty confident that they will remain so. Do yourself a favor and use them.

## NOTE TO TEACHERS

The title of Chapter 1, "A Brief History of English and American Courts," is somewhat misleading; it is more of an outline—a very selective outline—than a history of a complex course of institutional development. The chapter offers a rudimentary explanation of the distinctive power of common law courts, as distinct from those of civil law systems, to make substantive legal rules as well as to adjudicate cases. The nature of the subject matter and my own interest in legal history led me to recommend to the reader many of the works that I relied upon in writing the chapter and some others as well.

The order of Chapters 2 and 3, on jurisdiction and litigation, can be reversed if you wish. Although the material in the *Primer* is useful in any introductory course on law, it is intended primarily to supplement—not to replace—the casebooks usually assigned in introductory courses in constitutional law. One problem that most constitutional law casebooks present is that they begin with cases and discussions of the judicial power of American courts. The concepts of judicial power, jurisdiction, and justiciability are at once less familiar to new students of law than many issues of civil liberties and governmental powers—or than issues of contract and property law, for that matter—and yet more subtle than these issues of substantive law. Ironically, then, students must begin the course by confronting immediately some of the course's most difficult subject matter. Accordingly, I place the chapter on jurisdiction, which discusses this subject matter, before the chapter on litigation rather than after it, which might seem to some the more logical place.

The primary focus of the book is on American courts. To explain what courts *are* requires an account of what courts *do,* and it soon becomes clear that to discuss what courts do we must have some understanding of the course of litigation. This is the subject matter of Chapter 3. An understanding of the litigation process is also necessary in order to understand how cases get to appellate courts and the Supreme Court. Most law casebooks consist of excerpts from appellate court opinions; constitutional law casebooks are mostly excerpts from Supreme Court opinions. It is useful to know that many of the cases before the appellate courts have never been to trial: they have been "thrown out of court" on motions to dismiss or motions for summary judgment, and the appellants are simply trying to get back into the queue for trial, often to enhance their chances for a favorable settlement. The chapter on litigation is directed to providing the necessary information to accomplish both of these purposes.

If you assign Chapters 2 and 3 in reverse order, the accounts of the different federal and state courts (Chapters 4 and 5) follow smoothly from the discussion of jurisdiction, for the relationships between and among the different courts in a legal system can only be grasped through an understanding of the basic concepts of jurisdiction. The chapter on the Supreme Court gives readers of Supreme Court opinions information that they may need to understand those opinions a bit better. Hundreds of books have been and continue to be written about the Court, but I have refrained from recommending a sampling of this huge literature to students, preferring to leave that to you.

Although casebooks are and for some time will continue to be the foundation for courses in law, teachers of legal subjects are more and more relying upon the complete court opinions that are now available on the Internet for class assignments. Not only do web sites provide the up-to-the-minute legal developments that casebooks cannot, but it also seems that casebooks never have quite the perfect selection of cases and that the excerpts of the opinions are never edited exactly the way we wish them to be. Now we can easily take students straight to the source.

On the other hand, the length of many of the complete court opinions presents other difficulties. Selecting and then assigning only parts of a full opinion usually result in students having to read information that is a routine part of court opinions but that is usually edited out of the excerpts appearing in casebooks—namely, the procedural setting of the case, the lower court background, and the issues of jurisdiction and justiciability that are part of all litigation. These are precisely the issues that the *Primer* addresses.

It may be useful to have students read the appendix on "Finding and Citing Legal Sources" before they read Chapters 2 through 5 of the *Primer*. All references in these chapters are based on the citation forms explained in the appendix. The "Analyzing Opinions and Briefing Cases" appendix contains my own approach to briefing cases for class; your own approach may well differ, but the first part of the appendix is of general application. The discussion of "Theories of Judicial Decision-Making" is meant only to be an introduction to the subject, but I could not resist the urge to make some critical comments. The survey of "Additional Federal Courts" seemed appropriate in a book about American courts. The number of different state courts, of course, placed any such survey of state systems outside the limits of the *Primer*.

This book covers a wide and ever changing field of information, and I certainly cannot keep up with all of the changes as they occur. I would welcome new information through your comments, corrections, and suggestions. Email me at the following address: primeronthecourts@yahoo.com.

## FREQUENTLY USED SOURCES

All statistics cited in the *Primer* regarding the federal courts are taken from the annual reports issued by the Administrative Office of the United States Courts: *2003 Annual Report of the Director: Judicial Business of the United States Courts* (Washington, D.C.: U.S. Government Printing Office, 2004).

The Annual Reports and the Federal Judicial Caseload Statistics series, also published by the Administrative Office of the United States Courts, are valuable sources of information, both statistical and topical, about the federal courts. They are available via the "Library" tab at http://www.uscourts.gov. They provide the latest statistics relating to federal courts and also offer learned speculation about the reasons for significant changes in any of the statistical trends.

Statistics regarding the federal courts are, with some exceptions, gathered on the basis of a 12-month period from October 1 to September 30. Unless otherwise noted, all of the statistics on federal courts cited in this *Primer* are taken from the *2003 Annual Report* and refer to the year beginning October 1, 2002, and ending September 30, 2003. Supreme Court statistics are taken primarily from *United States Law Week* (U.S.L.W.).

All statistics on state courts are taken from B. Ostrom, N. Kauder, and R. LaFountain, *Examining the Work of State Courts, 2003: A National Perspective from the Court Statistics Project* (National Center for State Courts, 2004), at http://www.ncsconline.org/D_Research/csp/CSP_Main_Page.html. State court charts are taken from the Court Statistics Project, *State Court Caseload Statistics, 2003* (National Center for State Courts, 2004), at http://www.ncsconline.org/D_Research/csp/2003_Files/2003_SCCS.html. See also *State Court Organization, 1998,* a publication of the Bureau of Justice Statistics, United States Department of Justice (Wash., D.C.: 2000), http://www.ojp.usdoj.gov/bjs/abstract/sco98.htm. This publication and other publications of the National Center for State Courts available via their web site at http://www.ncsconline.org.

# Acknowledgments

I got a lot of help in putting this book together. I would like to thank the following scholars for reviewing earlier versions of the book and for offering valuable comments and suggestions, many of which have been included in this final version: Scott A. Comparato of Southern Illinois University at Carbondale, Jack Fruchtman of Towson University, William E. Kelley of Auburn University, Ashlyn Kuersten of Western Michigan University, Stephen Meinhold of the University of North Carolina—Wilmington, Robert M. Howard of Georgia State University, Philip Kronebusch of St. John's University, William D. Schreckhise of the University of Arkansas, David Van Heemst of Oliver Nazarene University, Dennis Pope of Fairleigh Dickinson University, Susan Thomas of Hollins University, and Chris W. Bonneau of the University of Pittsburgh.

I would like to thank especially three excellent litigation lawyers—Jay Barker, Kathleen McAllister, and "Hizzoner," Richard Ringell—for their careful review of Chapter 3 and their excellent suggestions; any errors that remain are strictly mine. For their cooperation and help, I also thank the wonderful people at the National Center for State Courts in both Rosslyn and Williamsburg, Virginia; the staffs of the Clerks of the United States Supreme Court, the United States Tax Court, and the United States Court of Appeals for the Armed Forces; and the library staffs of the Supreme Court, of Marymount University, and of the George Mason University law school. I also want to thank Eric Stano of Longman for his unfailing cooperation and encouragement and Melena Fenn and the WestWords staff for their patient competence. I would most of all like to thank Katherine and my four sons, Max, Matt, Pat, and Jake, for your love and continuing support; I could not have completed this without you.

Chapter **1**

# A Brief History of English and American Courts

## Chapter Outline

Why courts do what they do and what legal terms mean are questions requiring reference to historical origins and development. Even the practical no-nonsense questions about how legal systems really work must lead to historical investigation if our goal is comprehensive, not momentarily adequate, answers. Today in colleges and law schools, the emphasis is more on the "how" than on the "why": on immediately useful information—"efficient" causes, Aristotle would call them—than on the purposes that rules and institutions were formed to achieve, the "final" causes. Whether this emphasis results in a study of law that is less scholarly than technical and thus a study of law that is less "professional" in the older sense of that term is a question better discussed in another place. Here, let us simply assume that in order to understand the judicial institutions that exist in this country today, a review of the English and early American courts and institutions is helpful to understand the contemporary legal systems and then see if the assumption is warranted.

## THE UNITED STATES CONSTITUTION

New students of American courts might well assume that the authoritative definition of our federal courts is to be found in our founding documents—the United States Constitution and legislative enactments. Likewise, we would expect to find the institutional designs and purposes of state courts in state constitutions and statutes. When we turn to these materials, however, we find that the accounts of the judicial institutions are not nearly as complete as we anticipated. The federal and state constitutions, and the statutory enactments that were approved pursuant to the constitutions, rest upon silent assumptions about law and courts that can only be approached historically; that is, we must consider the institutions that existed at the time these constitutions and the statutes were drafted.

Article III of the Constitution of 1787, for example, is the shortest of the three articles establishing branches of the national government. Of its three sections, only the first two sections address the design of the federal judiciary; Section 3 is entirely concerned with the crime of treason. Section 1 authorizes the establishment of a supreme court, empowers Congress to establish other subordinate federal courts, and sets forth the terms of employment for federal judges. It says nothing about the number of judges on the Supreme Court nor does it spell out any age or citizenship qualifications, as Articles I and II do for members of Congress and for presidents. Section 2, Clause 1, sets forth the limits of federal court jurisdiction; Section 2, Clause 2, defines the original jurisdiction and the appellate jurisdiction of the Supreme Court; and Section 2, Clause 3, sets forth jury trial and venue requirements in criminal cases. Apart from the statement that there shall be "one supreme court" of unprescribed size and shape, the Constitution gives us no indication of the structure of the federal judicial system: the details, including the decision whether or not to have additional federal courts, were left to Congress.

More importantly for new students of court systems, we do not find much in the Constitution by way of description of what courts in general and what federal courts in particular are supposed to do. Section 1 and Section 2, Clause 1, speak in terms of the "judicial power," a term that is not defined. The term was suggested by James Madison and Gouverneur Morris as a substitute for the term "jurisdiction," which was the term in the draft language under consideration by the convention.[1] "Jurisdiction"

---

[1]See James Madison, *Notes of Debates in the Federal Convention of 1787*, 539 (August 27, 1787); also in 2 Max Farrand, *The Records of the Federal Convention of 1787*, 431, at http://memory.loc.gov/ ammem/amlaw/lwfr.html. All subsequent references to Madison's *Notes* will be to the dates on which the issues were raised. On the convention's discussions of the judicial power, see William Miller, *Cases of a Judiciary Nature*, 8 St. Louis U. Pub. L. Rev. 47 (1989).

tells us the types of cases courts may decide but does not tell us the methods that courts may or should use in deciding them.

The delegates to the Philadelphia convention spent relatively little time discussing such matters, although they did question the appropriate functions of judges when the convention was considering a proposal for a Council of Revision similar to the one established in the state of New York.[2] But with the exception of the Council of Revision debates, the essential judicial functions with which the debaters were familiar were neither thoroughly analyzed nor laid open for debate; rather, the functions were simply referred to as givens.

This lack of discussion about the basic judicial functions and procedures and the fact that more than 30 of the 55 delegates at Philadelphia and almost all of the active participants in the debates on the judiciary article and on the Council of Revision proposal were lawyers suggest the simple conclusion that the delegates did not discuss the basics because such matters were of such common knowledge—at least among attorneys familiar with courts and law—that the delegates did not have to hash them out anew. What this means for us today is that if we want to understand our judicial institutions as originally conceived, we must now attempt to acquire some familiarity with the legal systems contemporary with the Founders. To do this, we might examine first the legal systems of the newly independent states under the state constitutions and the Articles of Confederation, but this review would soon lead us to the English roots of the American courts. We shall therefore go directly to the English origins and then proceed forward in time to the American developments.

## ENGLISH ORIGINS

Lawyers usually use the term "common law" to denote legal rules that have been developed by judges in the course of deciding cases ("judge-made" law) as opposed to **statutes,** which are legal rules that have been enacted by legislators. The term "common law" also refers to one of the two great legal traditions—the other being the "civil law," or "modern Roman law," tradition—existing in the world today and to the individual legal systems that belong to the larger traditions. We focus here on this larger conception of common law.

Legal traditions and the individual legal systems within them are composed of more than legal rules; they are also made up of distinctive institutions, legal techniques, and, in advanced systems, sets of professionals who are trained in the rules, techniques, and institutions of their respective systems. If the fundamental purpose of both the common law and the civil law *traditions* is to provide justice, each individual legal *system* also includes a set of fundamental national or subnational purposes that articulate that society's understanding of justice.

The state and federal legal systems of the United States, with the notable exceptions of those of Louisiana and Puerto Rico, are common law systems, representing

---

[2]See the discussions on June 4, June 6, July 21, and August 15, 1787, in Madison's *Notes.*

the common law tradition for which England laid the foundation in the first three centuries after the Battle of Hastings. By the time the English exported the tradition to its colonies in North America, the common law had profited from several more centuries of development; but the common law in the seventeenth and even the eighteenth century was still a work in progress, even as it continues to be a work in progress wherever it has taken root.

We might best introduce the common law systems of the United States by examining the idea of "judge-made" law. **Litigation** refers both to court cases and to the process of having a dispute decided by a court. An **action** is another name for a court case, either criminal or civil, brought by one party against another. One common type of legal action filed in American courts, for example, is a "tort" action. A **tort** is a legal wrong, other than one based on contract, for which the courts offer the victim a remedy. One common type of tort is **negligence.** In a negligence action, a "plaintiff" seeks to prove that a "defendant" is **liable** (that is, responsible) for injuries of various kinds suffered by the plaintiff as a result of the defendant's failure to meet a certain duty of care to the plaintiff. In a negligence action, it is not necessary to prove that the defendant intended to harm the plaintiff; indeed, this lack of intent is the feature that distinguishes negligence actions from the large body of tort actions called "intentional torts."

Thus, the homeowner who fails to shovel the sidewalk may be sued for negligence by the plaintiff who slipped and fell on the ice. The homeowner should have foreseen that the slippery surface was going to be hazardous to pedestrians on the busy street, and she therefore had a duty to clear the sidewalk in a timely fashion after the snowstorm. The car owner whose SUV accidentally rammed into a parked sedan may be liable to the sedan's owner for the repairs because the brakes in the SUV had not been serviced in over 50,000 miles and thus could not stop the car within a reasonable distance. Owners have a duty to see that their cars function safely. Neither of these defendants intended to cause injury, yet the courts found both to be liable for the damages caused by their negligence.

Although the number of situations giving rise to tortious negligence is infinite, most negligence cases in common law systems have one distinctive feature in common: the legal rules that determine the defendants' duties and liabilities are common law rules, not statutory rules. There is probably no statute on the books that defines the duties of the homeowner to the icy fall victim or the duties of the SUV owner to the owner of the parked car and no statute that defines the scope of their liability to those who are injured. The rules are found instead in the court opinions rendered in cases arising out of similar factual situations. These opinions are called **precedents.** This is also true of most intentional torts, as well as of actions based on private contracts and of real property actions. The authority of courts—that is to say, the authority of *judges*—to make the rules in these and other actions that establish the standards and extent of legal liability is the earmark of our common law systems.

To understand a legal system that authorizes judges to make such rules, we must look at certain fundamental institutions and legal techniques that trace their origins to England in the twelfth, thirteenth, and fourteenth centuries: (1) the development of the royal courts (institutions), (2) the evolution of the modern cause of action out of the medieval writ (technique), and (3) the development of the jury trial (a technique that became an institution). This is not a history of nice, neat distinctions, yet our account must be brief, perhaps unconscionably brief. After all, Plucknett's *Concise History of the Common Law* runs more than 700 pages and Pollock and Maitland's classic *History of English Law Before the Time of Edward I* fills two volumes and 1,300 pages.[3] Still, the complexities of these three common law elements compel us to spend a little time on each one.

## The Royal Courts

When the Normans crossed the English Channel in A.D. 1066, they found in the Anglo-Saxon communities a set of social institutions and a set of tribunals for resolving disputes according to native English law. Anglo-Saxon England had developed the institutions of the borough, the vill or township, the hundred, and the county or shire. The **communal courts,** called "moots," of the vill, the hundred, and the county had emerged to resolve the legal disputes within these communities.

The moots, like the Anglo-Saxons themselves, were Germanic in origin. They consisted of an assembly of the men of the community called "doomsmen" making the judgments—"deeming the dooms"—in the cases before them. Sheriffs or other authorities would preside over the moots, but the doomsmen made the judgments. The law of the moots consisted primarily of local customs and rules that varied considerably throughout England. English law did include some royal rules, also called "dooms," announced from time to time by the Anglo-Saxon kings, but the great bulk of legal rules and norms that personally affected individuals was based on local custom. William the Conqueror and his immediate successors did not attempt to abolish or replace most English courts and English law.[4] In fact, in one of his early decrees, repeated in substance by his son Henry I, the Conqueror declared that "all shall keep and hold the law of King Edward" (the Anglo-Saxon king who ruled England from 1042 to 1066) with such additions as William made "for the benefit of the English people." What the Conqueror and his successors did do, however, was establish new tribunals that would enforce Norman law for the benefit of *their* people—the French-speaking Norman invaders.

---

[3]The following account of the English origins relies heavily on these two works as well as on Hogue's *Origins of the Common Law,* Van Caenegem's *Birth of the English Common Law,* Maitland's *Forms of Action at Common Law,* Hudson's *The Formation of the English Common Law,* Pound's *History and System of the Common Law,* and Rembar's *The Law of the Land.*

[4]Nor would he or any other new ruler be expected to effect a broad replacement of existing institutions. See, for example, Fritz Kern, *Kingship and Law in the Middle Ages,* 70–75, or Roscoe Pound, *The History and System of the Common Law,* 68–71. One immediate and significant change that William did make was the removal of matters involving church law (called "ecclesiastical law" or "canon law") from the communal courts to **ecclesiastical courts** presided over by archbishops, bishops, and abbots of the Church. Given the need to focus our brief history on the main elements of the common law tradition, we do not discuss the ecclesiastical courts. For an excellent history, see the three volumes of Robert Rodes's series, *This House Have I Built.*

## Table 1.1

### Kings of England During the Origins of the Common Law

#### Normans

| | |
|---|---|
| William I (the "Conqueror") | 1066–1087 |
| William II ("Rufus") | 1087–1100 |
| Henry I | 1100–1135 |
| Stephen (the period of the "Anarchy") | 1135–1154 |

#### Angevins (Plantagenets)

| | |
|---|---|
| Henry II | 1154–1189 |
| Richard I (the "Lion Hearted") | 1189–1199 |
| John | 1199–1216 |
| Henry III | 1216–1272 |
| Edward I ("Longshanks") | 1272–1307 |
| Edward II | 1307–1327 |
| Edward III | 1327–1377 |

The first set of these new courts was the **seignorial courts,** which were established to administer the rules of the feudal system among the Norman aristocracy. Feudalism, as imported from France by the Normans, was a system of social and political organization based upon grants by the king, as "lord," of estates to his military lieutenants, as "vassals," in return for their military support when the king demanded it. Eleventh-century England was an agricultural nation, and most of the estates granted by the king were large farms called "manors" that would support the vassals and provide them with income. Some of the land grants were so large that the vassals who received them directly from the king and who were called the "tenants-in-chief" could in turn grant some of their land to others and thus become lords to these latter grantees. The seignorial courts consisted of meetings of the feudal lords and their vassals for resolving disputes, especially disputes over possession ("seisin") and title ("right") of land, arising out of the new feudal order.

Because the feudal system provided the necessary support that the militarily active Norman monarchs and their successors, the Angevins, required, the kings took an interest in the activities of the seignorial courts that implemented the customary rules of the system—especially disputes over land. One of the priorities of the kings was uniformity or "common-ness" in the application of these feudal rules throughout England.

The lords of the estates were not only required to administer feudal law, however. If the estate consisted of one or more manors, the imposition upon the manor of the new Norman organization granted the Norman lord, like his Anglo-Saxon predecessors, rights to labor, products, and taxes from the manor's inhabitants. Along with these valuable rights, the lord acquired the additional right and duty, called "*sac*" or "*sac* and *soc*," to provide justice to the people of the manor by adjudicating their disputes and punishing their petty crimes. This right, too, was valuable because the fines he levied and the costs of administering justice through the manorial court went to the lord; but what is important to our study is that the disputes were resolved according to the local "custom of the manor," not according to feudal or royal laws. In the eleventh and twelfth centuries, the Anglo-Norman kings were not particularly interested in these disputes and did not attempt to provide any uniformity to the rules and procedures by which the disputes were resolved in the manorial courts.

The manorial courts existed primarily to address the problems that arose on the manors among the manorial population, most of whom were not free to leave the manor and avoid their inherited duties to their lord. These unfree "villeins," who constituted approximately 80 percent of the population of England during this time, could not go to the communal courts of the county and the hundred for justice; they had to go to the manorial courts. The communal courts provided an alternative source of justice for the small minority of the population called "freemen," some of whom may have lived on a manor but who were not legally bound to it and who could own land in their own right.

The second set of secular courts that the English monarchs established over time was the **royal courts,** which were rooted in the king's court, called *curia regis.* Like the Anglo-Saxon Witenagemot before it, *curia regis,* consisting of the king and his council, dealt with all manner of problems and policies facing the nation, including disputes between private individuals or between private individuals and the king that today we would characterize as "legal" disputes. The power of the king to resolve these disputes and administer justice to his subjects was supreme and rested ultimately upon the superior force that the Norman and Angevin kings could muster and upon the royal duties that they inherited from the Anglo-Saxons and that they assumed upon being crowned. These duties are reflected in the coronation oaths of many early monarchs, such as the oath of Edward II in 1308:

> "Sire, will you grant and keep and by your oath confirm to the people of England the laws and customs given to them by the previous just and god-fearing kings, your ancestors, and especially the laws, customs, and liberties granted to the clergy and people by the glorious king, the sainted Edward, your predecessor?" "I grant and promise them."
>
> "Sire, will you in all your judgments, so far as in you lies, preserve to God and Holy Church, and to the people and clergy, entire peace and concord before God?" "I will preserve them."
>
> "Sire, will you, so far as in you lies, cause justice to be rendered rightly, impartially, and wisely, in compassion and in truth?" "I will do so."
>
> "Sire, do you grant to be held and observed the just laws and customs that the community of your realm shall determine, and will you, so far as in you lies, defend and strengthen them to the honour of God?" "I grant and promise them."[5]

The different promises of the oath reflect the essentially customary nature of English law—the existence of Parliament as an institutionalized national legislature still lay in

---

[5]Stephenson and Marcham, *Sources of English Constitutional History,* 192; available at http://www.con-stitution.org/sech/sech_055.htm.

## *Curia Regis* or the King's "Court"

The words "court" and "*curia*" both originally referred to the place—the "courtyard"—where the officers, advisors, and chief subordinates of the king periodically gathered to conduct the business of the realm. Alongside this meaning, the term "*curia regis*" or "king's court" quickly came to refer also to the king's advisers that met at the court. Within the Norman and Angevin *curia regis,* also known as the king's "council," two groups were further distinguished: the king together with his tenants-in-chief—called "barons"—were referred to as the "great council." They met only periodically. The king, together with his closest administrative assistants—such as the justiciar, the chancellor, the chamberlain, the marshal, and others—who traveled with the king as part of his household, were referred to as the "small council." There was no fundamental difference in the legal authority of the great and small councils to do the king's business, and there was no formal separation of powers. The business included administrative, judicial, legislative, military, and political matters. Our present-day use of the term "court" to denote the county governments of some southern American states as well as to label executive (the "Court of St. James"), legislative (the "General Court of Massachusetts"), and judicial institutions (the "United States Supreme Court") reflects the original breadth of the term and the process of differentiation of governmental function that took place both in England and in the United States over the centuries.

the future—and the monarch's fundamental duties to enforce the laws fairly and to maintain law and order: the domestic tranquility that came to be known as the "King's Peace."

The king's willingness to do justice also rested upon his desire for money. Needless to say, the time of a busy king was valuable. The monarchs were naturally more interested in matters that directly concerned themselves, their income, or the disposition of the lands that they had directly granted to their tenants-in-chief than in matters more remote from royal interests, particularly disputes that arose between private individuals. Nevertheless, the English kings frequently did get involved in these private disputes as well. The former matters of direct interest, together with the violations of the King's Peace, were eventually gathered under the heading of the "pleas of the Crown"; the latter matters were denominated "common pleas." Like the manorial lords who held court, the king was paid for his judicial participation, and the money was then, as always, welcome.

While the kings were willing and able to provide legal justice for their subjects, the early monarchs were almost always on the move within England and in France, thus making it difficult for a litigant to be assured of the kings' personal—and therefore *authoritative*—involvement in any adjudication. With the king on his travels went his household, which included not only family but also the small council. It is this group of advisors, some of whom developed both a familiarity with and an expertise in adjudicating disputes, that became the root from which the royal courts grew.[6]

Many of the Norman and Angevin kings seem to have had a particular genius for administration and a sustained desire for effective government of their realm. The kings could not be everywhere at once, so they experimented with different administrative techniques to extend the royal presence and administrative control throughout the realm. King Henry I began a practice of sending out representatives, called "justiciars," from his court to see about the king's business, legal and otherwise. These justiciars were more than judges: they held the local officials accountable for their administrative and, especially, their financial duties to the king. The justiciars also decided legal cases, and their periodic appearance in the countryside was far more convenient to interested litigants than requiring litigants to pursue the royal household hither and yon across merry old England.

After the Anarchy, Henry II institutionalized the system of traveling justiciars, called **justices in eyre** ("eyre" from the French *errer*, to travel) to perform administrative and judicial functions, but he also developed several other tribunals expressly to handle judicial business. Though the exact development of these courts is veiled by time, it is clear that in the twelfth century the members of his small council who handled the finances of the kingdom regularly decided legal cases. Most of the cases heard by these officers, known collectively as the "Exchequer," or more strictly, the "upper Exchequer," involved financial disputes, but they decided disputes involving other subject matter as well. **The Exchequer,** which was the first distinct court to emerge from *curia regis* during the early centuries, traveled at first with the king.

By 1178 Henry had assigned to five additional individuals the sole function of judging legal cases, though not necessarily at a sole location. Forty years later, one of the demands addressed by the Magna Carta was the call for a fixed, and therefore readily accessible, location for this court, which by that time focused on common pleas and had come to be known as the **Court (or bench) of Common Pleas.**[7]

Above both of these courts were still the king and *curia regis,* who constituted the supreme authority of the kingdom and who continued to decide cases. In the course of the thirteenth century, the judicial functions of *curia regis* became more and more routine, and by the reign of Edward I they were institutionalized into the "Justices assigned for the holding of Pleas before the King himself," or simply the **Court of King's Bench.** This court heard pleas of the Crown and cases of alleged errors by the Court of Common Pleas. The King's Bench, of course, traveled with the king, who sometimes sat in on the adjudication.

These three royal courts—Exchequer, Common Pleas, and King's Bench—are known as the central courts or common law courts of England. These royal courts

---

[6]"The Court of Common Pleas, like its sister courts of King's Bench and Exchequer, was the result of a long process of gradual separation from a common parent stem." William Sharp McKechnie, *Magna Carta,* 312.

[7]Magna Carta, chapter 17: "Common pleas shall not follow our court, but shall be held in some definite place." That place was Westminster.

were not intended to, and never completely did, supplant the communal and seignorial courts. The royal courts emerged in the twelfth century into an unkempt garden of communal, seignorial, ecclesiastical, borough, and justiciars' courts characterized by "overlapping, uncertainty and confusion," according to Professor Van Caenegem, who also calls the first century of Norman rule in England a period of "crisis" for the judicial system, "a setback for the legal unification that was in full force in the old-English state."[8] Yet he concludes that by the late twelfth century, "the outline of this common law of England . . . was clear and the basic elements established for many centuries." By the middle of the thirteenth century, these common law courts were the dominant courts for freemen.

What were the main contributions of the early royal courts to the development of the common law? Initially the most important contribution was not a common set of substantive rules or laws that they originated and applied to the cases before them: the rules developed later. In the thirteenth century we do not yet see the courts functioning as the common law courts of today, creating new causes of action and articulating rules of law to serve as authoritative precedents. Rather the courts' importance rested more upon the fact that they (1) consisted of a common set of judges, (2) developed and used a common technical vocabulary, and (3) applied a set of common procedures to judicial business.

The judges of these courts, as we have seen, came from a cadre of individuals who were either part of *curia regis* or were personally known to and selected by the king and often personally instructed by the king on how to approach certain issues. Under Henry I and Henry II there developed a corps of professional judges who, whether they were deciding cases on eyre, far from the king himself, or in the society of other members of the royal household close to the king, understood and participated in the development of a common approach to legal disputes.

The royal courts conducted their business in a common language—namely, in the "King's English," which was French! For the first century of Norman rule, the native English of Anglo-Saxon stock and the conquering Normans constituted two separate social strata speaking two different languages, and this stratification continued into the reign of Henry II. The proceedings in the courts created by the Norman rulers—the seignorial and the royal courts—were conducted in French; the proceedings in the communal courts of the native English freemen were conducted in English. By the time the two races were assimilated sufficiently so that one could say there was only one English people, much of the courts' technical vocabulary, which is essential for efficient litigation, was already set.[9]

The early English common law, the law *common* to the realm, was more procedural than substantive: the rules of the early common law usually prescribed methods for resolving disputes rather than defined principles of liability. Thus, it was understood that the "common law" referred to "the custom of the King's Court"—the judi-

---

[8] R. C. Van Caenegem, *Birth of the English Common Law,* 3–17.

[9] See Pollock and Maitland, *History of English Law,* vol. 1, 81, for an extensive list of common legal terms of French origin, such as "plaintiff," "defendant," "judge," "juror," "tort," "contract," and "felony." Latin was the written language of the law.

cial approach that the royal courts routinely took toward particular types of cases. There was not yet a common law of England if by "common law" we mean a common set of substantive rules: the substantive rules were provided by local customs.

The procedural rules that these courts applied to the cases before them in the first two centuries originated with the king's royal writs, not with the judges themselves nor with Parliament, which was only beginning to emerge as a distinct institution in the latter half of the thirteenth century. The subject matter of these early writs reflected the main domestic concerns of the monarchy: money and crime. Taken together, the (1) royal proprietary interests, (2) royal financial interests, and (3) royal interests in maintaining law and order in the realm by punishing the felonies that were violations of the "King's Peace" constituted the substance of the Pleas of the Crown. This subject matter called for the development of common rules throughout the nation. In time, as the royal writs brought more and more subject matter before the royal courts, the common approach to those subjects taken by the common corps of royal judges yielded a set of common substantive rules. To understand the origins of this process of development, we must take a look at the early system of writs.

## The Writ System

As we saw above in the example of a negligence action, when we sue someone, we usually allege that the defendant is liable for some injury or injuries that we sustained and consequently should be required by the court to compensate us. The legal proceeding is called an "action"; the theory or rule of liability that we rely upon in the proceeding we call a **cause of action.** If during the proceeding we establish that the facts of the case fit the requirements of the cause of action, the defendant will be found liable and we will "recover damages," that is, we will be compensated to some extent for our injuries.

Not just any theory of liability, no matter how reasonable it may be, qualifies as a cause of action, however; only those theories that are accepted or recognized by the courts constitute causes of action. Although for centuries common law courts have accepted theories of liability that are based on judge-made as well as statutory causes of action, the royal courts were restricted early on to deciding only those cases that a royal command or "writ" directed them to hear. The **writ system** that originated and developed in the eleventh, twelfth, and thirteenth centuries is the second fundamental component of the common law system. Many of the judge-made *causes of action* that are recognized by common law courts today originated in the *forms of action* set forth in the medieval writs, and the practice and the authority of common law courts to manufacture causes of action can only be understood if we review the history of the writ system.

The simplest definition of a **writ** is that it is an official written command to someone to do something. The official issuing the command was usually the king (though later the courts themselves began issuing writs), and the use of royal writs in England was well established in the Anglo-Saxon kingdom when the Normans arrived. The Anglo-Saxon writ was a sealed letter that began with a formalized greeting identifying the sender and the individual(s) to whom the letter was sent. The rest of the letter contained directions regarding some administrative business. Anglo-Saxon England

# Anglo-Saxon and Early Norman Writs

**A Writ of King Edward the Confessor:** "King Edward sends cordial and friendly greetings to Bishop Wulfig and Earl Leofwine and all my thegns in Hertfordshire. And I inform you that Leofsi Duddesunu has given to Westminster, to Christ and to St. Peter, two and a half hides of land at Wormley with my permission and consent. God keep you."

**A Writ of King William I:** "William, king of the English, to Lanfranc, archbishop [of Canterbury], and Geoffrey, bishop of Coutances, greeting. See to it that *sac* and *soc,* as between Bishop Wulfstan and Walter, abbot of Evesham, are determined as they were on the day that, in the time of King Edward, geld was last taken for the building of a fleet. And for holding this plea, be you, Geoffrey, president (*praesul*) in my place; and be sure that Bishop Wulfstan fully has what is his right. Also see to it that the bishop justly has the houses in Worcester which he claims as against the abbot, and that all those who hold lands of him are always prepared for my service and his. Witness, Roger d'Ivry."[10]

in many ways was a more stable and more legally and politically developed society than was the Normandy homeland of the conquering heroes, but the Normans were quick learners. Recognizing the utility of Anglo-Saxon writs for administrative business, the Normans soon adopted this device and extended its use to judicial business as well.

The principal early use by Norman kings of writs in judicial affairs was to intrude into otherwise private legal business at the request of one of their subjects. The king's royal subjects were constantly badgering him and his council with complaints and petitions; after all, he had taken an oath to render justice to his subjects. If an individual was having legal problems in the county or the seignorial courts and if he was personally close enough to the king to persuade the king to get involved in the dispute and issue some order relating to the case, the individual might be able to *purchase* such aid in the form of a royal writ from the king, or rather from the Chancery, the office of the chancellor, where clerks drafted the royal writs at the king's direction. A variety of such aid was available. Writs that were "issued whenever applied for . . . and at a fixed sum" to address common legal disputes were known as "writs of course."[11] Other writs were tailored to the needs of the purchaser. The Writ of Right, set out in the next sidebar, is one example of these early writs.

---

[10]*Westminster:* Westminster Abbey; a *hide:* approximately 120 acres; *sac and soc:* the privilege or jurisdiction to try certain legal actions; *geld:* a tax or tribute rendered to an Anglo-Saxon king. The example of a writ of King Edward, which was issued sometime between A.D. 1053 and 1066, is taken from F. E. Harmer, *Anglo-Saxon Writs*, 355. The writ of William, issued sometime between A.D. 1079 and 1083, is from Stephenson and Marcham, *Sources of English Constitutional History*, 38; at http://www.constitution.org /sech/sech_019.htm.

[11]McKechnie, *Magna Carta*, 460. Since they were used to "originate" legal proceedings, they were known as "original" writs.

A second early use of writs was to instruct the royal justiciars who were sent out to do administrative and judicial business throughout the realm. Recall that the early courts and the justiciars were not limited exclusively to judicial functions as we generally understand these functions today. The courts and their officers had extensive administrative and financial responsibilities as well. Royal control over sheriffs and over the local courts, both communal and feudal, was primarily exercised not by enacting new laws but by calling the local officials to account and examining their books. The traveling justiciars, as we have already seen, were also authorized to decide legal disputes during their visits to the different shires. Writs were used, especially by Henry II, to instruct these justices how to resolve different kinds of legal disputes—that is, what general policies to follow and what procedures to observe. The Assize of Clarendon, part of Henry II's twelfth-century "war on crime," is an example of a broad, instructional writ addressing both administrative and judicial business.[12]

It was the author of the Assize of Clarendon, Henry II, who built on these two functions of writs in a systematic and effective way. In addition to the instructions to justiciars regarding criminal matters contained in the Assize of Clarendon, Henry II issued a number of writs that addressed a few types of property rights disputes that repeatedly occurred throughout the kingdom during his reign. These writs, called the "petty assizes"—there was probably a "grand assize," too, but it is unfortunately lost to us—were also available for purchase from the Chancery.

For example, one of these petty assizes, the Assize of Novel Disseisin, issued by Henry II in 1166, addressed the problem of individuals who claimed to have been recently (hence "novel") and improperly dispossessed ("disseised") of their land (their "freehold"). This form of royal writ required the assembling of a jury of neighbors in front of royal justices to determine who properly possessed the land.[13]

To the Assize of Novel Disseisin and the other petty assizes of Henry II were added other writs that dealt with common, recurring legal problems of medieval life. Usually the problems related to land. The actions based on these writs were brought in the royal courts, not in the county or seignorial courts. (Most early royal writs, such the Writ of Right *de recto,* were still directed to the county and seignorial, not the royal, courts.) In the course of the twelfth and thirteenth centuries, the number of royal writs that authorized actions in the royal courts increased dramatically. The monarchs encouraged individuals to purchase these writs and to look to the royal courts rather than the county and seignorial courts for justice, a policy that was addressed at the behest of the irritated barons in the Magna Carta. These writs gave

---

[12]See Stephenson and Marcham, *Sources of English Constitutional History,* 78–79, at http://www.constitution.org/sech/sech_031.htm, for the text of the assize. See also page 104 of the same work, at http://www.constitution.org/sech/sech_040.htm, for the text of Richard I's "Articles for the General Eyre" (1194) (commented upon by Pollock and Maitland, *History of English Law,* vol. 2, 520–522), an example of a charge to the traveling justiciars.

[13]"Assize," like "court," is a word that bears several related meanings all on its small back; in fact, one of the meanings of "assize" is "court." Other meanings include a session of a court, a decree or enactment taken by a court, and, as in the case of the Assize of Novel Disseisin that we discuss in the text, "the order creating the judicial action, the council from which the order issued, and the judicial action itself all shared a single lilting name: the Assize of Novel Disseisin." Charles Rembar, *The Law of the Land,* 129.

rise to the common law's "forms of action"—the legal remedies and procedures—that were available to injured litigants as long as they were freemen and not villeins.

---

# Original Writs

**Writ of Right** *(Breve de recto).* "The King to [a bishop, baron, or other lord of manor] greeting. We command you that without delay you do full right to A of one messuage with the appurtenances in Trumpington which he claims to hold of you by free service of [so much] *per annum* for all service, of which X deforceth him. And unless you will do this, let the sheriff of Cambridge do it that we may hear no more clamor thereupon for want of right."

**Writ of Right** *(Praecipe quod reddat).* "The King to the sheriff greeting. Command [*Praecipe*] X that [*quod*] justly and without delay he render [*reddat*] to A one messuage with the appurtenances in Trumpington which he claims to be his right and inheritance, and to hold of us in chief and whereof he complains that the aforesaid X unjustly deforceth him. And unless he will do this, and (if) the aforesaid A shall give you security to prosecute his claim, then summon by good summoners the aforesaid X that he be before our justices at Westminster [on such a day] to show wherefore he hath not done it. And have there the summoners and this writ."

**Assize of Novel Disseisin.** "The King to the sheriff greeting. A hath complained to us that X unjustly and without judgment hath disseised him of his freehold in Trumpington after [the last return of our lord the king from Brittany into England]. And therefore we command you that, if the aforesaid A shall make you secure to prosecute his claim, then cause that tenement to be reseised and the chattels which were taken in it and the same tenement with the chattels to be in peace until the first assize when our justices shall come into those parts. And in the mean time you shall cause twelve free and lawful men of that venue to view that tenement and their names to be put into the writ. And summon them by good summoners that they be before the justices aforesaid at the assize aforesaid, ready to make recognizance thereupon. And put by gages and safe pledges the aforesaid X or, if he shall not be found, his bailiff, that he be there to hear that recognizance. And have there the (names of the) summoners, the pledges, and this writ."

**Writ of Trespass** *vi et armis*—**Ejectment.** "The King to the sheriff greeting. If A shall [give you security to prosecute his claim,] then put by gages and safe pledges X that he be before our justices at Westminster on [such a day] to show wherefore with force and arms he entered into one messuage in Trumpington which M demised to the said A for a term which is not yet passed and ejected him, the said A, from his farm aforesaid; and other enormous things did, to the great damage of him the said A and against our peace: and have there the names of the pledges and this writ."[14]

---

[14]*Messuage:* dwelling house; *appurtenances:* land and buildings attached to a dwelling house; *freehold:* land that one owns; *make you secure:* give you something to guarantee; *tenement:* property of a permanent nature, such as land or an office; *chattel:* movable property; a *gage:* something deposited to secure

It is important to note what these original writs contained—and what they did not contain. The writ authorized the writ-holder to initiate official proceedings to resolve a particular legal dispute. Simultaneously, the writ authorized someone, or some court—county, seignorial, or royal—to resolve that dispute; in today's language, the writ gave someone or some court "jurisdiction" to decide the case. The writ also indicated the type of legal dispute that was to be judicially resolved and the procedure by which that dispute was to be resolved; if no procedure was indicated, the customary procedure was implied. In today's language, the writ made a dispute "justiciable."

The writ did not, however, command a particular outcome, *nor did it provide a rule or principle by which the dispute was to be decided or by which the theory of liability at issue in the case was defined.* In other words, the writ did not provide the substantive law, only the procedural law: it provided a "form of action," not a "cause of action." The first Writ of Right quoted in the sidebar simply demands that the feudal lord cited in the writ do justice to the claimant or else the sheriff of Cambridge will do so. The Writ of Right *praecipe quod reddat* commands the defendant to give back the disputed land or come to court and explain why not. The Assize of Novel Disseisin does rudimentarily identify the nature of the dispute and the legal remedy and thus states a legal principle: if the possessor ("tenant") of a freehold is turned out of possession ("seisin") by someone "unjustly and without a judgment," the possessor with this writ shall be placed back in seisin by the king's court. But "unjustly" is not specifically defined, nor is "seisin." A jury will determine who properly possesses the land. Finally, in the Writ of Trespass, the defendant is commanded to come before the royal justices and explain why he dispossessed the plaintiff of his land, but again no rule of possession is set out.

Note that the plaintiff, the one initiating litigation by means of the writ, had to purchase the appropriate writ or else be thrown out of court. The Writ of Novel Disseisin, for example, provided a remedy only to one who had been in possession of the land and had then been thrown out by the other party mentioned in the writ. If the writ holder had never been in possession of the land, the Writ of Novel Disseisin was not appropriate, even if the writ holder could claim that he and not the tenant was the true owner of ("had right in") the land. If proffered to the court, the writ would be "quashed" by the judges and the writ holder would leave without a remedy. By the sixteenth century, when original writs were no longer purchased from Chancery clerks but were drafted by plaintiffs' lawyers, the courts were, if anything, even more particular about the appropriateness of the writ for the action being brought. It was still important to choose at the outset the right writ for the particular kind of dispute.

Note also that the four writs, which are presented roughly in the chronological order in which they appeared, successively elbowed the seignorial courts aside in favor of the royal courts. The Writ of Right gave the seignorial courts first shot at resolving

---

performance (as in mort*gage*); *safe pledges:* surety given that a man shall appear on a certain day; *vi et armis:* force and arms. The language of the writs is taken from Maitland, *The Forms of Action at Common Law.* Alternative language for these and other writs is available in Stephenson and Marcham, *Sources of English Constitutional History,* 82–85; at http://www.constitution.org/ sech/sech_033.htm.

the dispute; if they did not resolve it, then there was recourse to the royal courts. The later Writ of Right *praecipe quod reddat* directly commanded the defendant to give back the land or appear before the royal justices to explain why he did not. The seignorial courts were not mentioned. Nor were they mentioned in the Assize of Novel Disseisin, yet initially matters of disputed land between vassals and subvassals were to be resolved in seignorial courts. The Writ of Trespass, about which we shall say more later, was issued in several forms, all of which provided a remedy for damages resulting from any kind of injury done to the plaintiff's person or his property as a result of defendant's use of violence—*vi et armis,* or "force and arms"—against him. The writ set forth here—"Ejectment"—related to land, but the claim of the royal courts to resolve disputes brought by Writs of Trespass was based on the violence that they recited, not on the fact that they were about land. The *vi et armis* indicated a violation of the King's Peace, a matter agreed on all sides to be within the King's judicial authority.

By the time the famous legal treatise attributed to Henry II's Justiciar Ranulf de Glanvill was written around 1190, about 39 original writs of course that were used to initiate actions in the King's Court were listed in the text. There were, of course, many more than 39 situations giving rise to legal disputes even in those simpler times when disputes over land were the principal business of seignorial and royal courts, *but the royal courts were soon limited to only those actions that were originated by royal writ.* The response of the monarchy in the thirteenth century to the demand for more and more varied writs was to authorize the Chancery to draft and issue more and more different writs to individuals who wished to initiate legal proceedings. By the end of the thirteenth century, the imaginative, innovative, and profitable Chancery and its staff had developed almost 500 forms of writs, and it appeared that a royal legal remedy was available for any legal wrong that one might have suffered in thirteenth-century England.

In the fourteenth century, however, under the pressure of the "barons," the lords who presided over the seignorial courts that were losing more and more judicial business to the central courts, the flood of new writs was reduced to a trickle, and the new writs that the Chancery did issue were almost all based on variations of the Writ of Trespass. Thereafter, English law in the royal courts formally proceeded on the basis of the existing writs for 500 years until nineteenth-century legal reforms eliminated them and fundamentally restructured the English legal system. The crystallization of the writ system into a set of several hundred forms of action that addressed the legal problems of the thirteenth century posed a major challenge to the courts: as time went on, new legal problems, unaddressed and perhaps unimaginable in the thirteenth century, begged for judicial attention. The courts met the challenge by extending these existing common law forms of action to new problems, bending and even distorting the original forms of action to fit new uses. The crystallization thus gave rise to the judicial creativity and law-making that is associated with the common law method.

## The Jury System

The third element of the common law developed by the Norman and Angevin kings—the jury—is also one of the main reasons that the royal courts eventually triumphed over the communal and the seignorial courts in their competition for valuable judicial business. A **jury** is a group of people assembled by an official and sworn to "recognize," or declare, the truth. Their statement of the truth, given in response to questions posed to them by the official and sometimes referred to as a "recognition," is usually called a **verdict** today.[15]

For the first 100 years after the Conquest, juries were rarely used as they are today: a group of people "trying," that is, determining, the facts of a legal case on the basis of evidence presented by other witnesses. Rather, the early jurors were themselves the witnesses. The Normans, following the Frankish kings before them, often used **inquests,** as juries and jury proceedings were called, to learn about all sorts of things. The inquest would be sworn and asked about who owned various lands, about who has allegedly committed crimes, and about what happened in particular legal disputes. William the Conqueror, for example, used inquests throughout England to gather the information that went into the *Domesday Book,* his inventory of manors and properties in England and the duties owed to him by the property holders.

In the time of Henry II, local juries would report to the traveling justiciars on the crimes that were violations of the King's Peace and that had been committed in the county. The people identified by these "presenting juries," or "juries of accusation" as Pollock and Maitland call them, would then have to stand trial. In this capacity, such juries are the forerunners of the modern **grand jury,** a group of people who, under the direction of a prosecutor, inquire into crimes and determine whether a bill of indictment, which is presented to them by the prosecutor and which charges an individual with a crime, is indeed a "true bill." If they so find, the individual charged in the indictment formally becomes a criminal defendant and must defend himself against the charges.

It was the use of **petty** ("petit") **juries** to testify about, and thus to determine, facts that gave royal courts the competitive advantage over the other courts in thirteenth-century England. To understand why litigants were attracted by the early "jury trial," we must understand a little of how guilt, innocence, and liability were determined before the jury method. Three methods were used.

For centuries throughout Europe, guilt, innocence, or legal liability was determined by **ordeals** of one sort or another. An ordeal was an act or test assigned to one of the parties and intended to invoke a supernatural judgment. Ordeals predated the Christianization of Europe, but as Christianity spread, the Church took over these earlier religious-judicial practices and, as the Church often did, gave them a Christian meaning and significance. The Church also administered the ordeals and received fees for its services.

For example, one accused of theft in the eleventh or twelfth century might have to undergo the ordeal of hot iron. During the holy Mass, the priest would give the accused the opportunity to confess. If he did not confess, he would have to carry a piece of iron, which had been heating up in a fire during the service, in one hand a distance of nine feet. After carrying the iron, the accused would have his hand bandaged. Three days later, the bandages would be removed and the hand inspected. If it was "clean," the

---

[15]Originally the French word *veirdit,* which in turn derives ultimately from the Latin words *vere dictum,* meaning "truly said."

---

# The Ordeals

**The ordeal of boiling water** was similar in some respects to the ordeal of hot iron. Both were used primarily for freemen. Here, during the Mass, the accused had to reach into a container of boiling water and take out a stone. His hand would then be bound. Three days later, the hand would be examined, and if it was clean, the accused was acquitted; if it was not clean, the accused was guilty.

**The ordeal of cold water** was also administered in the midst of the Mass but was mostly reserved for the unfree villeins (and later, of course, for witches). If the accused maintained her innocence even when the priest exhorted her to confess, the accused "went to the water." She was tied up and immersed in a creek or a pit of water that had been consecrated. If she floated, she was adjudged guilty because the floating was taken as a sign that the pure, blessed water was rejecting the impure individual.

**The ordeal of the cursed morsel** was reserved for the clergy. The accused was forced to eat a bite of food in which a feather or some such irritant was concealed. If the accused choked, he was guilty.

---

healing was taken as a supernatural sign of the accused's innocence; if it was not healing cleanly, the accused would be adjudged guilty, *and then be punished!*[16]

A later mode of proof that became more common than ordeals was the "wager of law" or method of **compurgation.** The accused individual—and by "accused" I do not mean only accused of a crime, but accused of doing any legal harm, civil or criminal—would have to "make his law." First, he would have to swear his innocence under oath. Then he would have to find a number of people, often 12, who were willing to take a solemn oath that the *accused's* oath was clean—that the accused had told the truth. These people, called "compurgators" or "oath-helpers," did not swear that the accused was innocent, nor did they swear to the facts, but only that the accused did not lie when he swore his oath. If the accused thus made his law, he was adjudged innocent. The reverence with which oaths to Almighty God were held provided the supernatural sanction of wager of law: if you deliberately lie to God, He will get you!

The Normans introduced a new method of proof—**battle**—that appealed to feudal knights' military orientation and machismo and that was initially used only in disputes between Normans. As it developed, trial by battle in criminal cases pitted the accuser against the accused in a duel. If the accused won, he was acquitted; if he lost, he would then be punished for the crime, often by hanging. In civil cases (that is, in cases other than crimes), the parties were permitted to have champions fight the battle for them. Some great landowners maintained permanent champions-in-residence; other parties could hire one of the traveling band of professional champions that followed the justices in eyre. Again, however, the mode of proof was given a religious

---

[16]There was variation throughout Europe in the details of these and other ordeals practiced in the Middle Ages.

significance: it was assumed that the winner of the duel won solely because of God's favor, not because of superior strength or skill.

All of these methods of establishing guilt, innocence, and liability relied upon the people's faith in divine justice for their legitimacy. But the Church was getting increasingly uneasy about its role in sanctioning and administering these modes of proof (didn't the ordeals sinfully tempt God?). Early in the thirteenth century, a church council forbade priests throughout Europe to administer the ordeals any longer.

Even earlier, the monarchs and litigants were also growing skeptical of the validity and the usefulness of the ordeals. As gruesome as they sound to us today, they were less so in times of callus-handed peasants, and they did not clearly tend toward findings of either guilt or innocence. One famous eleventh-century account describes the trial of 50 men accused of violating the laws of the forest. All were acquitted, and the king, who thus lost a tidy sum of fines, was not happy. A later statistical record from a thirteenth-century Hungarian monastery that regularly administered the ordeal of hot iron in that part of Europe reveals that out of 308 recorded cases, 130 defendants were found innocent, 78 were found guilty, 75 reached a settlement with their accusers, and 25 accusers withdrew their complaints.[17] Indeed, in England many *accusers* would offer to undergo the ordeal themselves rather than take the chance that the accused would get off the hook.

Again it was Henry II who played a leading role in the reform of English law. Henry II disliked compurgation, ordeals, and battle, and during his reign he took steps to discourage the use of each. For example, though not outrightly eliminating compurgation, he ordered in the 1166 Assize of Clarendon that some criminal defendants should no longer have the opportunity to make their law and that even those defendants who "make their law and are cleared by the law, if they are of very bad reputation, being publicly and shamefully denounced by the testimony of many lawful men, shall [nevertheless] abjure the lands of the king, so that they shall cross the sea within eight days unless they are detained by the wind . . . and thenceforth not return to England, except at the mercy of the lord king."[18]

In the petty assizes that we discussed above, Henry II offered civil litigants in the royal courts the opportunity to litigate certain property disputes by using inquests instead of the customary modes of proof. Inquests had been used to settle legal disputes—usually land disputes—before the reign of Henry II and even by the Anglo-Saxons, but the practice was not common. Henry II made it common by extending its availability to an increasing number of civil and criminal litigants; however, he also limited it to the royal courts. Thus litigants who wanted to use juries would have to pay the king. But pay they did: court records show an immediate demand for this method of trial.[19]

---

[17]R.C. Van Caenegem, *Birth of the English Common Law*, p. 68 (also referred to in Pollock and Maitland, *History of English Law*, vol. 2, 599n1).

[18]See the Assize of Clarendon, Chapters 12–14, in Stephenson and Marcham, *Sources of English Constitutional History*, 78–79, available at http://www.constitution.org/sech/sech_031.htm.

[19]Note also that the use of trial by jury in a civil case depended on a jury trial being prescribed by the writ. If the writ did not prescribe a jury, the traditional mode of proof was implicitly required.

These early trial juries did not listen to others present evidence and then form a verdict. Remember—the people called together and sworn to form a jury were essentially neighbors of the litigants and were those best placed to know personally the facts of the case. By asking for a jury trial, twelfth-century litigants were asking for a group of their peers to determine the truth of the case based on their own knowledge and then to present their verdict to the judge.

The development of juries in criminal cases was more complicated. Many criminal cases originated as accusations of one individual against another; such formal accusations were called "appeals" or "appeals of felony," and the accusers were called "appellors." The mode of proof in these cases was battle, but little by little in the twelfth century, parties in these cases were given the opportunity to purchase an inquest (that is, the right to use a jury procedure) from the king to establish the guilt or innocence of the accused rather than making the case hinge on the personal duel between the accuser and the accused.

In the criminal cases heard by the royal justiciars during their periodic circuits throughout England, the defendants were formally accused by "presenting juries" and not by individual appellors. Until the Fourth Lateran Council banned the use of ordeals in 1215, these defendants would be tried via the ordeal, but after 1215 another method had to be determined, and we see here another foreshadow of later common law judicial inventiveness. Henry III in 1219 instructed his justiciars to suspend use of the ideals, but did not at that time, nor later apparently, tell them how to proceed. The judges, rather than wait for royal instructions, proceeded on their own. They asked the members of the presenting juries or members of the neighboring communities for their opinion—their verdicts—on the guilt of the accused.

The royal judges in these early cases were not deterred by the apparent conflict of interest on the part of those jurors who first accused and were then asked also for their personal judgments (after all, who knew better the facts of a case than the neighbors of the victim and the accused?). Over time, however, there gradually emerged the idea of a disinterested and impartial jury weighing evidence presented by others. By the mid-fifteenth century, the jury trial as we understand it today—fact-finding by a group of individuals who consider the evidence presented by other witnesses—was clearly recognizable in the writings of contemporary observers.

## Development of the Common Law Method

Thus we have a selective and, I hope, not too misleading sketch of the development of the common law before the fourteenth century. But what happened between then and the colonization of America? In an even more summary account, we may point to the development of all three of the common law's basic components: the royal courts steadily proceeded to overwhelm the communal and seignorial courts and became the principal—but never the only!—courts of England; the writ system, frozen into a finite number of forms of action at common law, nevertheless provided the foundation for a dramatic enlargement of the subject matter addressed by the common law; and the trial by jury, popular and unpopular by turns with the English public, provided the impetus for much of the common law's development.

The development was a product of the interaction of these three components and of others besides, and the story is complex, but we may perhaps shed some light on it by keeping in mind an important legal-political point: with a few exceptions, the Crown and Parliament of England left the development of legal rights and duties and the development of legal procedure to the courts as long as the courts and Chancery did not overreach themselves. The courts, especially in the fourteenth century, did indeed mind their own business in order to enhance their fragile independence from politics; they devoted themselves more and more to engineering the technicalities of law. Thereafter, they proceeded slowly to expand the scope of the common law and to increase their own judicial business at the expense of other courts. Though the Norman and Angevin kings were instrumental in creating the first common law courts and in providing for the original writs that were the grist that those courts milled for several centuries, statutory incursions into substantive law and into litigation procedure were the exceptions, not the rule, for English government up to the colonization of North America. The further development of the writ system and the forms of action may best illustrate this.

The common law in the late thirteenth century consisted of some 500 original writs, and, reflecting its contemporary importance, land was the subject of most of the writs. Some nonland writs, such as debt and covenant, were among the original 500, but their scope was limited. The common law included neither commercial law (the "law merchant"), which today is perhaps the most important subject of civil law, nor canon law, which included much of what we might call "family law"—marriage, child custody, wills, and trusts—the volume of which rivals commercial litigation in today's state courts. For commercial matters, litigants had to go to communal courts, fair (as in "county fair") courts, and admiralty courts; for family law matters, litigants went to the ecclesiastical courts. Most matters of commercial and family law were still outside the common law at the time of England's North American colonization.

Even given the limited focus of the common law on land and on crimes—the breaches of the King's Peace—many of these early writs also became obsolete as the concrete situations that they originally addressed became less common over time. The royal judges' response to this situation was seemingly contradictory. On the one hand, the judges would accept no action that was not originated by the appropriate writ. An action mistakenly brought by the wrong writ would result in the writ being "quashed" and the litigant going home unremedied. Further, judges began to construe individual writs to apply only to certain, specific situations; thus, a knowledge of the custom of the king's courts rather than simple common sense was soon required to bring a successful action. This formalistic tinkering with the writs and with judicial procedure continued for centuries. According to Charles Rembar:

> Over the years, common-law procedure got cranky and tyrannical. The plaintiff had to find the single form of action proper to his case. The defendant had to make the proper answer. To the naked eye, any one of several forms might seem to suit the facts, but plaintiff had to pick the right one, else he could not stay in court. Or he

> might discover there was no form of action for his grievance, though it seemed in common justice he had been wronged.[20]

By the time England was colonizing North America, legal procedure was a mystery to most people. Again quoting Rembar:

> By the 1700s, English litigation was tragicomedy, comic in its pompous theater and its formulary rites, tragic in the poison to the law that emanated from it.[21]

This formalism and judicial nitpicking tended to limit the scope and appeal of the common law, especially since few new writs were being created.

Yet contrary to the centripetal force of formalism, the royal judges also worked to expand the scope of the common law in the centuries under review. As commerce and industry developed, a catalogue of writs that focused mostly on land prevented the common law courts from offering remedies suitable to new circumstances and from competing with other courts for judicial business. The fact that many of the existing writs required the old modes of proof rather than the increasingly popular trial by jury also spurred the judges to look for ways to reform the actions without unduly antagonizing the political interests that were jealous of the judges' power to create rights and duties and that might be tempted to interfere with the judges' control of the law. The judges were in a tight spot: increase business but do not create political controversy. Reform had to be incremental, not radical.

How was it done? We have already mentioned one method of expansion: the construing or engineering of particular writs to apply to particular situations which were not the situations originally contemplated by the drafters of the writs. As the writs took on more specific constructions, they came to define the elements of particular actions. In this way the technicalities and formalism of the common law more and more yielded a body of substantive rules.

Another method of expanding the common law was indeed the creation of new judicial writs. We said above that because of political pressure in the fourteenth century, the number of new writs slowed to a trickle. That trickle consisted almost entirely of variants of the Writ of Trespass. Remember that this writ came in several forms, addressing situations other than "ejectment" from land that we quoted in the example above. The element that placed trespass in the royal courts was not land but the breach of the King's Peace—the *vi et armis,* "force and arms," recited in the writ.

In the late thirteenth century, when the Chancery was already restricting the availability of new writs, Edward I responded to his subjects' requests for more common law actions by making a law that permitted the Chancery clerks to fashion new writs for situations that were *reasonably like* the situations contemplated in existing writs. Thus, the clerks could once again be creative, but within rather severe limits. The existing writ that most often served as the model for new writs created under this statute was the Writ of Trespass, and the spinoffs were called, collectively, Writs of

---

[20]Charles Rembar, *The Law of the Land,* 224.

[21]Ibid.

Trespass upon the Special Case, or Trespass on the Case, or simply "Case." Writs of Trespass on the Case provided judicial remedies for personal and property damage done to the plaintiff *without* violence. Over succeeding centuries, trespass on the case was the main instrument for the slow creation of common law contract and tort law, both of which were unknown to the old land-focused common law writs.

A third method was the use of "legal fictions": blatant and not-so-blatant false-hoods that the parties to litigation were forbidden to deny in court. For example, the Exchequer was originally limited to handling cases that related to royal finances— debts to and by the king. Debts and transactions between private individuals were not within its authority. But what if the plaintiff alleged that he could not pay his taxes to the king unless the defendant first paid his debt to the plaintiff: would that not make the private transaction a royal concern and thus a matter for Exchequer to hear? Apparently so, for Exchequer accepted this not-so-blatant stretching of logic— called *quo minus*—from a relatively early time.

The stretching reached the tearing point centuries later, however, when the common law courts, in order to snatch authority over cases of *foreign* commerce from the Admiralty court, accepted the fiction that the transactions that actually took place abroad and therefore outside the jurisdiction of the common law courts took place instead "in the parish of St. Mary-le-Bow in the ward of Cheap." Again, the defendant was barred from denying it.[22] Other more intricate fictions were aimed not at raiding other courts for business but at making ancient forms of action applicable to new situations demanding legal remedy. By the seventeenth and eighteenth centuries, the common law abounded with legal fictions that both expanded the jurisdiction of the common law courts and the scope of legal harms to which the common law writs applied.

Finally, the broader common law tradition benefited from the development of another body of law that is sometimes seen as a rival: **equity.** Though we have been discussing the methods of expansion employed by the common law judges, we must remember the formalism and the relatively strict limitations within which the judges operated. There were situations for which there was simply no common law remedy available, for which the remedy of monetary compensation was not sufficient, or for which the common law rules or remedy simply did not provide justice.[23] Then, too, there was considerable dissatisfaction with jury trials in the fifteenth century, for juries could be stacked, bought off, and intimidated.

Litigants who could not obtain legal satisfaction at common law would petition the king for other relief, and, though the practice of petitioning the king and his council is as old as the monarchy itself, in the fourteenth century the practice of referring cases to the chancellor for resolution grew abundantly. The chancellors' responses were not systematic at first. Common law judges were often consulted, and they cooperated and participated in the formulation of the chancellor's remedies. In

---

[22]Plucknett, *Concise History,* 663.

[23]Maitland recounts the alleged remark of a defendant's lawyer to the chief justice: "You must not allow conscience to prevent you doing law." Quoted in Plucknett, *Concise History,* 680.

# Equity

As the variety of forms of writs crystallized in the fourteenth century largely because of political pressure, there was also a significant change in the attitude of the common law judges toward the law. In the words of Professor Plucknett:

> The real question which [fourteenth century judges] had to face was how the future of the law should be developed. Was it to be a system of strict rule, mainly procedural, or was there to be a broader principle of conscience, reason, natural justice, equity? Plainly there were two points of view on this matter in the reign of Edward II, but it must have been fairly evident by the middle of the century that the stricter party had won. The law no doubt grew in content, but its growth was within a framework of technical doctrine and procedure instead of being the outcome of a broad principle of general equity.[24]

This constriction of the judicial function, the freezing of the variety of forms of writs, and the attempt of the judges to secure some greater degree of institutional independence from the king during this same period resulted in a limitation of the scope of the "law" and the "legal" remedies available to litigants and a demand for additional remedies to supplement and perhaps correct the law when necessary to do "justice." "Equity" is the name given to this supplementary body of law. Its institutional center was eventually the Chancery, the same office that dispensed the legal writs.

Equity was not a new creation by Chancery. Not only can we trace the idea of equity to Aristotle in the fourth century B.C., but we can already find in the early royal writs the kinds of remedies and the attention to fairness and justice at the expense of technical consistency that characterized later English equity.[25] Rather, as the common law courts and judges drew back from their broader conception of law-tempered-by-equity in the fourteenth century, the felt necessity for justice in addition to legal consistency was recognized by both the Chancery and the King's Council, who dispensed equitable remedies on an increasingly regular basis. One consequence of this was that in the later battles between Parliament and the Crown, equity was identified with the Crown while the common law was identified with Parliament. This identification is reflected in the hostility of many American Founders toward equity during the revolutionary era.

Though equitable remedies were at first tailored to specific situations and thus as Plucknett says, rather "fragmentary," the body of equity rules and principles eventually became as hardened and formulaic as law in later centuries, when a whole body of equity procedures, substantive rules, and courts developed alongside those of the common law.

---

[24]Ibid. Plucknett cites a maxim of the early lawyers that "they would tolerate a 'mischief' (a failure of substantial justice in a particular case) rather than an 'inconvenience' (a breach of legal principle)." See generally Plucknett, *Concise History,* 673–694.

[25]Aristotle, *Nicomachean Ethics,* 1137a31–1138a3.

the seventeenth century, the relation between the chancellor and the common law judges soured and symbolized the growing conflict between king and Parliament. With the restoration of the monarchy in 1660, equity rules and procedures became systematic and rigorous—as "cranky and tyrannical" as those of the common law—and equity became a truly distinct legal system within England. Yet the two systems never really lost touch with each other because many of the lawyers of England practiced before both set of courts and occupied both sets of judgeships.

Thus, at the outset of the colonization of North America, we are presented with a situation in which the greater common law *tradition* in England includes at least four significant bodies of law: the common law proper, equity, the "law merchant," and ecclesiastical law.

And what of the **doctrine of stare decisis**—the use of precedent for deciding legal disputes—that is one of the most distinguishing characteristics of modern common law? The answer to that question depends in part on a technology, in part on a uniform format for court reports, and in part on a hierarchical court structure that did not exist in the early developmental years of the common law and would not exist for another few centuries.

Clearly, reliance on the rules articulated by courts long ago or by courts in other parts of the country is all but impossible without reliable written reports that are available to attorneys and judges. The printing press was not invented until the fifteenth century; English common lawyers had to wait at least that long for a consistent and adequate supply of written reports.

Then, too, the reports of cases had to be regularized into a format that allowed readers to identify the rules that the judges relied upon to reach their decision. For centuries, judges were not expected to write up the rationale for their decisions themselves: they simply decided the questions brought to them, usually questions of pleading practice, and let others report the decisions if they wished. This practice did not significantly change until the seventeenth century.

The doctrine of precedent also distinguishes between the rulings of higher and lower courts, where the higher courts possess appellate jurisdiction and authority to correct the rulings of the trial courts below them. This formalization of a hierarchical court structure also did not exist in the early centuries of the common law courts, although it was anticipated by the authority of the Court of King's Bench to review decisions of the court of common pleas.

Even with the appearance of the three developments that we have indicated are necessary for the use of precedent in deciding cases, there must also be a recognition that cases—that is, the rules that are cited in the rationale for deciding a case—are authoritative *sources* of law. In the earlier days, cases were understood merely to exemplify the law, not to create or define it. As we have noted, the common law was often referred to as the "custom of the king's courts," the way the royal courts generally decided this or that type of legal dispute. The rules and principles of substantive law existed in the minds of the judges and the lawyers, a realm of existence that Oliver Wendell Holmes later mocked as a "brooding omnipresence in the sky."

Regardless of the mode in which the law may have existed, the early common law judges were clear that case law was not in itself authoritative and that they, the judges, were not bound by prior cases. Rather, the judges sought consistency in their decision of similar cases: the famous thirteenth-century legal commentator Bracton stated the principle: "If any new and unwonted circumstances . . . shall arise, then if anything analogous has happened before, let the case be adjudged in like manner, since it is a good opportunity to proceed from like to like."[26] Bracton cited many cases in his treatise, but often to show that they were wrongly decided—that they did *not* reflect the law—rather than to suggest that decided cases constituted or determined the law. This attitude that cases illustrated but did not determine the law was present in England and the United States until the nineteenth century.[27] Until cases were understood to be the *sources* and not just the reflections of law, the common law method of adjudication that we know today could not exist.

*          *          *

In these ragged swatches torn from the fabric of the history of the common law, we have seen the origination of the royal courts, the corps of royal judges, the original forms of action, and the method of trial by jury that are essential components of the common law. The story of the evolution of English common law between the fifteenth and the eighteenth centuries is a story of increasing complexity and technicality. These centuries present fascinating histories of the development of the fields of law—tort, contract, property, and wills and trusts—that we take for granted today, but that are far beyond the scope of this primer. Arduous training in the law became a necessity, and the subsequent costs kept most of the English population from seeking common law solutions to their legal problems. Thus, local courts, laws, and customs continued to flourish among the lower classes of English society, and the English colonists who settled America were drawn largely from these classes. It should not, therefore, surprise us that the common law and common law courts were not immediately established in the new English colonies of North America.

## COLONIAL AND EARLY STATE COURTS

The colonial charters, by which term we include the other founding documents of the English colonies as well, generally included several boilerplate clauses, a few of which are pertinent to our present purposes.[28]

First, the charters set forth basic structures of executive and representative power for the provinces. The principal officers were appointed, usually by name

---

[26]Quoted in Hogue, *Origins of the Common Law,* 200. Bracton went on to say that new and difficult decisions should be decided by the Great Council rather than the judges acting alone. See also Plucknett, *Concise History,* 342–350.

[27]But see *Anastasoff v. United States,* 223 F.3d 898 (8th Cir. 2000), *vacated as moot,* 2000 U.S. App. LEXIS 33247 (8th Cir. 2000)(en banc), where the court argues that "the doctrine of precedent was well-established by the time the Framers gathered in Philadelphia."

[28]See Benjamin Perley Poore, *Federal and State Constitutions, Colonial Charters, and Other Organic Laws of the States, Territories, and Colonies Now or Heretofore Forming the United States of America.*

from among the grantees, and the mode of selecting members to the representative institution was set forth in some detail.

Second, the grantees of the charters were given the power to make all laws and regulations for the good and happy government of the province and the power to execute and enforce those laws so long as the laws were not repugnant or contrary, so far as reasonable, to the laws of England. The king's Privy Council had the authority to determine repugnancy.

Third, the charters also contained a grant by the king to all of the subjects of the provinces of "all liberties and immunities of free and natural subjects within any of the Dominions of Us, our Heirs and Successors, to all Intents, Constructions and Purposes whatever, as if they and every of them were born within the Realme of England."

Finally, the settlers were also granted the power to establish "judicatories" or courts of law to try "all actions, suits and causes whatsoever, as well criminal and civil, real, mixed, personal, or of any other kind or nature whatsoever." The colonies could design their own courts within this broad grant of general jurisdiction.

Though the three latter charter provisions all depended to some degree on reference to the common law for their meaning, the charters did not explicitly require the establishment of the common law as the basis for colonial law, and in this the colonists were fortunate for several reasons.

For one thing, the common law of England and many of the English statutes, premised as they were upon an established commercial, as well as agricultural, society rooted firmly in medieval ideas and conditions, simply did not fit pioneer problems arising out of a primitive environment. The settlers were suspicious of the formalism and the technical language of the English common law procedures and often disliked the harshness of its rules.

Another reason why the common law did not take root immediately was that most of the settlers did not come from the English social classes that had most occasion to use the royal or common law courts in England. The law that the colonists were familiar with back home in England was the local law and custom that were still the basis of the legal order at the lower levels of English society in the seventeenth and eighteenth centuries. Besides, the commercial law relied upon by merchants and the law of marriage and personal property relied upon by nearly everyone were still outside the common law.

And finally, the colonies did not have the trained professional lawyers and the printed texts of opinions and statutes that are essential to a system of stare decisis. Printed reports of court opinions were all but nonexistent before the early years of the eighteenth century. In America, where lawyers were never popular, the few trained lawyers in the seventeenth century faced a situation that has been aptly summarized by Anton-Hermann Chroust:

> English law and English precedents often were neither followed nor used as a guide by the courts in the administration of justice with the result that the law, as well as the procedure, was constantly in a state of flux. The courts frequently were staffed or, at the very least, dominated by wealthy merchants, clergymen, governors or governor's deputies, politicians, favorites, or influential men who either had been appointed by the powers that were or had been elected by an ill-informed or ill-willed electorate.

Practically none of these judges had any legal training, and few were expected to be conversant in the law. The law itself often was extremely flexible and amateurish. In some instances, it was the highly questionable product of personal caprice, prejudice, or just plain ignorance. [29]

Supreme Court Justice Samuel Miller rendered a kinder judgment on the pioneer judges of the Amercian West two centuries later: the judges, he said, "did not know enough to do the wrong thing, so they did the right thing."[30]

Given these conditions, each colony developed its own court and legal systems and its own legal rules, borrowing where appropriate—and sometimes where inappropriate—from English models.[31]

It was not until the late seventeenth century, when colonial society had settled down a bit and colonial commerce was more prosperous and complex, that the virtues of the English common law and court procedures could be used to serve the interests of the American colonists. The number of professional lawyers, both home-grown and imported, increased, and the colonial courts took on a more recognizably English complexion. There was still a great variety throughout the colonies, but the English common law was taking hold of the colonies in fact as well as in principle.

For example, a 1683 New Jersey statute set up a "court of common right." The court was empowered "to hear, try and determine all matters, causes and cases, capital, criminal or civil causes of equity, and causes triable at common law." But the colonies created full batteries of special courts—courts of limited jurisdiction—as well. For the most part, the newly independent states carried over these courts. Some state constitutions also continued the practice of establishing as the highest state appellate court one of the branches of the legislature or the governor's council, even while expressly proclaiming the doctrine of separation of powers elsewhere in the constitution. This mixed appellate court was either described in the constitution or was established pursuant to a "sweeping" or necessary and proper clause. The mixed courts, of course, were themselves reflections of the appellate jurisdiction and veto power over colonial legislation that the king and privy council had held throughout the eighteenth century. So, too, did the dependence of the new state judges on the favor of the governor, the legislature, or both carry over from the earlier colonial era.

We should not be surprised by the mixing of legislative and judicial functions in these colonial and early state appellate courts. The separation of powers doctrine was still relatively new and untried. The doctrine emerged in England out of the tumult of seventeenth-century English politics and civil war and never took firm root in its

---

[29]*The Rise of the Legal Profession in America,* vol. 1, 26.

[30]Quoted in Roscoe Pound, *The Formative Era of American Law,* 11.

[31]It is important to note the profound influence of William Blackstone's *Commentaries on the Laws of England,* originally published in four volumes in England in the late 1760s, on the law of the new republic. Given the paucity of trained attorneys and judges as well as of legal texts, especially case reports, Blackstone's *Commentaries* provided a comprehensive and generally reliable survey of English common law for the American legal community, and it is said that more copies of the work were sold in the United States than in England. Sir Edward Coke's *Institutes of the Laws of England* was also influential.

native land.[32] The best, perhaps, that could be hoped for in eighteenth-century government was judicial independence, but that—at least at the local court level—was a long time in coming.

The common law—and the common lawyers—faced another early obstacle to their complete acceptance in the newly independent United States. The post revolutionary United States suffered through an economic depression in which many American debtors were thrown out of their homes and into debtors' prison. Only the creditors could afford to hire the available legal talent, and, following the age-old rule of killing the messengers of bad news, many Americans developed a powerful hatred of lawyers and of the English common law that the lawyers represented. Then, too, in the European struggle between the English and the French, there was strong American sentiment against their recent enemy and all things English and in favor of their recent ally and all things French, particularly the new French civil code. But attempts to establish and develop a civil law system in the United States never could overcome the deep cultural and political ties of the United States to England. Legal disputes continually arose and needed to be addressed, and the nation could not take a time-out to establish a radically new legal system and to train and retrain the professional lawyers and judges to implement it. In the end, the American states accepted the common law tradition as the foundation upon which to develop their own distinct legal systems, and the American systems—state and federal—continue to be parts of this tradition today.

## DEVELOPMENT OF THE FEDERAL COURTS

Under the first United States Constitution—the Articles of Confederation—no separate national court existed. Under Article IX the Congress served as "the last resort on appeal in all disputes and differences now subsisting or that hereafter may arise between two or more States concerning boundary, jurisdiction or any other causes whatever." Similarly, the Congress had final authority to decide "controversies concerning the private right of soil claimed under different grants of two or more States," if either party petitioned Congress to do so. In both of these situations, the Congress—or the delegates of the several states representing "the United States in Congress assembled"—did not actually sit as a huge court; Article IX provides that the Congress shall direct the creation of an ad hoc tribunal of "commissioners or judges to constitute a court for hearing and determining the matter in question." The tribunals were not permanent institutions.

The Virginia Plan proposed to change that. Presented to the 1787 Constitutional Convention in Philadelphia by Governor Edmund Randolph of Virginia and written largely by Virginia delegate James Madison, the plan's ninth resolution proposed "that a National Judiciary be established to consist of one or more supreme tribunals, *and of inferior tribunals to be chosen by the National Legislature*" (emphasis added). The proposal is close to, but not quite the same as, the language that now appears in

---

[32]See generally M. J. C. Vile, *Constitutionalism and the Separation of Powers.*

Article III, Section 1 of the Constitution: "The judicial Power of the United States, shall be vested in one supreme Court, *and in such inferior Courts as the Congress may from time to time ordain and establish*" (emphasis added). The difference between the two statements is significant and the reason for the difference worth noting.

The Virginia Plan would have required the national legislature to create one or more supreme tribunals *and* various subordinate courts; the language of the proposal implies a command—and the delegates understood it to do so—to create these courts. The final language of Article III explicitly commands the creation of only one supreme tribunal but merely authorizes the creation of subordinate courts *if the Congress so decides.*

This language of Article III reflects a compromise between two factions in a closely divided chamber. When the original proposal requiring the creation of both supreme and subordinate federal courts came up for consideration, John Rutledge of South Carolina moved to strike the clause requiring "*inferior* tribunals," arguing that state courts should "be left in all cases to decide in the first instance[,] the right of appeal to the supreme national tribunal being sufficient to secure the national rights [and] uniformity of Judgm<sup>ts</sup>."[33] Rutledge's motion narrowly passed. James Wilson and James Madison then immediately moved to give "a discretion to the Legislature to establish or not establish [inferior courts]." Their motion passed eight to two and was articulated in the first sentence of Article III. Upon the convening of the first Congress under the new Constitution in 1789, the Senate turned promptly to the question of the federal judiciary and, exercising its constitutional discretion, produced by September most of the language of the first Judiciary Act, which established a federal judiciary with supreme and inferior courts.

The language of Article III is the focus of another fundamental controversy, this one not resolved until the second half of the nineteenth century. Section 2 of the article lists the types of cases that the federal courts *shall* have the power to decide: "The judicial Power shall extend to. . . ." If we follow the usual meaning of the word "shall" in statutory language, Section 2 would seem to require Congress to vest all of the jurisdiction in the first paragraph of Section 2 in the federal courts that it creates. Yet the first Judiciary Act, which was the product of a Congress that included several of the Philadelphia delegates who wrote the Constitution, did not endow the federal courts with all of the Section 2 jurisdiction. Indeed, the opening category of jurisdiction in Section 2, "all Cases, in Law and Equity, arising under this Constitution, the Laws of the United States, and Treaties made, or which shall be made, under their Authority"—the so-called federal question jurisdiction—was not given to federal courts until 1875. If federal courts should be deciding any kind of cases, it would seem that they should be deciding this kind of case, in which, as John Rutledge put it, "national rights" are to be decided. Other bits of Section 2 jurisdiction were also withheld from the federal courts. What happened?

Robert Clinton argues persuasively and at length that the intent of the Framers— that the federal judiciary should indeed have jurisdiction over all of the classes of cases listed in Section 2—was defeated by a Federalist clique in Congress and by a

---

[33]Madison's *Notes,* June 5.

series of later, wrongly decided Supreme Court decisions.[34] Whether the "mandatory view" argued by Clinton was indeed the view of the Framers—and apart from the use of the term "shall," there is precious little evidence to be gathered from the reports of the debates at Philadelphia—the fact remains that the subsequent authoritative interpretation of Article III by Congress and the Supreme Court maintains that the jurisdiction set out in Section 2 is not the mandatory jurisdiction for the federal courts, but the maximum allowable jurisdiction that the federal courts may possess if Congress decides to give it to them. Congress may, however, decide not to give some or presumably all of the listed jurisdiction to the federal courts.

In the first Judiciary Act, Congress created a legal system consisting of three different courts.[35] In addition to the Supreme Court, which we shall discuss in greater detail in Chapter 5, the act established three "Circuit Courts" and thirteen "District Courts." The district courts were assigned permanent judgeships; the circuit courts were not. Rather, the semiannual sessions of each of the circuit courts were to be held by three judges: one district court judge and two Supreme Court justices who "rode circuit." The circuit courts were intended to be the principal federal trial courts, but they also were appellate courts, hearing appeals in some, but not all, cases from the district courts, which were exclusively trial courts. In possessing both trial jurisdiction and appellate jurisdiction, the circuit courts were like the Supreme Court. The cases heard by the new district and circuit courts were primarily admiralty cases, criminal cases, and diversity cases (cases in which plaintiffs from one state or country sue defendants from different states or countries). The circuit courts also heard cases in which the United

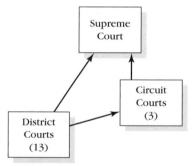

**Figure 1.1** Arrows indicate courses of appellate review available to litigants from lower courts to courts of appellate jurisdiction.

---

[34]Robert Clinton, *A Mandatory View of Federal Court Jurisdiction: A Guided Quest for the Original Understanding of Article III,* 132 U. Pa. L. Rev. 741 (1984), and *A Mandatory View . . . : Early Implementation and Departures from the Original Plan,* 86 Colum. L. Rev. 1515 (1986). The decisions are *Durousseau v. United* States, 10 U.S. (6 Cr.) 307, 3 L.Ed. 232, http://laws.findlaw.com/us/10/307.html (1810) and *Ex parte McCardle,* 74 U.S. 506, 19 L.Ed. 264, http://laws.findlaw.com/us/74/506.html (1868).

[35]Act of September 24, 1789, 1 Stat. 73.

States was a party. All the rest of the nation's litigation was brought in state courts, which, then as now, bore the greater share of the United States' civil and criminal cases.

This basic scheme of federal courts did not change until 1891, though there were alterations, some of which were significant, over the years. For instance, the Supreme Court justices almost immediately found the semiannual task of riding circuit across the eighteenth-century United States a nuisance. Already in 1792, Chief Justice John Jay asked President Washington to try to eliminate the circuit riding. The law was changed first to require only one justice to participate in the circuit court sessions: then, in the Judiciary Act of 1801 (the infamous Federalist "Midnight Judges Act"), the requirement was eliminated altogether.[36] But the Jeffersonians repealed the 1801 Act in 1802 and reinstated the requirement. The 1802 legislation, however, also provided that the circuit court sessions may be held by one district court judge, if other duties prevented Supreme Court justices from riding circuit, and this new rule took most of the burden off the justices. The circuit courts finally got their own judges in 1869 (one per circuit), and broader jurisdiction was conferred on both the circuit courts and the district courts in 1875.

The federal court structure was changed significantly in 1891 with the creation of Circuit Courts of Appeals—purely appellate courts staffed by judges from the circuit and district courts—and the elimination of the appellate jurisdiction of the circuit courts. (Figure 1.2.) The federal system now consisted of two separate sets of trial courts, a set of appeals courts, and the Supreme Court, which continued almost exclusively as an appellate court.

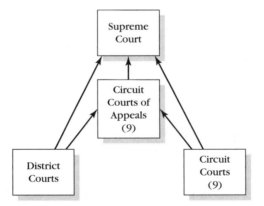

**Figure 1.2** Arrows indicate courses of appellate review available to litigants from lower courts to courts of appellate jurisdiction.

---

[36]The "Midnight Judges Act" was so called because the Federalist Congress and Federalist President John Adams enacted the law in the final moments of the Adams administration in 1801. In elections of 1800, Thomas Jefferson and the Jeffersonian party, the Democratic-Republicans, swept the Federalists from power in Congress and the presidency. The Act, in addition to making several substantive judicial reforms, created 16 new federal judgeships, which Adams and the Federalists attempted to fill with loyal Federalists such as William Marbury and thus to pack the judiciary until the Federalist return to power. The Federalists never did come back into power.

The circuit courts, which never possessed a distinct role in the federal system and which were now reduced to a set of courts parallel to the more numerous district courts, were finally abolished in 1911, when the federal system took on a shape quite similar to its present shape. (Recent developments in the structure of the federal judiciary will be discussed in more detail in Chapter 4.)

This brief history demonstrates the range of authority that the Congress (with, of course, the legislative participation of the president) has over the structure of the third branch of the federal government.

## DEVELOPMENT OF THE STATE COURTS

Until relatively recently, the courts of the various states were hardly ever organized as neatly or coherently as the federal courts have been since the very first Federal Judiciary Act. State court systems, according to Robert Tobin, did not develop into truly coequal third branches of government until midway through the twentieth century, despite looking like an independent third branch on paper:

> The judicial branch is not a coequal branch of government unless it has the ability and the authority to manage its internal operations, including its largest single component, the trial courts. When this important component is part of local government and local politics, there is no state judicial branch in any meaningful sense of the word.[37]

Before 1950, state court "systems" lacked precisely this internal cohesion.

State courts have always had two origins—the state constitutions and local government initiatives. State constitutions provided for a court of last resort and, perhaps, for an intermediate appellate court and a set of trial courts. State trial courts, however, were often created at the initiative of localities, funded from the proceeds of their own activities, and managed by practicing attorneys or by staff independently elected or drawn from other local government agencies.

The submersion of the trial courts in local politics was manifested in the quality of those selected or elected to serve as judges. Often individuals who were untrained in law but politically attractive to local politicians and voters were made trial court judges. Organizationally, local courts developed chaotically, and the multiplicity of locally required procedures, coupled with the lack of accountability to higher courts, resulted in the absence of an authoritative common law for the state.

Under the banner of "court unification," the court reform movements, supported by state judges and bar organizations, promoted unitary systems of courts that replaced the hodgepodge of local courts with a set of county courts of broad, general jurisdiction that were presided over by legally trained judges. A number of states also added intermediate appellate courts to relieve the highest court of some of its increasing appellate caseload. These courts were state-funded and professionally staffed. The reform movement has been widely successful, though the court organizations of some states, such as Tennessee and Georgia, still reflect the prereform era.

---

[37]*Creating the Judicial Branch: The Unfinished Reform,* 21. "State supreme courts were like heads without bodies." Ibid., vii. The authoritative history of American law is Lawrence Friedman's excellent and most readable *History of American Law.*

Today, though still suffering to a degree from "a resentful inferiority complex" regarding their federal court brethren and fighting to protect their turf from encroachment by federal courts in various forms over state court jurisdiction, the state courts are increasingly recognized for the quality of their judges and the importance of their adjudication.[38] As we shall stress when we take up the discussion of state courts and their functions in Chapter 4, most of the nation's litigation takes place in state courts, and the kinds of cases that state courts decide do not significantly differ from those decided by federal courts.

## Selected Bibliography and Recommended Readings

Blackstone, William. *Commentaries on the Laws of England.* 4 Vol. Oxford: Clarendon Press, 1765–1769. The first edition is available via Yale Law School's Avalon Project at http://www.yale.edu/lawweb/avalon/blackstone/blacksto.htm#intro. An American edition, edited and with additional commentaries by St. George Tucker (Philadelphia: Birch and Small, 1803), is available via the Liberty Library of the Constitution Society at http://www.constitution.org/tb/tb–0000.htm.

Chroust, Anton-Hermann. *The Rise of the Legal Profession in America.* 2 Vol. Norman: University of Oklahoma Press, 1965.

Coke, Sir Edward. *Institutes of the Laws of England.* 1628–1644. Selections from the four Institutes are presented in volume 2 of *The Selected Writings and Speeches of Sir Edward Coke,* ed. Steve Sheppard (Indianapolis: Liberty Fund, 2003), available also at http//oll.libertyfund.org.

Farrand, Max. *Records of the Federal Convention of 1787.* New Haven: Yale University Press, 1911. Available via the Library of Congress web site, "Thomas: Legislative Information on the Internet," at http://memory.loc.gov/ammem/amlaw/lwfr.html.

Fifoot, C. H. S. *English Law and Its Background.* London: G. Bell and Sons, 1932.

Friedman, L. M. *History of American Law.* New York: Simon and Schuster, 1973.

Harmer, Florence E. *Anglo-Saxon Writs.* Manchester, England: Manchester University Press, 1952.

Hogue, Arthur R. *Origins of the Common Law.* Bloomington: Indiana University Press, 1966. Reprint, Indianapolis: Liberty Press, 1985.

Holt, J. C. *Magna Carta.* 2d ed. New York: Cambridge University Press, 1992.

Hudson, John. *The Formation of the English Common Law.* London: Longman, 1996.

Kern, Fritz. *Kingship and Law in the Middle Ages.* Translated by S. B. Chrimes. Oxford: Blackwell, 1939.

Madison, James. *Notes of Debates in the Federal Convention of 1787.* Edited by Adrienne Koch. Athens: Ohio University Press, 1966. Reprint, New York: Norton, 1987.

Maitland, Frederic William. *Forms of Action at Common Law.* Edited by A. H. Chaytor and W. J. Whittaker. Cambridge: Cambridge University Press, 1954.

---

[38] Ibid., 18.

Merryman, John Henry. *The Civil Law Tradition.* 2d ed. Stanford, CA: Stanford University Press, 1985.

Milsom, S. F. C. *Historical Foundations of the Common Law.* London: Butterworth's, 1969.

Plucknett, Theodore F. T. *Concise History of the Common Law.* 5th ed. Boston: Little, Brown and Co., 1956.

Pollock, Sir Frederick, and Frederic William Maitland. *History of English Law Before the Time of Edward I.* 2d ed. New York: Cambridge University Press, 1898; reprint, 1978.

Poore, Benjamin Perley, compiler. *Federal and State Constitutions, Colonial Charters, and Other Organic Laws of the United States.* Washington, D.C.: Government Printing Office, 1878. (Relevant excerpts from a later edition, compiled and edited by Francis Newton Thorpe in 1906 and printed by the Government Printing Office in 1909, are available via the Yale University Avalon Law Project web site at http://www.yale.edu/lawweb/avalon/states/statech.htm#ge.)

Pound, Roscoe. *The History and System of the Common Law.* New York: P. F. Collier and Son, 1939.

_____. *Formative Era of American Law.* New York: Little, Brown, 1938; reprint 1959.

Rembar, Charles. *Law of the Land: The Evolution of Our Legal System.* New York: Harper and Row, 1980.

Rodes, Robert E., Jr. *Ecclesiastical Administration in Medieval England : The Anglo-Saxons to the Reformation.* Vol. 1, *This House I Have Built.* Notre Dame: University of Notre Dame Press, 1977.

Stephenson, Carl, and Frederick George Marcham, eds. *Sources of English Constitutional History.* New York: Harper and Row, 1937. Available via the Liberty Library of the Constitution Society at http://www.constitution.org/sech/sech_.htm.

Stubbs, William, ed. *Select Charters and Other Illustrations of English Constitutional History.* 9th ed. Revised by H. W. C. Davis. Oxford: Oxford University Press, 1921.

Supreme Court of the United States. *History of the Supreme Court of the United States.* Vol. 1, *Antecedents and Beginnings to 1801,* by Julius Goebel, Jr. New York: Macmillan Publishing Co., 1974, c. 1971.

Tobin, Robert W. *Creating the Judicial Branch: The Unfinished Reform.* Williamsburg, VA: National Center for State Courts, 1999.

Van Caenegem, R. C. *The Birth of the English Common Law.* 2d ed. Cambridge: Cambridge University Press, 1989.

_____. *Royal Writs in England from the Conquest to Glanvill.* Vol. 77, Selden Society. London: Bernard Quaritch, 1959.

Vile, M. J. C. *Constitutionalism and the Separation of Powers.* 2d ed. Indianapolis: Liberty Fund, 1998.

Wright, Charles Alan. *The Law of Federal Courts.* 3d ed. St. Paul, MN: West Publishing, 1976.

# Chapter 2

# Jurisdiction

## Chapter Outline

The creation of a court system is in large part the allocation of different kinds of jurisdiction to different courts; it is this distribution of jurisdiction that determines the relationships between and among the courts in the system. If we are to acquire a basic understanding of the American court systems, we must first understand the relevant concepts of jurisdiction. Further, since jurisdiction is essentially the power to do something, we must understand what it is that the courts in question may do; in other words, what functions do they have the power to perform?

The answers to these and related questions will enable us to understand the structure of American court systems in general and the United States Supreme Court in particular.

# THE FOUR J'S: JUDICIAL POWER, JURISDICTION, JUSTICIABILITY, AND JUDICIAL REVIEW

## Judicial Power

The term **judicial power** refers to the functions that law courts perform. The primary function of Anglo-American courts, and particularly of the federal courts, is deciding cases and controversies and ordering the appropriate remedies.[1] State courts may have additional powers, such as rendering **advisory opinions** to state government officials or administering certain statutes.[2] The functions of courts may therefore be different in different judicial systems, but the core judicial power common to American courts is the power to decide legal disputes in a manner similar to that of the English courts that served as the models for the original courts in the United States.

## Jurisdiction

In general, the **jurisdiction** of a public institution or official is the power or authority of that institution or official to do something.[3] The jurisdiction of courts is their

---

[1]According to the Supreme Court in the case of *Muskrat v. United States,* 219 U.S. 346, 31 S.Ct. 250, 55 L.Ed. 246, http://laws.findlaw.com/us/219/346.html (1911), this is the only function that federal courts may perform:

> It is . . . apparent that from its earliest history this court has consistently declined to exercise any powers other than those which are strictly judicial in their nature.
>
> It therefore becomes necessary to inquire what is meant by the judicial power thus conferred by the Constitution upon this court, and, with the aid of appropriate legislation, upon the inferior courts of the United States. "Judicial power," says Mr. Justice [Samuel] Miller, in his work on the Constitution, "is the power of a court to decide and pronounce a judgment and carry it into effect between persons and parties who bring a case before it for decision." Miller, Const. 314.
>
> As we have already seen, by the express terms of the Constitution, the exercise of the judicial power is limited to "cases" and "controversies." Beyond this it does not extend, and unless it is asserted in a case or controversy within the meaning of the Constitution, the power to exercise it is nowhere conferred.
>
> . . .
>
> By cases and controversies are intended the claims of litigants brought before the courts for determination by such regular proceedings as are established by law or custom for the protection or enforcement of rights, or the prevention, redress, or punishment of wrongs. 219 U.S. at 356-57, 31 S.Ct. at 253-54, 55 L.Ed. at 250.

[2]An **advisory opinion** is a judicial opinion that is requested not to decide a case or controversy, but to provide guidance or advice to government officials or private parties. According to the National Center for State Courts, in 2002 the supreme courts of 12 states and Puerto Rico had the authority to render advisory opinions. Court Statistics Project, *State Caseload Statistics, 2003* (National Center for State Court, 2004), see http://www.ncsconline.org/D_Research/csp/2001_Files/2001_SCCS.html. On the federal courts and advisory opinions, see John E. Nowak and Ronald D. Rotunda, *Constitutional Law,* 6th ed., Hornbook Series (St. Paul: West Group, 2000), § 2.12(b).

authority to exercise judicial power; thus, in light of the foregoing description of the judicial power, a court's jurisdiction generally refers to the kinds of cases and controversies that a court may decide.[4] For both historical and practical reasons, the jurisdiction of each court is limited to certain kinds of cases. No American court, state or federal, has the authority to resolve every kind of legal controversy.

Congress and the state legislatures assign jurisdiction to the federal and the state courts, respectively, within the bounds established by the federal and state constitutions. Courts of law, like all American governmental institutions, are creatures of the constitutions and statutory enactments.

The jurisdiction of the state and the federal courts is often outlined in the respective state and federal constitutions and statutes, but the constitutions and statutes seldom, if ever, explain in detail what the judicial power is or how it is to be performed.[5] This is probably because the functions included in the judicial power are assumed to exist on the basis of what English and American courts have generally done in the past. Thus, the jurisdiction of the courts is their authority to exercise the judicial power in certain defined circumstances.[6]

---

[3]We often hear the term "jurisdiction" used to refer to a particular geographical territory. For instance, we might say that a murder committed in Virginia is in the jurisdiction of the Virginia courts and law enforcement agencies, while a murder committed in another state is outside of their jurisdiction. Certainly, territory is one of the factors that definitions of court jurisdiction often include, but the jurisdiction of courts and of other government institutions is more than simply a territorial allocation of authority. Jurisdiction is the legal authority to perform a particular function, and it may or may not be limited to a particular territory.

[4]The close relationship between the terms "jurisdiction" and "judicial power" is reflected in the motion at the 1787 constitutional convention in Philadelphia by James Madison and Gouverneur Morris to strike the phrase "the jurisdiction of the supreme Court" from an earlier draft of Article III and replace it with "the judicial Power." Madison's *Notes,* August 27, 1787. This change conformed the language of the Constitution to the usage described above: "jurisdiction" describes the kinds of legal disputes to which the "judicial power" of a court may be applied.

[5]Article III of the federal constitution exemplifies this. After first describing in the barest of terms the possible outlines of a federal judiciary and the terms of employment of federal judges (Section 1), the text turns abruptly to the jurisdiction of a federal judiciary: "The judicial Power shall extend to all cases," whereafter follows an enumeration of the kinds of cases and controversies to which the federal judicial power might apply (Section 2). There is no textual discussion of how the federal courts are to go about their business, nor do the notes of the 1787 convention reflect any detailed discussion of the nature of the judicial power. See Miller, *supra,* chapter 1, note 1, 71–72 (1989).

[6]This general assumption by American constitution makers that the judicial function is to be identified with the functions traditionally performed by the Anglo-American courts is reflected in the fact that the Framers of the federal Constitution in 1787 discussed the development of Article III and the powers of a new national court system on only 9 out of 75 days of discussion during that summer in Philadelphia. It is true, however, that they did discuss the proper and improper functions of federal judges during the debate over the proposed Council of Revision and the seating of federal judges on it. But when reading Madison's *Notes,* one gets the impression that the speakers assumed that the delegates understood what law courts did and, further, that law courts would continue to function much as they functioned in the eighteenth century.

# Justiciability

One necessary condition for the exercise of judicial power is the existence of a justiciable dispute. **Justiciability** is the quality of being a *judicially* resolvable dispute.[7] We noted in the discussion of the early English courts in Chapter 1 that not all injuries or wrongs were actionable in the royal courts because the royal writs did not cover all possible wrongs for which people wanted legal remedies. We also noted that even if a particular injury was remediable by the courts, not all theories of liability were acceptable to the courts; the litigant had to obtain and proceed under the proper writ. These early relationships between what is judicially remediable and what is "legal" foreshadowed the issues addressed by the present-day concepts of justiciability.

In today's legal usage, the term "justiciability" has two senses, one broad and one narrow. There are all sorts of disputes among people and all sorts of harms that can be suffered, but not all are *legal* disputes. The dispute over who shall sit in which chair at the family dinner table is a real dispute. The harm that one inflicts by snubbing someone at a party is surely a real harm, but typically the courts will not settle the dinner table dispute nor will they entertain a suit for damages by the slighted partygoer. We commonly say that these are not "legal" disputes or that the parties in these cases have no "legal" rights to court-imposed remedies. A justiciable dispute must first be a legal dispute. This is justiciability in the broad sense.

Nonlegal disputes may be transformed into legal disputes. How? American and English courts recognize two principal methods. First, of course, a government may enact a statute relating to dinner table seating. Disputes arising under that statute would then be legal because the legislature determines them to be so, and the primary function of our courts, as we indicated earlier, is deciding cases and controversies that arise under the laws of the land.

Second, in common law countries the courts themselves may establish a cause of action—for example, a suit for damages caused by the judicially recognized harm of being snubbed at a party. The harm and the consequent right and cause of action, here a tort, would probably be narrowly defined at first on the basis of existing common law principles, but no legislative action would be necessary to establish this new cause of action.

Thus, the question of whether a particular dispute is a legal dispute is usually answered in the first instance by reference to the statute books or the law reports. But even if a dispute is recognized as a legal dispute—as a cause of action—it may still not be a *justiciable* legal dispute because there are additional constitutional and prudential conditions to bringing a suit in court. Issues of justiciability in this narrower sense are a major concern of all courts and are our major concern in this chapter. The judicial power to decide cases or controversies, as articulated in the *Muskrat* case, has repeatedly been held to apply only to "concrete" cases or controversies—not abstract, philosophical, or generalized grievances. Is there a real conflict at the time that the lawsuit is filed, or does the plaintiff simply believe that there will probably be

---

[7]"Nonjusticiability," said the Supreme Court in *Baker v. Carr,* is "the inappropriateness of the subject matter for judicial consideration." 369 U.S. 186, 198, 82 S.Ct. 691, 7 L.Ed.2d 663, http://laws.findlaw.com/us/369/186.html (1962).

a dispute in the near future? If there is a real conflict at the time the suit is brought, the case is said to be **ripe;** if the conflict has not yet occurred, the case is not ripe for adjudication—it is not justiciable.[8] On the other hand, is the plaintiff complaining about a harm or a conflict that no longer exists? Or is it the kind of dispute for which a court of law cannot fashion an effective remedy? If so, the case may be **moot**—no longer resolvable by a court.[9]

Is the dispute one that is usually, or is properly, resolved by other governmental institutions or by the elective political process?[10] If so, the dispute presents a **political question,** and the courts, though they are essentially governmental and hence "political" institutions themselves, will decline to resolve the dispute and will defer to the other governmental agencies or to the political process.[11]

Finally, has the dispute been brought to court by the appropriate plaintiff? Is the plaintiff actually involved in the conflict, or is the plaintiff simply interested emotionally or intellectually in the conflict? If the plaintiff has not personally suffered a harm that was caused by the action or condition about which the plaintiff is complaining, the plaintiff will not have **standing to sue** (or simply **standing**), and the court, on the motion of the defendant, will dismiss the case because it is not justiciable.[12]

An example of an issue of standing may be helpful. Suppose that a neighbor of yours pays someone $100 to mow her yard every week while she goes on a month's vacation. As a matter of fact, during that month the worker only mows the yard once, the day before the neighbor returns. Under these circumstances, the neighbor could probably bring a breach of contract suit against the worker to recover some or all of

---

[8]On ripeness, for example, see *United Public Workers v. Mitchell,* 330 U.S. 75, 67 S.Ct. 556, 91 L.Ed. 754, http://laws.findlaw.com/us/330/75.html (1947), discussed in Ronald D. Rotunda and John E. Nowak, *Treatise on Constitutional Law: Substance and Procedure,* 3d ed., vol. 1 (St. Paul: West Group, 1999), 207–214. The federal Declaratory Judgment Act, 28 U.S.C. §§2201–2202, which provides litigants with the opportunity to get a judicial determination of their rights and duties under a questioned federal statute *before* a legal injury has been suffered, provides that an action for declaratory judgment may be brought "in cases of actual controversy." This apparent exception to the ripeness requirement was upheld in *Aetna Life Insurance Co. v. Haworth,* 300 U.S. 227, 57 S.Ct. 461, 81 L.Ed 617, http://laws.findlaw.com/us/300/227.html (1937).

[9]See, for example, *DeFunis v. Odegaard,* 416 U.S. 312, 94 S.Ct. 1704, 40 L.Ed.2d 164, http://laws.findlaw.com/us/416/312.html (1974), and the discussion in Rotunda and Nowak, *supra,* 185–207. Mootness should be distinguished from the problem posed by a statute of limitations. Common sense tells us that a victim who suffers a legally recognized injury does not have to sue the injurer while the injury is taking place: that may well be impossible. In their **statutes of limitations,** each state and the federal government give victims a certain amount of time to bring suit for damages. Mootness typically applies to *equity* situations in which the plaintiff is asking for relief from a continuing or ongoing situation that has, at the time the case is brought, come to an indefinite end. The victim whose equity suit is moot may still have a good claim for compensation at *law* in the form of money damages for the harm caused by the previous conduct.

[10]By the elective political process, I mean the practice of throwing out the bums who made or who favor the law and electing enlightened candidates who will change the laws in an appropriate manner.

[11]See *Baker v. Carr, supra,* note 7.

[12]See, for example, *Allen v. Wright,* 468 U.S. 737, 104 S.Ct. 3315, 82 L.Ed.2d 556, http://laws.findlaw.com/us/468/737.html (1984), and *Lujan v. National Wildlife Federation,* 497 U.S. 871, 110 S.Ct. 3177, 111 L.Ed.2d 695, http://laws.findlaw.com/us/497/871.html (1990).

the $100. Your neighbor, however, has other concerns and decides simply to forgive and forget. You, on the other hand, recognize in this instance the terrible depths of man's injustice to man and decide to sue the worker on behalf of your neighbor. Do you have standing to sue the worker for breach of contract? You do not. You, personally, have not suffered a legally recognized harm as a result of the worker's conduct.

A less trivial example of the standing issue is the line of cases in which individuals have gone to court to challenge or prevent some government program or policy and have argued that they have standing to sue by virtue solely of their status as taxpayers. After all, it is their money that the government is spending: the government is injuring them by misspending it. In *Frothingham v. Mellon,* the Supreme Court initially refused to recognize the sufficiency of "taxpayer standing" as legally sufficient, but then indicated a change of heart in *Flast v. Cohen,* only to draw back from the *Flast* decision in *Valley Forge Christian College v. Americans United for Separation of Church and State.*[13]

All of these aspects of justiciability—ripeness, mootness, political questions, and standing to sue, as well as the refusal to issue advisory opinions—are rooted in the constitutional requirement that the judicial power of federal courts be applied only to "actual" cases and controversies.[14] State courts may have different criteria for standing, ripeness, and mootness, and we have already noted that a number of state supreme courts have the authority to render advisory opinions.

## Judicial Review

Finally, the three "J's" that we have been discussing must be distinguished from the fourth "J" of constitutional significance—judicial review. **Judicial review** is the power of courts to declare a statute or governmental action invalid because it conflicts with the United States Constitution.[15] Notice that it is "the power of courts," not just the power of the Supreme Court, the federal courts, or any other particular courts. Unless the statute establishing an American federal or state court actually prohibits it from considering constitutional arguments, every judicial court in the land has the power to invalidate a particular law or governmental action if the law or action contravenes the Constitution.

---

[13]*Frothingham v. Mellon,* 262 U.S. 447, 43 S.Ct. 597, 67 L.Ed. 1078, http://laws.findlaw.com/us/262/447.html (1923); *Flast v. Cohen,* 392 U.S. 83, 88 S.Ct. 1942, 20 L.Ed.2d 947, http://laws.findlaw.com/us/392/83.html (1968); *Valley Forge Christian College v. Americans United for Separation of Church and State, Inc.,* 454 U.S. 464, 102 S.Ct. 752, 70 L.Ed.2d 700, http://laws.findlaw.com/us/454/464.html (1982). See also *Doremus v. Board of Education,* 342 U.S. 429, 72 S.Ct. 394, 96 L.Ed. 475, http://laws.findlaw.com/us/342/429.html (1952).

[14]See *Muskrat v. United States, supra,* note 1. In addition to the constitutional component of the justiciability requirement, there is also a nonconstitutional or "prudential" component. See Rotunda and Nowak, *supra,* note 9, at 174 *et seq.*

[15]The term "judicial review" may also refer simply to the power of courts to review the decisions of other tribunals. See, for example, *Reno v. Catholic Social Services,* 509 U.S. 43, 113 S.Ct. 2485, 125 L.Ed.2d 38, http://laws.findlaw.com/us/509/43.html (1993).

This is true because the Supreme Court, in the case of *Marbury v. Madison,* ruled that the Constitution is not only the political instrument that constituted the fundamental institutions of the American government, but is also a *law,* and as a law, it is subject to interpretation and application by courts.[16] Moreover, the court said that the Constitution is superior to all other laws in the United States. Whenever it conflicts with other laws, the other laws must give way.[17]

The power to exercise judicial review is part of the judicial power of all United States courts and not a separate grant of jurisdiction to the courts. As such, the power to exercise judicial review is also subject to the requirements of jurisdiction and justiciability that were discussed above.

# TYPES OF JURISDICTION

Now that we have surveyed the legal concepts most closely related to the concept of jurisdiction, we shall focus on the concept itself by looking at several different aspects of jurisdiction. These aspects are represented by several pairs of concepts that provide important distinctions in judicial authority.

## Original and Appellate Jurisdiction

**Original jurisdiction** is the authority to consider a case from its initial entry into the judicial system, that is, from its *origins.* Courts of original jurisdiction, called **trial courts,** have authority to decide cases and controversies that require a determination of the pertinent facts and the application of the appropriate legal rules. **Appellate jurisdiction** is the authority to review rulings of other courts. Courts with appellate jurisdiction, called **appellate courts** or **courts of appeals,** have authority to decide cases and controversies that arise from the parties' disagreement over whether another court—a lower trial court or intermediate appellate court in the same legal system—properly determined and applied the legal rules. A particular court may have both original and appellate jurisdiction. The best example of such a court is the United States Supreme Court, the jurisdiction of which is set forth in Article III of the Constitution and is discussed in Chapter 5.

Resolving a legal claim or dispute requires us to (1) determine the facts, (2) determine the appropriate rule or rules to apply to the dispute, and (3) resolve the dispute in accordance with the proper rules. The principal difference between trial courts and appellate courts is that trial courts must perform each of these functions, whereas appellate courts directly perform only the second and third: they decide whether the trial courts determined and applied the rules properly.

---

[16]*Marbury v. Madison,* 5 U.S. (1 Cranch) 137, 2 L.Ed. 60, http://laws.findlaw.com/us/5/137.html (1803). See the Supremacy Clause in Article VI of the Constitution.

[17]The Supreme Court's opinion in *Marbury* closely followed the reasoning of Alexander Hamilton in *Federalist* 78.

Appellate courts may generally review only judicial *rulings* that are alleged by one of the parties to be incorrect and to have significantly affected that party's chance to win at trial. Appellate courts do not find facts. They take no evidence: no witnesses testify and no evidence, verbal or otherwise, is presented to appellate courts for them to "try." The findings of fact made by the trial court—either by the jury in a jury trial or by the judge in a **bench trial,** which is a trial without a jury— are accorded great respect and will not be disturbed unless the appellate court finds them "clearly erroneous."[18] Appellate courts have before them the complete record of the earlier proceedings, which includes all of the pleadings in the case and the transcripts of the trial and hearings. The issues for review are always couched in the formulaic question, "Whether the trial court (or the lower appellate court) erred when it ruled in this particular way or that particular way."

In discussing the functions of appellate courts, we must not assume simply that they decide "appeals," for in this context this term has two distinct meanings, a general and a specific one. Generally, to "appeal" a case is to ask, or to petition, an appellate court to review certain rulings that one of the parties, usually the losing party, believes to be incorrect. Specifically, however, an **appeal** is one particular legal procedure for obtaining appellate court review. This particular legal procedure is also referred to as an **appeal as of right,** signifying that the **appellant,** the party seeking review, has a right to such review and that the appellate court must in fact review the ruling; consider arguments from the appellant and the opposing party, the **appellee** (by which we almost always mean "arguments from the *attorneys* of the parties involved"); and decide the case on the merits. Appellate courts that *must* review the **merits**—that is, the issue(s) that the appellant wants the appeals court to decide—of the cases before them are said to have **mandatory appellate jurisdiction** over those cases.

Parties to a lawsuit do not always have the right to have an appellate court review a ruling. Sometimes the rulings are simply not reviewable at all, and sometimes appellate courts do not have an absolute obligation to review the merits, although they have the authority to review it if they wish to do so. In the latter situation, we say that the appellate courts have **discretionary appellate jurisdiction** over some or all of their cases. This means that the litigant, here called the **petitioner,** who wants the appellate court to review the questioned rulings has only the right to request or petition the appellate court to review the merits. A court exercising discretionary appellate jurisdiction must first determine whether or not to review the case. If the court decides not to review the case, it will render no decision on the merits and the lower court decision will stand as is. Because the decision not to review the case is not a decision on the merits, it cannot serve as formal legal precedent on the legal issues presented for review, even though the practical effect of the

---

[18]Thus, a verdict as such is not reviewed on appeal because a verdict is not a ruling of the court. The effect of appealing or reviewing a verdict is achieved by appealing the judgment that the judge enters upon the verdict. Where the verdict is a general verdict, the judgment usually, but not always, confirms the verdict.

decision not to review the lower court decision is to let the latter decision stand, just as would a decision to affirm the decision.

If, on the other hand, the court decides to accept the case for review, it will then address the arguments of the petitioner and the opposing **respondent** concerning whether the questioned rulings were correct or incorrect, and prejudicial or harmless, and will render a decision on the merits. This decision, whether to "affirm," "reverse," or dispose in some other way of the lower court decision, may then be accompanied by an opinion providing the court's rationale. This opinion may serve as precedent in future similar cases.

The sharp distinction between "appeal" and "review" is often blurred in legal discussions. The term "appeal" is commonly used to refer to "appeals as of right" as well as to the whole practice of asking an appellate court to review a ruling. Accordingly, throughout our discussions we shall generally use the terms "appeal" and "review" synonymously, taking care to distinguish the two when necessary.

Since very few of the cases that are filed in courts of original jurisdiction ever proceed as far as a trial, we ought also to mention several other important functions of trial courts. Many of the rulings made by judges are made in **hearings,** nonjury proceedings in which one or both of the parties make formal requests, called **motions;** orally argue about motions; and perhaps present evidence that the judge hears and responds to. The motions range over a great array of matters. For example, attorneys for a criminal defendant may **move**—make a motion—to prevent the prosecutor from presenting certain evidence at trial because they argue that it was improperly obtained. The court must decide the issue and rule on it, and that ruling may be reviewable.

The point here is that each time a judge responds to a motion, each time he resolves a disputed issue, the court *rules,* and the party who opposed that particular ruling may be able to ask an appellate court to review the ruling. Many of these rulings are made not during a trial but during pretrial proceedings.[19]

We have noted above that not all rulings are reviewable. This fact reflects the general principle that due process does not generally necessitate a right to appeal a ruling or even to petition for its review to a court with appellate jurisdiction.[20] The notion of a hierarchical court structure with some courts occupied exclusively with reviewing the decisions of other courts for mistakes is relatively recent. Maitland commented on the status of appellate review in the early centuries of the common law:

> We must not here introduce the notion of an "appeal" from court to court, for that is a modern notion. In old times he who goes from court to court does not go there merely to get a mistake put right, to get an erroneous judgment reversed; he goes there to lodge a complaint against his lord or the judges of his lord's court, to accuse his lord of having made default in justice . . . , to accuse the judges of having

---

[19]The rulings in question might also be issued in response to motions made after the trial, which are called "posttrial motions."

[20]See, for example, *Smith v. Robbins,* 528 U.S. 259, 270n5 120 S.Ct. 746, 145 L.Ed.2d 756, http://laws.findlaw.com/us/528/259.html (2000).

pronounced a false judgment; he challenges his judges and they may have to defend their judgment by their oaths or by their bodies. Still the king has here an acknowledged claim to be the supreme judge over all judges, and this claim can be pressed and extended, for if it profits the king it profits the great mass of the people also.[21]

Thus, the Court of King's Bench from early in its development reviewed the decisions of the Court of Common Pleas, but a more extensive system of appellate review took centuries to develop. Even in 1789 in the first Judiciary Act, Congress did not provide for appellate review of federal criminal cases!

Today, however, not only one, but two levels of appellate review for each case usually exist in American court systems. Where this is true, the "lower court" whose rulings are being appealed to a "higher court" may itself be a court of appellate jurisdiction. Thus, in the federal system, the principal trial courts are the United States district courts, whose appealable rulings can usually be appealed as of right to an intermediate appellate court, called a United States Court of Appeals for a particular circuit. The rulings or decisions of the court of appeals may then be reviewable by the United States Supreme Court, the court of last resort in the federal system. Federal litigants thus get three bites at the apple.

---

## Examples of Federal Court Appellate Jurisdiction

### United States Courts of Appeals

28 U.S.C. § 1291: The courts of appeals (other than the United States Court of Appeals for the Federal Circuit) shall have jurisdiction of appeals from all final decisions of the district courts of the United States, the United States District Court for the District of the Canal Zone, the District Court of Guam, and the District Court of the Virgin Islands, except where a direct review may be had in the Supreme Court. The jurisdiction of the United States Court of Appeals for the Federal Circuit shall be limited to the jurisdiction described in sections 1292(c) and (d) and 1295 of this title.

### United States Supreme Court

28 U.S.C. § 1258: Final judgments or decrees rendered by the Supreme Court of the Commonwealth of Puerto Rico may be reviewed by the Supreme Court by writ of certiorari where the validity of a treaty or statute of the United States is drawn in question or where the validity of a statute of the Commonwealth of Puerto Rico is drawn in question on the ground of its being repugnant to the Constitution, treaties, or laws of the United States, or where any title, right, privilege, or immunity is specially set up or claimed under the Constitution or the treaties or statutes of, or any commission held or authority exercised under, the United States.

---

[21]Maitland, *Forms of Action at Common* Law, 11. *By oath:* compurgation; *by their bodies:* in trial by battle.

State litigants may get four bites. States with two levels of appellate courts resemble the federal system just described, but some decisions of the state courts of last resort, typically but not always called the "state supreme courts," may be reviewed by the United States Supreme Court.

Appellate review has two aspects. We have thus far viewed it from the perspective of a litigant, for whom an appellate court may correct a judicial wrong that the litigant has suffered in the legal system. We must also view the appellate function from the perspective of the highest court, or court of last resort, in a legal system. From this point of view, we see appellate review as the means by which the courts in the system provide uniform justice to all litigants and thus cohere into a single, hierarchical system. An appellate court usually reviews the rulings of a number of different judges and sometimes a number of different judicial institutions. Using the principle of stare decisis, the principle that similar cases should be decided according to the same legal rules, appellate courts sit as monitors of the courts below them. By reviewing the rulings and affirming or reversing the judgments of the lower courts, the appellate courts supervise them and assure uniformity throughout the system. If the system has more than one appellate court directly reviewing trial court rulings—as, for example, the federal system has with its more than a dozen United States courts of appeals—an even higher appellate court, the court of last resort, performs the same supervising and unifying function on the intermediate courts of appeals that are below it. Thus, many decisions of the United States Supreme Court are intended to put all of the United States courts of appeals on the same page by providing these intermediate appellate courts with the legal rules that they, in turn, are obligated to apply in the cases brought before them from the federal trial courts. In this way, a degree of uniformity is imposed on the system.[22]

Review by *higher* courts of rulings of *lower* courts is called **direct review** or direct appeal. Federal and state trial courts may also review state court criminal proceedings by means of writs of habeas corpus. This type of review is called **collateral review**—authoritative review not by a higher court in the same system but by a trial court in the same or in another system. Collateral review is discussed in more detail in Chapter 3.

## Exclusive and Concurrent Jurisdiction

Authority of one court or legal system, to the exclusion of other courts, to decide certain cases is **exclusive jurisdiction.** Authority that is shared with other courts is **concurrent jurisdiction.** Exclusive and concurrent jurisdiction are concepts that describe both the relations between courts in a particular judicial system, be it one of the state systems or the federal system, as well as relations between courts in different systems, notably between state courts and federal courts.

Within the federal judiciary there are several courts of original jurisdiction—the United States district courts, the United States Court of Federal Claims, and the United States Court of International Trade, to name just three.

---

[22]But only a degree; there is never complete uniformity throughout a system.

## Examples of Concurrent Jurisdiction in Federal Trial Courts

### U. S. District Courts and Court of Federal Claims

28 U.S.C. §1346(a): The district courts shall have original jurisdiction, concurrent with the United States Court of Federal Claims, of:

(1) Any civil action against the United States for the recovery of any internal-revenue tax alleged to have been erroneously or illegally assessed or collected, or any penalty claimed to have been collected without authority or any sum alleged to have been excessive or in any manner wrongfully collected under the internal-revenue laws.

See also 28 U.S.C. §1491(b)(1): Both the Unite[d] States Court of Federal Claims and the district courts of the United States shall have jurisdiction to render judgment on an action by an interested party objecting to a solicitation by a Federal agency for bids or proposals for a proposed contract or to a proposed award or the award of a contract or any alleged violation of statute or regulation in connection with a procurement or a proposed procurement. Both the United States Court of Federal Claims and the district courts of the United States shall have jurisdiction to entertain such an action without regard to whether suit is instituted before or after the contract is awarded.

Sometimes the federal jurisdiction over a particular matter is concurrent, that is, it is shared by more than one court. (See the sidebar above.) Thus, the original jurisdiction over many civil cases in which the United States is a defendant is held concurrently by the United States district courts and the United States Court of Federal Claims. On the other hand, some jurisdiction of the district courts over cases in which the United States is the defendant is exclusive, while in certain commerce and antitrust matters the district court is excluded from jurisdiction: the court of international trade exercises exclusive jurisdiction.

To take an example from state law, in Pennsylvania **probate jurisdiction**—the authority to determine or prove the validity of a will—was once possessed exclusively by "orphans' courts" in counties that had such institutions; in counties without them, the courts of common pleas exercised probate jurisdiction as part of their general, original jurisdiction. The statute below expresses the current basic allocation of original jurisdiction among Pennsylvania courts.

The appellate jurisdiction of a court may also be exclusive or concurrent. Thus, the United States Court of Appeals for the Federal Circuit and the other 12 territorial United States courts of appeals each exercise exclusive appellate jurisdiction over certain federal cases. The jurisdiction of the United States courts of appeals for the first through eleventh circuits and the District of Columbia circuit is exclusive on most appeals because no other federal court has been given the jurisdiction set forth in 28 U.S.C. §1291; the jurisdiction of the Court of Appeals for the Federal Circuit is exclusive because of explicit statutory language in §§1292 and 1295 granting such

# The United States District Courts, Court of International Trade, and Court of Federal Claims Jurisdiction

Great care is taken to delineate the boundaries between the jurisdiction of these three trial courts. Several statutes exclude the United States district courts from jurisdiction possessed by the court of international trade. For example, 28 U.S.C. §1337(a) and (c); see also 28 U.S.C. §1340. 28 U.S.C. §1491(c) similarly excludes the court of federal claims from the jurisdiction of the court of international trade. Finally, Sections 1581–84 of Title 28 set forth the jurisdiction of the court of international trade, all of which is exclusive and therefore makes questionable the need to indicate separately the exclusions in §§1337(c) , 1340, and 1491(c).

28 U.S.C. §1337: (a) The district courts shall have original jurisdiction of any civil action or proceeding arising under any Act of Congress regulating commerce or protecting trade and commerce against restraints and monopolies. . . .

(c) The district courts shall not have jurisdiction under this section of any matter within the exclusive jurisdiction of the Court of International Trade under chapter 95 of this title.

28 U.S.C. §1491(c): Nothing herein shall be construed to give the United States Court of Federal Claims jurisdiction of any civil action within the exclusive jurisdiction of the Court of International Trade, or of any action against, or founded on conduct of, the Tennessee Valley Authority, or to amend or modify the provisions of the Tennessee Valley Authority Act of 1933 with respect to actions by or against the Authority.

# Example of Exclusive and Concurrent Jurisdiction in *State* Trial Courts: Pennsylvania

### Courts of Common Pleas

42 Pa.C.S. § 931. Original jurisdiction and venue.

(a) General rule.—Except where exclusive original jurisdiction of an action or proceeding is by statute or by general rule adopted pursuant to section 503 (relating to reassignment of matters) vested in another court of this Commonwealth, the courts of common pleas shall have unlimited original jurisdiction of all actions and proceedings, including all actions and proceedings heretofore cognizable by law or usage in the courts of common pleas.

(b) Concurrent and exclusive jurisdiction.—The jurisdiction of the courts of common pleas under this section shall be exclusive except with respect to actions and proceedings concurrent jurisdiction of which is by statute or by general rule adopted pursuant to section 503 vested in another court of this Commonwealth or in the district justices.

---

# Example of Exclusive Jurisdiction in Federal Appellate Courts

### United States Court of Appeals for the Federal Circuit

28 U.S.C. §1292(c) reads as follows:

> (c) The United States Court of Appeals for the Federal Circuit shall have exclusive jurisdiction—
>
> (1) of an appeal from an interlocutory order or decree described in subsection (a) or (b) of this section in any case over which the court would have jurisdiction of an appeal under section 1295 of this title; and
>
> (2) of an appeal from a judgment in a civil action for patent infringement which would otherwise be appealable to the United States Court of Appeals for the Federal Circuit and is final except for an accounting.

(28 U.S.C. §1295 enumerates 14 grants of exclusive jurisdiction for the Court of Appeals for the Federal Circuit.)

---

jurisdiction, and because of the language in §1291 expressly limiting the federal circuit's jurisdiction.

Again using an example from Pennsylvania, the two Pennsylvania intermediate appellate courts, the Superior Court and the Commonwealth Court, also possess exclusive appellate jurisdiction over different kinds of cases under Pennsylvania law.

The distinction between exclusive and concurrent jurisdiction also helps to explain the relations between federal and state courts. While this area of law, like so many others, is intriguingly (not to say *lucratively,* from an attorney's point of view) complex, there are several principles that serve as good points of departure.

Federal courts do not generally have jurisdiction over matters arising purely out of state law unless the case satisfies the requirements of §1332 diversity jurisdiction. If no diversity jurisdiction exists, state court jurisdiction over state law issues is exclusive of the federal courts. The corresponding exclusivity is not true of federal court jurisdiction over cases arising purely under federal law: the Constitution, federal statutes, and federal treaties. In these cases, jurisdiction is presumed to be concurrent: "[S]tate courts may assume subject-matter jurisdiction over a federal cause of action absent provision by Congress to the contrary or disabling incompatibility between the federal claim and state-court adjudication."[23] This rule is cast in terms of a **presumption**—a fact that the courts assume to be true unless the presumption is **rebutted,** or over-

---

[23]*Gulf Offshore Co. v. Mobil Oil Corp.,* 453 U.S. 473, 477–78 101 S.Ct. 2870, 69 L.Ed.2d 784, http://laws.findlaw.com/us/453/473.html (1981), citing *Dowd Box Co. v. Courtney,* 368 U.S. 502, 82 S.Ct. 519, 7 L.Ed.2d 483, http://laws.findlaw.com/us/368/502.html (1962).

# Examples of Exclusive Jurisdiction in State Appellate Courts: Pennsylvania

### Pennsylvania Superior Court

42 Pa.C.S. §742. Appeals from courts of common pleas.

The Superior Court shall have exclusive appellate jurisdiction of all appeals from final orders of the courts of common pleas, regardless of the nature of the controversy or the amount involved, except such classes of appeals as are by any provision of this chapter within the exclusive jurisdiction of the Supreme Court or the Commonwealth Court.

### Pennsylvania Commonwealth Court

42 Pa. C.S. § 762. Appeals from courts of common pleas.

(a) General rule.—Except as provided in subsection (b), the Commonwealth Court shall have exclusive jurisdiction of appeals from final orders of the courts of common pleas in the following cases:

1. Commonwealth civil cases . . .
2. Governmental and Commonwealth regulatory criminal cases . . .
3. Secondary review of certain appeals from Commonwealth agencies . . .
4. Local government civil and criminal matters . . .
5. Certain private corporation matters . . .
6. Eminent domain . . .
7. Immunity waiver matters . . .

(The numbered sections explain the named types of cases in more detail.)

come, by other evidence. "In considering the propriety of state-court jurisdiction over any particular federal claim, the [Supreme] Court begins with the presumption that state courts enjoy concurrent jurisdiction" with the corresponding federal courts. That presumption in favor of state-federal concurrent jurisdiction over cases arising out of federal law can be rebutted, but the presumption is a strong one.[24]

---

[24] The Court in *Gulf Offshore Company* points to three grounds for rebutting the presumption in favor of concurrent jurisdiction in federal cases. First, an "explicit statutory directive" will defeat the presumption. For example, in cases involving admiralty or maritime jurisdiction, the federal jurisdictional statute states that "the district courts shall have original jurisdiction, exclusive of the States." See, for example, 28 U.S.C. §1333. Second, the presumption will be defeated by "unmistakable implication from legislative history"— for example, a clear, unopposed statement in a congressional committee report or in the record of the floor debate in the Senate or House that exclusive jurisdiction is intended. A third basis for rebutting the presumption, says the Court, is "a clear incompatibility between state-court jurisdiction and federal interests." This ground will be determined by the courts on the basis of the arguments of counsel.

State courts routinely adjudicate claims of federal constitutional rights raised in criminal cases and in civil rights cases. State courts also routinely interpret and apply federal statutes in cases before them. It is definitely *not* true that state courts handle only cases arising under state law and that federal courts handle only cases arising under federal law: state courts often decide cases arising under federal law, and federal courts, exercising §1332 diversity jurisdiction, often decide cases arising under state law.

## General and Limited Jurisdiction

The English-American courts developed within the common law tradition, as explained in Chapter 1. Those courts that have jurisdiction over any case or action that was recognized at common law are called courts of **general jurisdiction.** On the other hand, those courts that are created to adjudicate only certain types of cases, as determined by their jurisdiction over the subject matter or over particular classes of parties, are called courts of **limited** or **special jurisdiction.** In the United States, states have courts of general jurisdiction.[25] States may also create courts of limited jurisdiction.

Federal courts created pursuant to Article III of the Constitution alone are courts of limited jurisdiction because Article III, Section 2, specifies the limits of federal jurisdiction. Thus, the only jurisdiction that these federal courts have is the jurisdiction granted to them by Congress in federal statutes that are based on Article III. Because Article III does not contain a grant of jurisdiction over cases arising purely under state law, these federal courts do not have such jurisdiction.

As we shall see in Chapter 4, Congress can create courts to serve as courts of general jurisdiction for United States territories, and Congress has granted some of these territorial courts Article III jurisdiction as well. The general jurisdiction of such courts comes not from Article III but from the power of Congress under Articles I and IV to provide the necessary rules and regulations for the District of Columbia and the other territories belonging to the United States.

We noted above that no single court in the United States has jurisdiction over every kind of case, nor does any particular court have jurisdiction over every single action recognizable at common law. This does not mean that no true courts of general jurisdiction exist. States may take away from courts of general jurisdiction the jurisdiction over certain classes of cases, yet the court is still a court of general jurisdiction. This is reflected in one very practical consequence. In courts of general jurisdiction, the court assumes that it has jurisdiction over every case brought before it unless a party brings the court's lack of jurisdiction to the court's attention. In courts of limited jurisdiction, the court assumes that it does not have jurisdiction over a case

---

[25]For example, see the Pennsylvania statute, 42 Pa.C.S. §931, quoted in the sidebar, "Example of Exclusive and Concurrent Jurisdiction," *supra,* that creates the state's court of general jurisdiction, called the court of common pleas.

brought before it, and thus the party seeking the jurisdiction of the court must specifically plead—that is, must explicitly indicate—the statutory basis of jurisdiction. In cases brought in federal court, the first thing in the complaint filed with the court is a jurisdictional statement, usually a reference to a federal statute, explaining the basis of federal jurisdiction.

A more significant incident of general as opposed to limited jurisdiction is the traditional and inherent—perhaps "traditionally inherent" or "inherent by tradition" would be more apt—power of common law courts of general jurisdiction to expand the law by recognizing new causes of action and exercising the consequent power of remedying new legal harms without legislative action.

## Jurisdiction of the Subject Matter and Jurisdiction over the Parties

A useful distinction when reviewing the federal court jurisdiction outlined in Article III of the Constitution is that between jurisdiction of the subject matter and jurisdiction over the parties. Both of these terms refer to the kinds of cases a court may decide. Jurisdiction of the subject matter, or **subject matter jurisdiction,** refers to the nature of the dispute: subject matter jurisdiction is the authority to adjudicate certain cases on the basis of the topics or questions at issue and not on the basis of who the plaintiffs or defendants are. **Jurisdiction over the parties** refers to the nature of the parties: it is the power to adjudicate certain cases because of who the parties are, not because of the nature of the legal issues.[26]

Article III, Section 2, of the Constitution outlines the potential jurisdiction of federal courts in terms of these two categories of jurisdiction. The opening clause of Section 2 reads, "The judicial Power shall extend to all Cases, in Law and Equity, arising under this Constitution, the Laws of the United States, and Treaties made, or which shall be made, under their Authority." This statement refers only to the classes of questions presented in the cases. It makes no reference to the nature of the parties and is therefore an example of subject matter jurisdiction. The clause in Section 2 that follows—"to all Cases affecting Ambassadors, other public Ministers and Consuls"— makes no mention of the types of questions: it grants jurisdiction because of the identity of the parties. The next clause is again an example of subject matter jurisdiction, ("to all Cases of admiralty and maritime Jurisdiction"), and the one that follows ("to Controversies to which the United States shall be a Party") exemplifies again jurisdiction over the parties.

---

[26]"Jurisdiction over the parties," in this limited context, must not be confused with the more common legal concept of **personal jurisdiction** or jurisdiction over the person. A court generally cannot render a judgment against someone unless that person or party has been properly notified of the action and of the opportunity to defend himself. The power of the court to render a judgment against a particular individual is personal jurisdiction. It is discussed in greater detail in Chapter 3.

## CONCLUSION

This outline of the different concepts of court jurisdiction will be helpful in understanding the structure of any American judicial system and particularly of the federal system. Though the relations between federal courts are often explained by the use of charts made up of boxes and arrows, a sound understanding of the structure requires a basic understanding of the types of jurisdiction—original and appellate, exclusive and concurrent—that Congress grants to each court in the system.

# Chapter 3

# Litigation

## Chapter Outline

This chapter outlines the basic steps of judicial procedure at the trial and the appellate levels, paying particular attention to those steps at which a trial court is routinely called upon to make rulings that may be challenged on appeal. The appellate review of such rulings is the substance of most of the decisions and opinions that appear in legal casebooks.

# CIVIL CASES AND CRIMINAL CASES

In the common law courts, there are two broad categories of cases—criminal and civil—and before we attempt to understand the general procedures common to both categories, we should have a basic idea of the nature of each kind of litigation. A criminal case pits the government, represented by a **prosecutor,** against a **defendant.** The prosecutor alleges that the defendant is **guilty** of violating one or more criminal laws. The purpose of the litigation is to determine **beyond a reasonable doubt** whether the defendant has done so, and if so, to have the court impose a penalty. Usually, the penalty is a monetary fine paid to the state, some sort of restriction on the convicted defendant's liberty, or both. A defendant found guilty beyond a reasonable doubt is **convicted** of the crime.

In civil litigation, which at this point we may define as all litigation other than criminal, a **plaintiff,** who may be a government or a private party, sues, or brings an action against, a defendant, who also may be a government or a private party. The plaintiff alleges that the defendant caused a legal harm to the plaintiff and that the court should order the defendant to provide the **relief** or remedy that the plaintiff requests. The purpose of the litigation is to determine the defendant's **liability,** or legal responsibility, for the plaintiff's legal injuries. To do this, the court must find by a "preponderance of the evidence" or, in some cases, by the higher measure of "clear and convincing evidence" that the plaintiff's allegations are true and that the defendant has no valid reason to be excused from liability. If these requirements are met, the defendant is found "liable."

Civil cases can be further divided into two kinds: **legal actions** and **equitable suits.**[1] Relief in legal actions is usually in the form of money, called **money damages** or **compensatory damages,** to compensate the plaintiff for the injury. In cases where the defendant has been found liable for particularly harmful or blameworthy behavior, the court might also award the plaintiff additional money, called **punitive** or **exemplary damages,** in order to punish the defendant and deter others from similar behavior. Apart from the fact that they are paid to the plaintiff, who in a civil case is also the victim of the defendant's legally wrong actions, and not to the state, punitive damages are often a lot like the fines imposed on defendants in criminal cases.

Relief in equitable suits is usually in the form of the court ordering the defendant to perform or to refrain from performing some action. The court may order **specific performance** to require a defendant to do something, such as transfer property, or it may issue a **temporary restraining order** or **preliminary injunction,** followed by a **permanent injunction,** to **enjoin,** or prevent, a defendant from doing something.

To recap, in a criminal case, a prosecutor attempts to prove a defendant guilty of violating one or more criminal laws. If found guilty beyond a reasonable doubt, the defendant is convicted of the crime and is punished in terms of either losing property or losing personal freedom. Compensating the victim for injuries is not the pur-

---

[1]The use of the term **action** to refer to civil litigation in law and the term **suit** to refer to civil litigation in equity, while correct, is often not followed, and lawyers and laymen alike often talk about any kind of litigation as a "lawsuit" or a "legal action."

pose of a criminal prosecution, although **restitution,** restoring to the victim some or all of what was lost because of the crime, is often ordered. In a civil case, a plaintiff seeks to prove a defendant liable for the plaintiff's injuries. If found to be liable by a preponderance or a clear and convincing standard, the defendant is ordered to compensate the plaintiff-victim for his injuries or, in an equity suit, to do something or to cease doing something in order to remove the cause of the plaintiff's injuries.

One notable difference between criminal and civil cases is the attitude of the various American legal systems toward nontrial settlements of the underlying disputes out of which litigation arises. It is a well-established principle that in civil cases the law encourages voluntary settlements of the disputes "out of court," meaning without a trial. Settlement avoids the uncertainty of jury determinations and also the great expense of trial attorney fees. There may be such a thing as an "open and shut case," but juries often seem to have difficulty grasping the concept, and this makes any trial risky for both parties. The overwhelming majority of civil cases—and criminal cases, too, as we shall see—that are filed in court are settled by the adverse parties, or dropped by the plaintiffs, or "thrown out" of court on motions to dismiss or motions for summary judgment before the cases reach trial. Our state and federal legal systems depend on these high rates of attrition. If the proportion of trials to settlements, in particular, were to increase by just a few percent, the additional demand for trials would gridlock the courts.

The law encourages settlements of criminal cases, too, but criminal cases pose a more complicated situation. Prosecutors have the legal authority, if they can stand the political pressure, to stop a case ("drop the charges") against a defendant for various reasons. In the case of less serious crimes and in cases in which the prosecution must rely primarily upon the testimony of the victim to prove guilt, the prosecutor may drop the charges against a suspect if the victim refuses to "press charges"—that is, to testify against the defendant and to otherwise cooperate with the prosecutor. If the charges are dropped sufficiently early in the litigation, the prosecutor may have the opportunity to file the same or amended charges against the defendant at a later date. But once the formal trial process begins, the prosecutor might be barred by the Fifth Amendment guarantee against double jeopardy from dropping the charges and then refiling charges later.

The defendant, of course, has much less control over the process. Defendants may offer to plead guilty to some charges in exchange for (1) the prosecutor dropping other, usually more serious, charges and (2) the prosecutor's recommendation to the judge that a particular sentence be imposed on the defendant. Such **plea bargains** may benefit the defendant, who then will have a good idea of how the case will come out and what the ultimate sentence will be, and they benefit the prosecutor, who avoids the time, expense, and unpredictability of trials. But the judge in the case does not have to accept the bargain arrived at by the prosecutor and the defendant, in which case the two parties may try to bargain anew or may decide to take the case to trial. The parties' control over the settlement is limited.

A criminal defendant may seldom successfully offer to do something—for example, compensate a victim for any alleged injuries he might have caused—in return for having the charges dropped. And never may the two parties—prosecutor and defendant—determine guilt and punishment exclusively between themselves, even if the defendant willingly concedes that all of the charges against him are true and is willing to accept any punishment the prosecutor may choose. In such cases, as in all criminal cases, only the court, in formal session, has the authority to sentence a defendant to a particular punishment.

With this background in mind, let us look at typical procedures in civil and criminal cases, and then turn to appellate procedure in general, for appellate courts generally follow the same procedures in both civil and criminal cases. We will also examine "collateral review" in the form of federal habeas corpus procedures.

Our discussions will make some references to different sets of federal rules of procedure—specifically, the Federal Rules of Civil Procedure ("Fed.R.Civ.P.") and the Federal Rules of Criminal Procedure ("Fed.R.Crim.P.")—but each of these general sets of rules is similar to the corresponding rules of the judicial systems of the various states.[2] Thus, familiarity with one set of rules will be helpful to one who is trying to understand another. This does not mean that a lawyer may safely disregard the specific requirements of the system in which he is litigating, however; within the framework of the general rules, each forum—each circuit, each local court, and even each judge—has its own rules and procedures that an attorney must follow. In all litigation, adherence by the parties' counsel to the procedural rules is essential to maintaining the action and presenting the defense.

# CIVIL PROCEDURE

## Pleadings

A civil case is formally begun when the plaintiff files an official court document—a **pleading**—often called a **complaint**.[3] In state courts that follow the older **fact pleading** approach, the complaint must allege the specific facts that constitute the legal harm of which the plaintiff complains. In other state courts and in the federal courts, which follow the **notice pleading** approach, less factual detail must be set out. The complaint must merely give enough facts to convey to the defendant the nature of the legal action brought against him by the plaintiff in order that the defendant may take the necessary steps to develop a defense.

The function of notifying the defendant about the nature of the legal action, a function that is necessary in both the fact and notice pleading approaches, leads immediately to a second requirement for beginning a lawsuit: actual notification of the defendant (Rule 4). This requirement is referred to as obtaining **personal jurisdiction** or **in personam jurisdiction** over the defendant. It often requires serving

---

[2]These rules and the Federal Rules of Appellate Procedure ("Fed.R.App.P.") are available at the following Web sites: Fed. R. Civ. P. at http://www.law.cornell.edu/rules/frcp/overview.htm, Fed. R. Crim. P. at http://www.law.cornell.edu/rules/frcrmp/ and Fed. R. App. P. at http://classaction.findlaw.com/research/frap.pdf.

[3]Fed. R. Civ. P. 3. All subsequent references to the Federal Rules of Civil Procedure in this section of the chapter will be referred to simply as "Rule," such as "Rule 3," "Rule 4," and so on.

the defendant in person with a copy of the complaint. Sometimes, the defendant cannot be found and therefore cannot be served. This may be because the defendant is intentionally avoiding being served or because the plaintiff, through no fault of his own, does not know where to find the defendant. It may also be because the defendant is too far away from the territory over which the court has jurisdiction. Generally in such cases, the lawsuit stalls until the defendant can be properly served.[4]

The notice function of the complaint and the personal jurisdiction requirement are logical consequences of an adversarial legal system that determines the legal rights and liabilities of parties by requiring that they present, or have the guaranteed opportunity to present, their best arguments to a neutral authority. Sometimes, however, the courts are willing to take action on behalf of a plaintiff before and without hearing from the defendant. Such proceedings in equity, called **ex parte** proceedings, though rare, occur in situations in which a present and continuing harm is taking place or will imminently take place unless the court restrains or enjoins the defendant from acting. Even then, however, reasonable efforts must be made to notify the defendant and give him the opportunity to appear before the court.

Another function of the complaint filing requirement is to meet the **statute of limitations** deadline. With few exceptions, civil cases must be filed within a certain statutorily defined period of time following either the occurrence or, perhaps, the discovery of the alleged harm. Actions that are not filed within the limitations period may be dismissed.

Having been served with the complaint, what can the defendant do in response? The rules provide a number of alternatives. One is to do nothing. In this case, the plaintiff, having proved to the court that the defendant was properly served with the complaint and was thus given an opportunity to defend the suit, may win a **default judgment:** the court will consider all of the allegations in the complaint to be true and may rule in favor of the plaintiff and award some or all of the relief prayed for by the plaintiff (Rule 55).

Secondly, the defendant can challenge the jurisdiction or the venue of the court in which the complaint has been filed.[5] All courts are limited by law with regard to the range of cases that they have authority to decide. In a court of limited jurisdiction, the plaintiff must indicate in the complaint the basis of the court's jurisdiction. If the plaintiff is not correct, a federal court, for example, may *sua sponte*—on its own initiative—question its jurisdiction and dismiss the case if it decides the necessary jurisdiction is lacking. In a state court of general jurisdiction, it is up to the parties— the defendant in this case—to bring to the attention of the court the issue of jurisdiction. **Venue** refers to the propriety of the geographical location of the court in which the complaint has been filed.

---

[4]Another aspect to personal jurisdiction is the fact that not everyone may be hailed into a particular court to defend himself against a lawsuit even if he is served. If a party is sued, constitutional due process requires a certain minimum contact by the party with the state in which the court is located. See *International Shoe Co. v. Washington*, 326 U.S. 310, 66 S.Ct. 154, 90 L.Ed. 95, http://laws.findlaw.com/us/326/310.html (1945).

[5]Rule 12(b) provides a variety of grounds to attack the complaint.

Thirdly, the defendant may file an answer in response to the plaintiff's complaint (Rule 12(a)). In the **answer**—the main responsive pleading to the complaint—the defendant may concede or deny any or all of the allegations in the complaint, or may offer **affirmative defenses,** which are legally recognized excuses to the legal harm set forth in the complaint. For example, the defendant may offer the defense that the action is barred by a statute of limitations—in other words, the defense that the action was brought too late.

The defendant may also go on the offensive and bring an action, called a **counterclaim,** against the plaintiff; may add other parties who are not named in the plaintiff's complaint but are involved in the underlying transaction that gave rise to the plaintiff's suit (called "**joinder,**" or joining other parties); or may bring actions, called **crossclaims,** against other defendants.[6]

At this stage of the proceedings, legal issues begin to develop that require resolution by the trial court. For example, in response to a complaint, a defendant may want to make a "motion to dismiss" or "motion to dismiss for failure to state a claim."[7] This motion says, in effect, that even if everything in the complaint were true, the allegations still fail to show a legal wrong for which judicial relief is available to the plaintiff. The plaintiff, in turn, faced with the motion, will probably argue that the allegations do indeed show a justiciable legal wrong. The disagreement constitutes an **issue or question of law**—"Does the complaint state grounds upon which relief can be granted?"—upon which the court must rule. If the court rules that the defendant is correct, the plaintiff will often have an opportunity to amend the complaint, but sometimes the court will dismiss the complaint. In that instance, the plaintiff is out of court and might wish to appeal the ruling in order to get back into court. If, on the other hand, the court rules in favor of the plaintiff, the defendant will not be allowed to appeal immediately, but instead will have to go ahead and file an answer to the complaint, reserving objections to the complaint till a later date.[8]

---

[6]See Rules 13 and 19.

[7]Rule 12(b)(6). This is called a **demurrer** in some state courts.

[8]The rules for determining when and which rulings may be appealed are based primarily on a concern for economy and efficiency in litigation. With some exceptions, parties may only seek appellate review after the trial court has issued a **final judgment** that would otherwise terminate the litigation. In the example of the motion to dismiss, the ruling that the defendant is correct and that the plaintiff's suit is dismissed is clearly a final judgment because unless the plaintiff can persuade the appellate court to reverse the trial court, the plaintiff's suit is dead.

On the other hand, a ruling against the defendant on a motion to dismiss—that is, a ruling that the complaint does indeed contain allegations establishing a claim upon which relief can be granted by a court—does not terminate the litigation: it allows the litigation to continue. This ruling, then, is not a final judgment, and an appeal at this stage of the litigation would be an **interlocutory appeal**—an appeal taken in the middle of an ongoing legal action rather than after a final judgment has been entered in the case. To permit this and other interlocutory appeals to be brought before appellate courts immediately would significantly prolong the litigation because the proceedings in the trial court would have to be held in abeyance until the appellate court resolves the issue raised by the appeal. Litigation punctuated by interlocutory appeals might stretch on interminably, and therefore reforms of legal procedure over the last century have severely curtailed the number of permissible interlocutory appeals.

The defendant's answer also is a major source of legal issues. For example, suppose a plaintiff alleges that the defendant speeded through a red light and hit the plaintiff's car broadside: the defendant denies the light was red. This disagreement—namely, whether the defendant's car did indeed run a red light—presents an **issue or question of fact** that the trier of fact (the judge or a jury) must ultimately determine based upon the evidence presented by the parties at trial.

Or suppose that the defendant answers that the plaintiff filed the complaint one day too late under the applicable statute of limitations; the plaintiff replies by arguing that the defendant is citing the wrong statute and that the complaint was indeed filed in time under the appropriate statute. This question of which statute of limitations is the appropriate one gives rise to an issue or question of law that the court must resolve by a ruling after it gives both parties an opportunity to present their arguments in writing, at a hearing, or through both.

As in the case of motions to dismiss, the ruling on the statute of limitations question can be appealed if the court finds for the defendant, for then the plaintiff will be out of court and the ruling will be a final judgment. The defendant cannot appeal the ruling if the court rules for the plaintiff. We must also note that given the liberal approach of the federal courts to amending incorrect or incomplete pleadings, if the problem with the plaintiff's (or the defendant's) pleading can be corrected by rewriting it, the losing party may well be permitted to file an amended pleading and to continue the case (Rule 15).

## Pretrial Procedure

Assuming that the parties have survived any challenges to the pleadings, the case enters a new stage of development—**discovery.** The pretrial discovery phase of litigation has one overriding purpose: the determination of just exactly what material facts, if any, are in dispute between the parties. **Material facts** are facts that are directly relevant to proving the plaintiff's causes of action or proving the defendant's legal defenses. Do the parties disagree about what happened? Or do the parties agree on the facts but disagree on their legal significance? At this stage of litigation, the parties—encouraged and to some degree directed by the court—attempt to investigate and discover the facts in an effort to determine the issues on which they cannot agree. In addressing these questions, the discovery process enables the parties and the court to decide whether a trial is necessary in order to resolve any significant factual disputes or, if there are no disagreements about the facts, whether a hearing on the legal questions alone will be sufficient.

The discovery phase often begins with a case management conference with the parties and the judge in the case. The judge may then issue an order plotting in some detail the course of the subsequent discovery, the deadlines for pretrial motions, and the date for the pretrial conference. Although Rule 26 of the Federal Rules *requires* the parties to disclose to each other several categories of information and documents relevant to the case, the parties often send additional requests for the production of documents to the other parties as well as sending them a set of written questions, or **interrogatories,** that the parties are required to answer. Document production is often the key to subsequent discovery.

## Table 3.1

### General Stages of Discovery

1. Case management conference or order
2. Rule 26 compulsory document production
3. Request for production of documents (Rule 34)
4. Written interrogatories (Rule 33)
5. Depositions (Rules 27–32)
6. Motions for summary judgment (Rule 56)
7. Hearing on summary judgment
8. Pretrial conference

Once the written discovery has been substantially completed, the attorneys may take depositions of the parties and witnesses relevant to the case.[9] A **deposition** resembles a formal interview at which a witness is sworn in and questioned by the attorneys. Depositions serve several purposes in addition to investigating the facts. Because deposition witnesses answer the questions under oath, any departure from their deposed statements at trial or during later formal proceedings might constitute the criminal act of perjury or at least may damage their credibility when testifying at trial. Then, too, since the witnesses have been examined and cross-examined during the deposition, their statements may be admissible as evidence at trial if they themselves are not available to appear.

Witnesses and parties may also be examined by having them answer **written interrogatories** either at a formal deposition or more often in the privacy of their own attorney's office and out of the presence of opposing counsel (Rule 33). In

---

## The Use of Depositions

Usually there are half truths and large amounts of misinformation on both sides. Personalities can be key and a deposition is a great opportunity to evaluate the other side. That is why we do both. We get the documents, we ask the written questions in the form of interrogatories and then we have the tools we need to legally dissect the witness from a variety of standpoints. Does he look good? Can he talk? Does he lie? Is his version credible? How does he stand up against your own witnesses? What is it that he is holding back? And perhaps the best reason is to have just one more writing where the witness has the golden opportunity to contradict or impeach himself.

—Trial attorney Kathleen McAllister of the Pittsburgh firm of Dibella Geer McAllister Best

---

[9]See Rules 27–32 on depositions.

depositions, the attorneys have greater freedom to ask questions than they would have at trial, where stricter rules of evidentiary relevance are enforced. Written interrogatories might be required where the questions must be framed with great care to avoid falling into an area of legally impermissible inquiry. Then, too, written interrogatories are a simpler and cheaper device than formal depositions for establishing a witness's testimony; but interrogatories limit the attorneys' ability to pursue lines of questioning by preventing them from spontaneously following up on points of interest in the witness's response to the preceding question.

Parties may decide to use expert witnesses in the case (Rule 26). Experts may be deposed, and their reports are subject to discovery by the other side. They are also usually expensive. Parties may also ask the court to order opposing parties to submit to a physical or mental examination if necessary in order to establish relevant evidence in the case (Rule 35).

Cooperation between the parties during discovery may be ultimately assured by court orders (Rule 37) and by the court's issuance of **subpoenas** requiring the presence of witnesses at depositions and hearings or requiring the submission by witnesses of requested materials (Rule 45); however, judges generally are loathe to interfere in the discovery process and encourage the parties to resolve their discovery differences among themselves. In the course of the discovery process, which may take weeks or perhaps months to complete, judicial rulings may be sought and received by parties who seek to pursue particular methods of investigation that are opposed by the other party or by the targeted witnesses themselves. In principle, these rulings are reviewable on appeal, but the federal rules give the trial judge broad discretion over matters of discovery, and the appellate courts are not likely to overturn trial court orders in these matters. Also, because it is by nature not final but interlocutory, any appeal must generally be reserved until after a final judgment on the merits is entered. The effect of this delay is to magnify the considerable discretion that trial courts already have over the discovery process.

The discovery process is followed by a submission of motions for summary judgment by each of the parties. The **motion for summary judgment** is an extremely important judicial tool, the purpose of which is to determine whether a "genuine issue of material fact" exists after all of the "pleadings, depositions, answers to interrogatories . . . admissions on file, together with affidavits" have been reviewed.[10] If no genuine issue of material fact exists, that is, if no purely factual dispute exists, then the dispute boils down to one of law that can be decided by the judge without a trial—without witnesses, testimony, evidence, and so on.

---

[10]Rule 56(c). Summary judgment as a means of identifying the specific factual issues or disagreements in a case has been emphasized by the Supreme Court a number of times and particularly in three 1986 cases: *Anderson v. Liberty Lobby,* 477 U.S. 242, 106 S.Ct. 2505, 91 L.Ed.2d 202, http://laws.findlaw.com/us/477/242.html; *Matsushita Electrical Industries v. Zenith Radio Corporation,* 475 U.S. 574, 106 S.Ct. 1348, 89 L.Ed.2d 538, http://laws.findlaw.com/us/475/574.html; and *Celotex Corporation v. Catrett,* 477 U.S. 317, 106 S.Ct. 2548, 91 L.Ed.2d 265, http://laws.findlaw.com/us/477/317.html. The three cases "signaled to the lower courts that summary judgment should be relied upon to weed out frivolous lawsuits and avoid wasteful trials." 10A Wright, Miller, and Kane, *Federal Practice and Procedure* §2712 (1998).

Keep in mind that almost every lawsuit alleges several different causes of action, just as most appeals allege several judicial errors. A motion for summary judgment may result in the removal or resolution of some, but not all, of the causes of action in the complaint and the counter- and cross-claims; the rest of the causes of action may then go to trial.[11] Although the overwhelming majority of cases filed in court are settled by the parties without a trial, cases in which one party succeeds in getting the other party's action dismissed by one of the pretrial motions, such as summary judgment, often wind up in the appellate court. Thus, the appellate courts review many cases that have never been to trial.

Finally, both parties will file a pretrial statement prior to a meeting between the attorneys in the case and the judge called the **pretrial conference** (Rule 16). The statement will include an account of the case, a list of the facts and the expert witnesses that may be called to testify, a list of the exhibits to be entered into evidence at the trial, and sometimes a discussion of novel legal issues posed by the case. (In a given case, the judge might require such meetings also during the course of the discovery period to monitor the progress of the parties or might schedule more than one such conference at the conclusion of discovery.) If the case has survived motions for summary judgment, material factual issues have been shown to exist. The judge and the parties are also sure to address the possibilities for settlement in the case and the status of any ongoing settlement negotiations now that the focus of a trial and the basic game plans of the parties are clear to all.

## Trial

The purpose of a trial is to resolve issues of fact by having a trier of fact—either a jury or a judge—determine, on the basis of evidence presented, just what occurred. *If there is no disagreement about the material facts, there is no trial.*

In the United States today, trial courts must withstand tremendous pressure upon the finite amounts of time, space, and personnel at their disposal, and judges are constantly alert to ways of reducing the demand for trial time. We have already noted the high rates of settlement in both civil and criminal cases. Additionally, we have just seen that in a civil trial, the factual issues have been distilled during the summary judgment briefing and pretrial conference, and the judge and both parties know exactly which points of fact are in disagreement and exactly how the other party will attempt to persuade the trier of fact by using legal **proof**—admissible evidence—that his version is correct. In other words, there should be no Perry Mason surprises to either party or to the judge during the trial. Though essentially adversarial, the trial should be a highly choreographed co-presentation aimed by the parties at persuading the trier to accept their respective views of the facts over their opponents'.

Courts—and the parties—may seek to shorten trials even further by agreeing to present mutually agreeable statements of factual evidence (known as **stipulations**)

---

[11]In the year ending September 30, 2003, of the 252,197 civil cases in United States district courts that were terminated, *only 1.7 percent, or 4,206 cases, had reached trial!* Over 41,000 ended without any court action at all, and another 186,472 ended before formal pretrial proceedings.

to the trier of fact in order to eliminate the time that the normal eliciting of such testimony would otherwise take. The trial might also be "bifurcated"; that is, the liability stage of the trial might be conducted first in order to determine whether the defendant will be found liable. If the defendant is found liable, then the damages stage will be conducted. If the defendant is not found liable, there will be no need for a trial on how much damages the plaintiff suffered.

If the case is to be tried to a jury, the jury must first be selected by the attorneys. In this day of ultra-specialization, the attorneys may hire jury consultants to assist them with this task. Then the plaintiff presents his case first, calling witnesses and introducing evidence by questioning those witnesses through **direct examination** in an effort to establish that the plaintiff's version of the facts is correct. During the plaintiff's presentation, the defendant's counsel has the opportunity to question the plaintiff's witnesses (**cross examination**), but not to call witnesses or introduce evidence. Both parties may wish to **impeach** or call into question the character and credibility of the witnesses: the defendant may impeach the plaintiff's witnesses, after which the plaintiff, on **re-direct examination,** may attempt to repair any damage that has been done.[12] Increasingly, counsel in the courtroom are employing high-tech software and equipment to display evidence and assist in the examination of witnesses.

At the conclusion of the plaintiff's case, when evidence on each of the factual issues has been introduced, the plaintiff rests and the defendant usually moves for a **judgment as a matter of law** (Rule 50), which in the federal rules was formerly called, and in many state courts is still called, a **directed verdict.** If, as is usually the case, the motion is denied (remember, there should be no surprises), the defendant then presents his case, calling witnesses and introducing evidence, defending if necessary the character and credibility of those witnesses, and trying to persuade the trier of fact that the defendant's version of the facts is true. The plaintiff, as was the case with the defendant during the plaintiff's case, is restricted to cross-examining the defendant's witnesses.

At the close of all evidence, but before the instructing of the jury by the judge, either party, or both, may again move for a judgment as a matter of law (or a directed verdict). Although the causes of action initially brought by the parties have been weeded out to some extent at the summary judgment stage before trial, the trial proceeds on the basis of several remaining causes of action. Motions for judgments as a matter of law at the close of all evidence provide another opportunity for the court to narrow the case by judicially determining that a party has failed to sustain its burden of proof on one or more causes of action during the trial and that the case should not go to the jury on those theories of liability.

On the other hand, the courts rarely grant motions for directed verdicts where the ruling would dismiss the whole case and all of the causes of action, even in cases where such motions appear to be warranted because of considerations of time and

---

[12]**Re–cross examination,** or further questioning by one party of a witness called by the other party, is also possible in some situations.

expense: if the court does grant a motion for a directed verdict and is then reversed on appeal, the reversal may well be based on the argument that real issues of fact existed in the case, upon which the jury should have deliberated. The court will probably have to retry the case in order to send it to the jury. Why not, then, do what courts routinely do and deny motions for directed verdicts at the close of all evidence, allow the jury to have its say, and then entertain a motion for a judgment as a matter of law? If the ruling for a judgment as a matter of law is reversed on appeal, the appellate court can simply reinstate the jury verdict and save time and money.

The applicable standard of proof determines the threshold of persuasion for the parties. The general rule in a civil case is that the plaintiff must prove his case, and hence his version of the facts in question, by a **preponderance of the evidence.** This means that the plaintiff must prove his version is "probably true" or "true more likely than not." It is probably futile to attempt to reduce the standard to any mathematical or other equally precise formula, such as the "50 percent +" standard that one sometimes hears. In some actions and on some issues, the standard is one of proof by **clear and convincing evidence,** a higher but even more difficult standard to measure. (In criminal cases, of course, the standard is that of proof beyond a reasonable doubt.)

Rulings that may be reviewed on appeal are generated at trial in a number of ways. Perhaps the one most familiar to viewers of courtroom dramas on television and in the movies is the objection by one attorney to the other's question to a witness. The objection elicits a ruling of "sustained" or "denied," perhaps after short statements of reasons by the lawyers in support of their respective positions.

These rulings can, indeed, be the basis of an appeal and request for a new trial, but the appellate court must find that the ruling was both wrong and **prejudicial,** that is, that the outcome of the trial might well have been affected by the erroneous ruling, either when taken alone or as a part of a larger pattern of erroneous rulings. Appellate courts will not reverse a trial court judgment if the errors they find are merely **harmless errors;** they must find **prejudicial errors.**

As a second source of appealable rulings, an attorney might object to the admissibility of certain evidence at trial and move to exclude it; this motion provokes a responsive ruling from the judge. In the modern civil trial, the course of the trial and the issues of admissibility are thoroughly reviewed and argued at the pretrial conference. Evidentiary issues that will likely emerge at trial will probably be submitted to the judge in writing—**in limine**—prior to trial so that they may be resolved expeditiously. The rulings, of course, may later be appealed no matter how expeditiously they were handled at trial.

A third source concerns the jury. Verdicts—jury determinations of the disputed material facts—cannot be directly appealed for the simple reason that they are not court rulings. The court, however, must enter a judgment upon the verdict rendered by the jury, and this judgment, which is a ruling, can be reviewed. The judgment may be a ruling that the verdict is sufficiently supported by the evidence. In cases in which the verdict that has been rendered appears to be arbitrary and capricious and to run clearly against the weight of the evidence, the losing party, before the court enters judgment, may renew its motion for a judgment as a matter of law, which at

## Stages of Civil Litigation

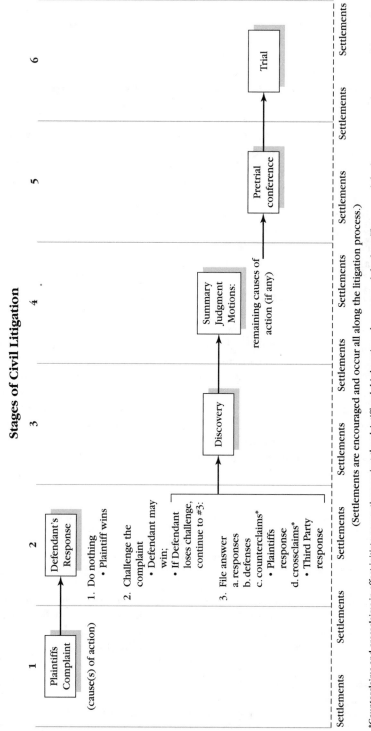

**Figure 3.1**

*Counterclaims and crossclaims in effect initiate new actions against the plaintiff and third parties, who are now defendants. These new defendants must treat the counterclaims and crossclaims just as the initial defendants treated the complaint, namely (1) by doing nothing, (2) by challenging them, or (3) by filing answers.

67

this stage of the litigation was formerly called a **judgment notwithstanding the verdict** (or "judgment n.o.v.") in the federal rules. This motion asks for a judgment counter to the verdict (Rule 50). The ruling on this motion may then serve as the basis for an indirect attack on the verdict.[13]

Another significant source of appellate rulings is the instructions that the court gives to a jury charged with returning a **general verdict** in a case: a verdict that determines the facts and then applies the law to the facts.[14] Before sending the jury out to deliberate, the court instructs the jury about the law. The attorneys for both parties may suggest instructions for the judge and may object to instructions that the judge delivers. Because these instructions are themselves interpretations of the law, they provide a relatively straightforward issue for the reviewing court to decide.

In a bench trial, the judge's findings of fact and conclusions of law replace the jury's verdict and the judge's instructions to the jury.

Finally, any event during the trial that casts doubt upon the ability of the parties to obtain a fair resolution of their conflict may serve as the basis for a motion for mistrial. The denial of the motion may later be reviewed.

## CRIMINAL PROCEDURE

Litigation procedures in civil cases and criminal cases are similar enough to permit many American lawyers (and English barristers) to practice both civil and criminal law. But there are procedural differences, and some of them are important. Criminal proceedings may destroy people's lives by legally sanctioning ruinous fines and forfeitures, devastating imprisonment, and the ultimate penalty of death. It may well be that our constitution would not have been ratified but for the promise that the first order of business of the first Congress would be a bill of rights that included several guarantees of criminal procedure. James Madison and the First Congress kept that promise by proposing the constitutional amendments that are known as the Bill of Rights. It is primarily these constitutional requirements that distinguish criminal procedure from civil.[15]

---

[13]The motion for a judgment as a matter of law here is comparable in purpose to the defendant's motion for a judgment as a matter of law (directed verdict) at the close of the plaintiff's case and a judgment as a matter of law at the close of all evidence (Rule 50). These motions, made at different stages in the litigation process, force the question of whether the parties, even in light of the evidence that the parties have presented at trial, have sufficiently proven the essential facts required by the specific legal actions and defenses that are being tried.

[14]**Special verdicts** and **special interrogatories** are sometimes used to elicit the jury's determination of particular facts or of whether particular parties are liable and, if so, to what degree of liability.

[15]The Constitution contained individual legal rights and guarantees when it issued from Philadelphia in September 1787, leading Alexander Hamilton to argue in *Federalist* 84 that a "bill of rights" was already included in it. Article I guarantees the right to habeas corpus proceedings in peacetime and prohibits bills of attainder and ex post facto laws, Article III guarantees jury trials and appropriate venue for federal criminal cases, and Articles II and III address the crime of treason in more detail than most any other subject within the Constitution.

To emphasize their importance, the following discussion of criminal procedure will refer primarily to constitutional provisions and to cases that have interpreted them rather than to particular rules of the Federal Rules of Criminal Procedure.

The constitutional procedural rights address each stage of criminal procedure. Prior to trial, Fourth Amendment standards govern lawful searches and arrests; the Fifth Amendment requires indictments for the initiation of felony cases and prohibits double jeopardy and forced self-incrimination; the Sixth Amendment requires a speedy trial, initial notice to the defendant of the charges, assistance of counsel in some circumstances, and the power of a defendant to subpoena witnesses; finally, the Eighth Amendment protects against courts setting excessive bail.

Regarding the trial itself, the Fifth Amendment prohibition of forced self-incrimination applies to the questioning of defendants who testify in their own behalf at trial, while the Due Process Clause of the Fifth Amendment sets the overarching standard of fairness that goes beyond the more specific constitutional requirements.[16] The Sixth Amendment applies principally to trials. It requires public trials, impartial judges and juries, the convenient location of trials ("venue"), the ability of defendants to confront their accusers and witnesses at trial, and the assistance of counsel for the defendant.

Finally, postconviction proceedings are addressed by the Eighth Amendment, which prohibits the imposition of excessive fines and cruel and unusual punishment upon convicted defendants.[17] Postacquittal proceedings are the subject of the Fifth Amendment Double Jeopardy Clause, which prohibits a second trial for the same offense.[18]

## Pretrial Proceedings

Like civil procedure, the pre-trial stage of criminal procedure requires the prosecution to indicate clearly the precise charges against the defendant, allows both sides to engage in discovery, albeit a more limited discovery than in civil litigation, and requires the defendant to give notice to the prosecution of the planned use of certain defenses, such as alibi or insanity.[19] The defendant does not file a responsive pleading, such as an "answer"; rather, the defendant simply pleads "guilty" or "not guilty" in an arraignment in open court.[20]

The criminal pretrial process does not attempt to focus the issues as narrowly as the civil process by requiring the defendant to admit to or to concede any of the

---

[16]The Fifth Amendment Due Process Clause applies only to federal courts. The same function regarding state courts is supplied by the Due Process Clause of the Fourteenth Amendment. Both clauses also apply to civil trials and to other government proceedings.

[17]In a line of cases beginning in 1925, the Due Process Clause of the Fourteenth Amendment has been interpreted to require most of these rights, originally intended to apply only to the federal government and federal courts, to be applied to state governments and state courts. This is referred to as **incorporation:** many guarantees in the Bill of Rights have been "incorporated" into the Fourteenth Amendment Due Process Clause.

[18]Once the jury has been sworn in, or, in a nonjury trial, once the first witness has been sworn in, "jeopardy attaches" and the defendant may raise a Fifth Amendment double jeopardy claim in any subsequent criminal proceeding that prosecutes a violation of the *same* criminal statute. See *Crist v. Bretz*, 437 U.S. 28, 98 S.Ct. 2156, 57 L.Ed.2d 24, http://laws.findlaw.com/us/437/28.html (1978).

[19]Court systems differ from one another on which defenses require notice.

[20]States may permit other pleas, such as "nolo contendere" or no contest, by which a defendant does not formally admit guilt, but accepts punishment without trial.

allegations of the prosecution—the Fifth Amendment right against self-incrimination guarantees that the defendant need not admit anything. Confessions and incriminating statements by the defendant that are made to the police without sufficient voluntariness, awareness of consequences, or adequate legal assistance, should the defendant so desire counsel, might be ruled "inadmissible" as trial evidence at a pretrial **suppression hearing.**[21]

## Arrests and Investigations

Constitutional requirements also apply to the opening steps of criminal litigation, which, in the United States, present a variety of ways to initiate a case.

A criminal case may begin by (1) the police who witness a crime, making an immediate arrest; (2) a prosecutor, as a result of an investigation, filing a written accusation called an **information** with the court or presenting an indictment or bill of indictment to a grand jury; (3) a special grand jury investigating a crime and handing down an indictment; or (4) in some states, a private individual filing a complaint against the defendant(s). In the case of the latter three alternatives, if the defendant is not yet under arrest at the time of the filing of the information, indictment, or complaint, the next step is the issuance of an arrest warrant to be executed by the police.

State and federal systems differ significantly from one another in prescribing the procedural steps that must follow an arrest, but there are certain general principles of constitutional law that govern the preliminary stages of all American legal systems. In particular, arrests are governed by the Fourth Amendment, which requires probable cause to make an arrest, with or without a warrant.

Cases may begin with a warrantless arrest made by police officers who witness a crime or attempted crime by a suspect. Upon **arrest,** the suspect may then be placed in **custody,** that is, his freedom of movement is restricted by the police. In the light of the Fourth Amendment, the arrest of an individual is a seizure of a person and therefore must be accomplished in a reasonable manner.[22] What "reasonable" means within the context of the Fourth Amendment is indicated by the term **probable cause,** which appears in the second half of the amendment: a reasonable arrest is one that is based upon probable cause, which roughly means that the officers have sufficient demonstrable reason to believe that the defendant probably committed a crime. Compared to the "beyond a reasonable doubt" standard required for a criminal conviction, the probable cause standard is quite low.

Where an officer or a prosecutor attempts to obtain an arrest warrant *before* an arrest, he must provide a judge or magistrate, who is legally presumed to be neutral and

---

[21]At a suppression or exclusion hearing, the court hears arguments on the defendant's motion(s) to suppress or exclude unlawfully obtained evidence from trial.

[22]The Fourth Amendment provides:

> The right of the people to be secure in their persons, houses, papers, and effects, against unreasonable searches and seizures, shall not be violated, and no Warrants shall issue, but upon probable cause, supported by Oath or affirmation, and particularly describing the place to be searched, and the persons or things to be seized.

detached and therefore to be a guardian of the constitutional rights of the person to be arrested,[23] with sufficient information to persuade "a prudent man in believing that the [suspect] had committed or was committing an offense at the time of the arrest."[24] The information in the complaint, said the Court, must provide the magistrate with a basis for finding probable cause: "It must provide the affiant's answer to the magistrate's hypothetical question, 'What makes you think that the defendant committed the offense charged?'"[25] The credibility of the "affiant," the individual who swears that the information in the affidavit or statement is true, is also subject to question.[26]

If a defendant can successfully prove to the court that he was arrested *without* probable cause, the consequent evidence turned up on the basis of the invalid arrest may be challenged by the defendant and, at a suppression hearing, deemed to have been invalidly obtained and therefore inadmissible as evidence during the trial. Evidence that is obtained pursuant to an unreasonable search—one without probable cause—or as a result of improperly conducted questioning can also be suppressed. Incriminating evidence is often crucial to the prosecution, and its loss can weaken or cripple the case, especially, for example, drug crime cases. There is no direct counterpart to this exclusion of improperly obtained evidence in civil cases.

## Detention and Charging

In the case of a warrantless arrest, the police may keep the arrestee in custody for only a limited time before they must either justify the custody to a magistrate by

---

[23]See *Aguilar v. Texas*, 378 U.S. 108, 84 S.Ct. 1509, 12 L.Ed.2d 723, http://laws.findlaw.com/us/378/108.html (1964), quoting Justice Robert Jackson's opinion in *Johnson v. United States*, 333 U.S. 10, 13–14, 68 S.Ct. 367, 92 L.Ed. 436, http://laws.findlaw.com/us/333/10.html (1948):

> The point of the Fourth Amendment, which often is not grasped by zealous officers, is not that it denies law enforcement the support of the usual inferences which reasonable men draw from evidence. Its protection consists in requiring that those inferences be drawn by a neutral and detached magistrate instead of being judged by the officer engaged in the often competitive enterprise of ferreting out crime.

The *Aguilar* Court continued:

> Although the reviewing court will pay substantial deference to judicial determinations of probable cause, the court must still insist that the magistrate perform his "neutral and detached" function and not serve merely as a rubber stamp for the police. 378 U.S. at 111, 84 S.Ct. at 1512, 12 L.Ed.2d at 726–727.

[24]*Beck v. Ohio*, 379 U.S. 89, 91, 85 S.Ct. 223, 225, 13 L.Ed.2d 142, http://laws.findlaw.com/us/379/89.html (1964). If the magistrate issues a warrant, the defendant may later challenge its validity on the grounds that the requesting police officer or prosecutor lied or even made an honest mistake about the information, or that the judicial officer mistakenly or intentionally issued a warrant upon insufficient information.

The Fifth Amendment selfincrimination clause and the Sixth Amendment assistance of counsel clause apply even to prearrest, investigatory questioning under some circumstances. *Miranda v. Arizona*, 384 U.S. 436, 86 S.Ct. 1602, 16 L.Ed.2d 694, http://laws.findlaw.com/us/384/436.html (1966).

[25]*Jaben v. United States*, 381 U.S. 214, 224, 85 S.Ct. 1365, 14 L.Ed.2d 345, http://laws.findlaw.com/us/381/214.html (1965).

[26]Id.

showing probable cause or bring formal charges against the arrestee.[27] Following the decision in *County of Riverside v. McLaughlin*, the time limit for holding someone who was arrested without a warrant in custody without charging him with a crime is presumptively 48 hours.[28]

At this preliminary hearing, the magistrate may also set bail and inform the defendant of the right to counsel. The defendant may also challenge the basis of his arrest, and if no probable cause is established, the defendant must be freed.

If the defendant was arrested pursuant to a warrant, a magistrate already found probable cause before issuing the warrant; the preliminary hearing may then focus on bail and right of counsel functions.

How are arrest warrants obtained from a magistrate? The Fifth Amendment provides that a grand jury indictment (or presentment) must be issued in order to charge an individual with a "capital, or otherwise infamous crime" under federal law.[29] This has been interpreted to mean that indictments are positively required for capital crimes (those punishable by death), but the requirement may be waived by the defendant in other felony cases. No indictment is necessary in a federal misdemeanor case. The grand jury indictment requirement of the Fifth Amendment has not been made applicable to the states through Fourteenth Amendment incorporation: most states do not require, but do permit, indictments in any felony cases, capital or noncapital.

All states and the federal government provide for criminal informations—formal written accusations by a prosecutor, filed with a magistrate, that charge a defendant with a crime. The magistrate must then determine whether the information rests upon probable cause.[30] The information may be challenged at the preliminary hearing.

There are two remaining ways for initiating an arrest: a special grand jury indictment and, in some states, a complaint filed by a private citizen. Special grand juries are sometimes convened to investigate criminal matters and to initiate indictments, not simply to judge bills of indictment presented by the prosecutors. In such cases, the probable cause is established by the grand jury and cannot be attacked at a preliminary hearing.

Citizen complaints should either establish probable cause before a magistrate issues an arrest warrant based on the complaint, or probable cause in the form of

---

[27]"Maximum protection of individual rights could be assured by requiring a magistrate's review of the factual justification prior to any arrest, but such a requirement would constitute an intolerable handicap for legitimate law enforcement. . . .

"Under this practical compromise, a policeman's on-the-scene assessment of probable cause provides legal justification for arresting a person suspected of crime, and for a brief period of detention to take the administrative steps [the "booking"] incident to arrest. *Once the suspect is in custody, however, the reasons that justify dispensing with the magistrate's neutral judgment evaporate. . . . [T]he Fourth Amendment requires a judicial determination of probable cause as a prerequisite to extended restraint on liberty following arrest." Gerstein v. Pugh*, 420 U.S. 103, 95 S.Ct. 854, 43 L.Ed.2d 54, http://laws.findlaw.com/us/420/103.html (1975) (emphasis added).

[28]*City of Riverside v. McLaughlin*, 500 U.S. 44, 111 S.Ct. 1661, 114 L.Ed.2d 49, http://laws.findlaw.com/us/500/44.html (1991).

[29]Only grand juries may issue an **indictment** against, or "indict," defendants.

[30]*Note*: An information or an indictment may be required prior to issuing an arrest warrant, or it may be required after a suspect has been arrested without a warrant and has been subjected to a preliminary hearing.

an information or indictment testable at a preliminary hearing must follow the arrest.

## Discovery

As we discussed above, the main purpose of discovery in civil litigation is to eliminate surprises at trial and to determine exactly what facts are in dispute. To achieve this end, the parties are authorized to share all relevant evidence, identify all possible witnesses, and ask and obtain from the opposing parties any admissions against the interests of those parties.

Discovery in criminal trials is not nearly so broad. Defendants need not share their exculpatory evidence (evidence that tends to prove innocence) with the prosecutor, but the prosecutor must share such evidence with the defendant's counsel. Surprise witnesses at trial are possible. And, of course, the defendant need not admit anything—need not answer any questions—to the prosecutor.

## Trial

Trial proceedings in criminal cases, apart from the constitutional guarantees already indicated above, are similar to civil proceedings, especially tort proceedings.[31] As noted above many trial lawyers do both civil and criminal trial work.

The principal differences between civil and criminal litigation are, in criminal trials, (1) the elevated standard of proof for conviction (that is, proof beyond a reasonable doubt rather than preponderance of the evidence or clear and convincing evidence), (2) the inability of the prosecutor to place the defendant on the stand as a witness, and (3) the inability of the judge to reverse a jury verdict of acquittal (though the judge may enter an acquittal even if the jury finds the defendant guilty).

The "beyond a reasonable doubt standard" of proof is not specifically required by constitutional language, but is part of the traditional due process applicable to criminal trials.[32] Regarding the defendant as witness, the prosecutor not only may not call the defendant as a witness (as the plaintiff may call the defendant in a civil case), but also may not comment on the defendant's refusal to take the stand in his own defense. Finally, the jury verdict of acquittal is final, though, as stated above, a judge can enter a judgment of acquittal over a jury verdict of guilt.

## APPELLATE PROCEDURE

Courts may have the authority to review rulings of other courts in two ways: (1) **appellate review,** sometimes called "direct review" or "direct appellate review"; and (2) **collateral review,** usually in the form of a **habeas corpus** proceeding. We shall take up these two processes in turn.

---

[31]Most all criminal behavior is also tortious behavior. Thus, homicide is both a crime and a tort. The O. J. Simpson cases, first the criminal proceeding, then the civil—are a good example of this dual nature of many legal harms.

[32]See *Cage v. Louisiana*, 498 U.S. 39, 111 S.Ct. 328, 112 L.Ed.2d 339, http://laws.findlaw.com/us/498/39.html (1990).

## Direct Appellate Review

Appellate procedure in federal courts is generally the same for both civil and criminal cases and is equally important to all litigants: the United States courts of appeals throw out as many cases, if not more, on procedural grounds as they decide on the merits. The party seeking appellate review must first file a notice of appeal within the time limits set by the rules of the appropriate appellate court, and the other party or parties to the case must receive notice of the appeal.[33] Copies of the record of the case—the pleadings and exhibits, a transcript of the proceedings (or of the relevant portions thereof), and the docket entries—must be ordered at the appellant's expense for use by the appellate court (Rules 10, 11, and 30). And steps must be taken to assure that neither party will unduly benefit from the mere pursuit of appellate review. For instance, if a civil litigant has been found liable for a monetary award of damages and decides to appeal, that litigant-appellant does not want to pay the damages before learning what the appellate court decides. On the other hand, the winning party does not want the appellant to benefit from the lapse of time caused by the appeal by otherwise disposing of the assets that will be used to satisfy the judgment. In such a case, the appellant will move for a "stay" of the trial court's judgment pending appeal; thus, the damages will not be due until after the appellate court rules. But the appellant will also have to post a bond, called a "supersedeas" bond, to secure the appellee's right to eventual payment, if necessary (Rule 8). In a criminal case, the defendant-appellant will usually want to be released from custody pending appeal: Rule 9 provides the procedure to seek such release.

The key variable in describing appellate procedure in general is whether the jurisdiction in question is mandatory or discretionary. Since 1990, for example, over 99 percent of the cases docketed in the Supreme Court are filed under the court's discretionary appellate jurisdiction. In contrast, all appellate jurisdiction of the United States Courts of Appeals over final judgments of federal trial courts is mandatory, but their jurisdiction over appeals from government agency tribunals and over interlocutory appeals is discretionary. The allocation of mandatory and discretionary appellate jurisdiction to state appellate courts varies from state to state and is often a combination of both kinds of jurisdiction. What does the distinction between mandatory and discretionary mean for the litigant?

A court with discretionary appellate jurisdiction over a case has the discretion, or choice, to review the allegedly erroneous rulings of the lower court or not to review them; a court with mandatory appellate jurisdiction must review the rulings of the lower court and must itself rule on the arguments of the appellant and appellee. Accordingly, in discretionary review cases, the petitioner begins the process by notifying the respondent and by filing, within a period of time defined by statute,

---

[33]Fed.R.App.P. 3 and 4. The Federal Rules do distinguish between civil and criminal cases in the deadlines they set for filing appeals. Incidentally, the other party or parties in the case may also "cross-appeal." (All subsequent references to the Federal Rules of Appellate Procedure in this section of the chapter will be referred to simply as "Rule"—e.g., Rule 3.)

a document called a **petition** with the court. (See, for example, Rule 15.) In many courts the petition asks for a writ of some sort to be sent to the court that has rendered the decision in question. (In the Supreme Court of the United States, the petition is for a **writ of certiorari,** which, if granted, commands the lower court to send up a certified copy of the record of the case.)

The petition does not present the party's arguments on the merits, that is, the alleged errors in the rulings of the lower court; the petition presents arguments aimed only at persuading the appellate court that the case before them is a good one to review because of the timeliness of the issues, the general need for a resolution of such issues, or other such prudential reasons. The respondent's reply also addresses only the question of whether the case is a good one to review, and typically the respondent, who has won below, argues that there is no good reason to disturb the lower court rulings.

Based on these documents, the court must decide whether or not to review the case—whether, that is, to grant or deny the writ. If the petition is dismissed, that is generally the end of the direct appellate review process within that legal system: the lower court ruling stands (though a seldom-granted motion or petition by the petitioner for reconsideration of the petition may be filed).

If the writ is granted, the lower court record is sent up and the court then asks for written statements, called **briefs,** of the arguments that the petitioner is relying upon to persuade the court that the lower court erred when it ruled as it did. These are called the **briefs on the merits.** The petitioner's brief succinctly presents arguments and prays that the appellate court **reverse** or **vacate** the lower court judgment, which was based on the erroneous rulings. Again, the respondent usually argues that the lower court rulings were not in error and that the appellate court should approve and **affirm** the judgment of the lower court.

If, on the other hand, the appellate jurisdiction is mandatory, the petitioning process is deleted, and the parties have an appeal as of right. The appealing party—the appellant—typically begins the procedure by filing a notice of appeal, which is then served on the appellees, and by filing a brief on the merits with the court.

In both discretionary and mandatory review, the court, after receiving the briefs on the merits, may decide the case with or without oral argument. **Oral argument** usually consists of a period of time, often one hour equally divided between the two parties, during which each party's attorneys have the opportunity to explain their arguments in more detail and respond to any questions that the judges might have. In the United States courts of appeals, the rules weigh strongly in favor of oral argument, although the court has the ultimate authority to decide whether to allow it in a particular case (Rule 34). That said, in 2003 the courts of appeals decided twice as many cases *without* oral argument as with it.

We must emphasize again the crucial importance of observing the procedural rules regardless of whether the appellant is seeking review in a court exercising discretionary or mandatory appellate jurisdiction. Failure to observe procedural rules such as deadlines and proof of service requirements often results in the case being dismissed and the opportunity for review lost. In 2003, more cases were terminated procedurally in the United States courts of appeals than were decided on the merits.

## Decisions and Opinions

After oral argument, the court considers the case again and takes a preliminary vote on how to decide the case. The decision is made according to majority rule. The court then considers whether to issue a **per curiam** ("by the court") decision or a signed written opinion of the court. A per curiam opinion usually contains a bare statement of the issue and the court's holding. If the court decides to issue a signed opinion, it must then decide who among the majority will write the opinion, which is a full statement of the rationale for the decision.

These two aspects of the court's action—the decision and the opinion—should be carefully distinguished. Intermediate appellate courts, particularly the United States courts of appeals, usually assign cases to panels of three appellate judges for decision, and the panel decides the case by majority rule. The **decision,** which may also be referred to as the **disposition of the case,** is the judgment of the appellate court. It is the statement that the judgment, disposition, or decision of the lower court is affirmed, reversed, vacated, reversed and remanded, or vacated and remanded. The **opinion** states the rationale for the court's decision: why the court affirmed, reversed, and so on. Any justice may also write a separate opinion, called a **concurring** opinion when it is in agreement with the majority and a **dissenting** opinion when it is not. A majority opinion is potentially an authoritative precedent.

Just as a majority must agree to decide the case, a majority must agree on a rationale in order for there to be an "opinion of the court." If a majority cannot agree on the reasons for the judgment, and this is a common if not frequent occurrence on the Supreme Court in recent decades, there can be a decision but no "opinion of the court." Instead, there may be a **plurality opinion,** along with several concurring opinions. If a judge or justice agrees with the *decision* of the majority but does not agree with the *opinion* of the majority or plurality or anyone else, his opinion will begin with words such as "Justice White, **concurring in the judgment.**" This means that the judge is concurring only in the judgment (i.e., the decision) and not in the opinion. If the justice agrees with the opinion of the majority but wishes to add a few, or many, separate comments, the opinion will simply state something like "Justice White, concurring."

In many cases, if the appellate court agrees with the petitioner that the lower court erred, mere reversal of the lower court judgment is not enough. The court might decide that the lower court must hold a new trial or take other further action, and thus the appellate court reverses or vacates and **remands** the case to the lower court for further action consistent with the appellate court's judgment.

After the appellate court renders its judgment and opinion, the losing party has the opportunity to petition the court for a rehearing. In cases in which the initial decision was made by a three-judge panel, the losing party might ask for a rehearing *en banc,* a hearing before the full membership of the appellate court. Seldom are these petitions granted, but when they are granted, the decisions of the full court carry great authority and outweigh the decisions of any of the court's three-judge panels.

## Collateral Review

The **writ of habeas corpus** is a means of challenging the legality of one's detention.[34] Although use of the writ is not limited to contesting criminal detention, the greatest number of applicants for the writ in the federal system is prisoners, state and federal, who wish to test the legality of their incarceration and, in consequence, the legality of their very conviction.

Habeas corpus has a long history in England and the United States, and its significance as a means by which a lone individual can challenge the power of the government to detain him is symbolized by its inclusion in Article I, Section 9, of the Constitution: "The Privilege of the Writ of Habeas Corpus shall not be suspended, unless when in Cases of Rebellion or Invasion the public Safety may require it."

One may apply or petition for the writ to state courts, federal courts, or both.[35] Typically, the procedure in a criminal case is as follows: a defendant who is convicted and sentenced to prison may directly appeal the conviction as of right to at least one appellate court. In some states, the defendant has an appeal as of right to the intermediate appellate court and to the state court of last resort; in other states and in the federal system, the defendant has one appeal as of right and a subsequent right to petition for discretionary review from the court of last resort, which in the federal system is the United States Supreme Court. Reversals of lower court rulings may, of course, lead to one or more retrials and subsequent appeals until there is a final judgment in the case.

If the final judgment on direct review affirms the defendant-appellant's conviction and prison sentence, the prisoner may then apply or petition to a state court for a writ of habeas corpus to review particular aspects and rulings of the trial process again. If the trial court denies the application, the denial may be appealable to state appellate courts. If the state courts finally reject the prisoner's application, he may then apply to the United States district court and ask it to review the legality and constitutionality of specified rulings of the state courts. This resort to a different legal system for review of a court ruling is called **collateral review**.[36] Again, denial of the

---

[34]See *Fay v. Noia*, 372 U.S. 391, 83 S.Ct. 822, 9 L.Ed.2d 837, http://laws.findlaw.com/us/372/391.html (1963); Charles Alan Wright, *Handbook on the Law of Federal Courts*, 3d ed. (St. Paul, MN: West Publishing Co., 1976), Sec. 53; Victor E. Flango, *Habeas Corpus in State and Federal Courts* (Williamsburg, VA: National Center for State Courts, 1994), 1; and generally Macklin Fleming, *The Price of Perfect Justice* (New York: Basic Books, 1974).

[35]The federal statutes in question are 28 U.S.C. §§2241–2255. Each state has its own habeas corpus statutes for use in the state courts.

[36]The term "collateral" suggests a directional imagery. Thus, on "direct appeal," the appellant takes the case "up" on appeal, and the appellate court reviews the "lower court's" rulings. Also, levels of appellate courts are often referred to as "intermediate" and "high" or "highest courts." "Collateral" suggests a sideways move, such as a state prisoner asking the federal court to review the state court proceedings. (It should be clear by now that the federal court system is not superior to, or "higher" than, the state court systems, but rather coordinate to the state systems.) Collateral review is also available within the same legal system: prisoners convicted in state courts may seek a writ of habeas corpus from a state court, as federal prisoners may seek the writ from a federal court. In this context, the term "collateral" is used simply to distinguish the procedure from "direct" appellate review.

application by the district court may be appealed to the United States Court of Appeals, and, if the denial is affirmed by the appellate court, may be reviewed by the United States Supreme Court upon petition by the prisoner. As one can see, review of a criminal conviction can rattle around the state and the federal legal systems for a long time; indeed, for a 20-year period after 1963, the denial of one application did not bar a subsequent application by the same prisoner in the same case. [37]

Consequently, applications by state prisoners to federal courts for writs of habeas corpus constitute a significant number of the cases filed in federal courts each year. From the early 1940s to about 1963, such applications amounted to hundreds. In

---

## Example of Collateral Review via Habeas Corpus

*Schlup v. Delo,* 513 U.S. 298, 115 S.Ct. 851, 130 L.Ed.2d 808, http://laws.findlaw.com/us/513/298.html (1995), provides an example of the extended litigation made possible by collateral review in the form of habeas corpus relief before the federal statute was amended in 1996 by the Antiterrorism and Effective Death Penalty Act ("AEDPA"), Pub.L. 104-132, 110 Stat. 1218 (1996). The effect of the AEDPA on the volume of collateral review remains to be seen. Defendant Schlup was convicted in a Missouri state court of murder and was sentenced to death. On direct review, the Missouri Supreme Court affirmed the conviction, and the United States Supreme Court denied his petition requesting direct appellate review. Schlup then applied to the Missouri state courts for a writ of habeas corpus. The state courts, including the Missouri Supreme Court, rejected this request for collateral review, and Schlup, representing himself, filed for federal habeas corpus relief in the United States district court. The district court rejected his application; he appealed. The United States court of appeals affirmed the district court, and again the United States Supreme Court denied his petition for appellate review of the judgment by the court of appeals. Schlup began again. Represented by an attorney, Schlup again applied to the United States district court for habeas corpus relief and was again denied. He appealed to the United States court of appeals, which again affirmed the district court and denied a request for a second hearing. This time his petition to the Supreme Court was successful. The Court, in a 5–4 decision, vacated the court of appeals decision and remanded the case to the United States district court with orders to conduct an evidentiary hearing using the criteria that the Supreme Court announced in its opinion. As a result, the district court granted Schlup's petition for habeas corpus, finding that Schlup received "ineffective assistance of counsel" in his capital murder defense. Schlup's release from custody under the death sentence did not release him from prison, however; he remained incarcerated to serve a life sentence for a separate conviction of assault in the first degree.

---

[37]Drafting applications for writs of habeas corpus became a major prison industry with "jailhouse lawyers" working on their own and on fellow prisoners' applications. See Macklin Fleming, *supra,* and Victor Flango, *supra,* note 34.

1963, the Supreme Court, in a series of cases, reinterpreted the federal habeas corpus statute in a way that liberalized its availability to state prisoners. Thus encouraged, state prisoners began applying in ever greater numbers—from a total of 1,408 in the year preceding the 1963 rulings to 9,063 in 1970 and almost 19,000 in 2003.[38] The total number of prisoners in state prisons exploded from less than 200,000 in 1962 to more than 650,000 in 2002.[39] Applications by federal prisoners, a significantly smaller population than that of the state prisoners, to federal courts amount to less than one-quarter of the state prisoner volume.

Very few of the prisoner applications are granted, although in recent years a half dozen or so of the Supreme Court's decisions each term are entered in cases brought by state prisoners via habeas corpus in federal courts. This is not an insignificant amount. The implicit superior authority of federal courts to review their fellow state jurists' rulings has understandably provoked resentment by state judges over the years, and several serious attempts to statutorily limit federal court habeas corpus jurisdiction were considered by Congress.

In the 1990s, the Supreme Court construed the federal statute in ways that made it more difficult for state prisoners to obtain federal habeas relief, and in 1996 Congress enacted the Antiterrorism and Effective Death Penalty Act (AEDPA), which was intended to further limit the availability of federal habeas corpus relief to state prisoners.[40] The ingenious prisoners, however, many of whom have considerable amounts of time at their disposal, have increasingly channeled their efforts into tort suits against the state prisons under federal civil rights statutes. In 2003, almost 23,000 such actions were filed in the United States district courts.

# EXPEDITED CONSIDERATION OF CONSTITUTIONAL ISSUES

The foregoing description of the civil litigation process reveals several points at which appealable rulings may be made. If we focus for a moment on United States Supreme Court decisions, we should note that the Court might be asked to review (1) rulings that interpret or apply substantive rules of law, (2) rulings that apply court procedural rules to the proceedings in question, and (3) rulings that determine the constitutionality of statutes or actions in the case. The latter type requires further examination.

Challenges to the constitutionality of a statute might emerge at any stage of litigation, including trial, but normally they occur much earlier. Indeed, if the defendants

---

[38]See Flango, *supra*, note 34, 14.

[39]Flango makes the point that the rapid and consistent increase of such applications throughout the 1960s occurred at a time when the number of state prison inmates *decreased* by 20,000. The steady increase in state prison population only began in 1973 and has not been marked by as dramatic an increase in prisoner applications. See Flango, *supra*, 14. For prison population statistics, see *Sourcebook of Criminal Justice Statistics Online*, http://www.albany.edu/sourcebook/1995/pdf/t614.pdf.

[40]Pub.L. 104-132, 110 Stat. 1218 (1996). The habeas corpus statute is 28 U.S.C. §§2254 and 2255.

to a civil action question the constitutionality of the statute or legal rule out of which the case against them arises, the challenge, in the form of an affirmative defense or a motion to declare the statute void on its face or as applied to the defendants in the case at hand, may be made shortly after the complaint is filed.[41] The trial court's rulings may then be appealed as of right to the intermediate appellate court of the federal system—the United States court of appeals—the judgments of which are then reviewable by the United States Supreme Court under its discretionary appellate jurisdiction. If the trial court is a state court, its rulings are subject to at least one and probably two state appellate courts before the parties can petition the United States Supreme Court to review the case. The complete process usually takes several years.

On the other hand, a party might bring an action for the sole purpose of challenging the constitutionality of a statute. In these cases, the litigation follows a different course. The suit may be equitable in nature; that is, the plaintiffs may ask the court to enjoin the government or some other party from enforcing the allegedly unconstitutional statute. Alternatively, the action may be at law and ask the court to decide upon the constitutionality of the statute and to render a judgment accordingly.

Up until 1976, in the federal system such direct challenges to the constitutionality of state and federal laws would require the convening of a **three-judge district court**.[42] The 1976 legislation repealing these jurisdictional provisions left to three-judge district courts only jurisdiction over certain challenges to issues of legislative apportionment under the Voting Rights Act of 1965. This jurisdiction has been enlarged from time to time. A decision of a three-judge district court was appealable directly to the Supreme Court and still is today; indeed, such decisions are the only cases remaining in the Court's mandatory appellate jurisdiction.[43] Thus, consideration of the constitutional issues by a three-judge district court may expedite litigation considerably by eliminating the appellate review of the United States courts of appeals; the case goes straight from the three-judge district court to the Supreme Court.

The litigation might also be hastened along by the narrow focus of the constitutional issues. If only the constitutionality of the law is in question, there will perhaps be no factual issues, and therefore no need for an evidentiary trial at all. Even if there are facts other than the statutory language that need to be brought before the court, these facts may be agreed to in stipulations, thus enabling counsel to direct their remarks to the legal issues. This also saves considerable time.

---

[41]For example, in the case of *McCulloch v. Maryland*, 17 U.S. (4 Wheat.) 316, 4 L.Ed. 579, http://laws.findlaw.com/us/17/316.html (1819), defendant McCulloch attacked the constitutionality of the Maryland law that was being applied to him. In the Guaranty Clause case of *Luther v. Borden*, 48 U.S. (7 How.) 1, 12 L.Ed. 581, http://laws.findlaw.com/us/48/1.html (1849), the plaintiff sued the defendant law enforcement officials for trespass. The defendants replied that their entry into the plaintiff's house was not trespass because they were authorized to enter by certain military orders. The plaintiff then attacked the validity and constitutionality of the orders.

[42]28 U.S.C. §2281 (repealed, 1976) covered challenges to state laws; 28 U.S.C. §2282 (repealed, 1976) covered federal laws. For the present jurisdiction, see 28 U.S.C. §2284.

[43]See 28 U.S.C. §1253.

Because the three-judge district court procedure promises a saving of time and because the constitutionality of controversial legislation is sometimes of momentous importance, Congress occasionally includes in the legislation provisions that enable parties wishing to challenge its constitutionality to proceed by filing an action with a three-judge district court. Congress sometimes even adjures the three-judge court or the Supreme Court to act as quickly as possible!

For example, the Cable Television Act of 1992 provides that civil actions "challenging the constitutionality of section 534 or 535 of this title or any provision thereof shall be heard by a district court of three judges convened pursuant to section 2284 of Title 28."[44] So, too, the Telecommunication Act of 1996[45]; the Bureau of the Census provisions in the 1998 Commerce, Justice, State Appropriations Act[46]; and the Bipartisan Campaign Reform Act ("McCain-Feingold")[47] provide for initial three-judge district court jurisdiction. The McCain-Feingold legislation provides specifically for a three-judge district court in the District of Columbia to have original jurisdiction. By contrast, the Line Item Veto Act of 1996 provides for direct appeal to the Supreme Court from the United States District Court for the District of Columbia, but does not specify a *three-judge* district court.[48] The 1998 Commerce, Justice, State Appropriations Act; the McCain-Feingold Act; and the Line Item Veto Act all proclaim it the duty of the district court and the Supreme Court "to advance on the docket and to expedite to the greatest possible extent the disposition" of the case before them.[49]

We must remember that any challenge in the federal courts to the constitutionality of a statute or government action requires a justiciable case or controversy—an

---

[44]The Cable Television Consumer Protection and Competition Act of 1992, Pub. L. No. 102-385, 106 Stat. 1460, 47 U.S.C. §555(c)(1). Section 555(c)(2) provides for direct appeal from the district court to the United States Supreme Court. See *Turner Broadcasting System v. Federal Communication Commission*, 512 U.S. 622, 114 S.Ct. 2445, 129 L.Ed.2d 497, http://laws.findlaw.com/us/512/622.html (1994).

[45]Pub. L. No. 104-104, §561, 110 Stat. 56 (1996), 47 U.S.C. §223 note. See *Reno v. American Civil Liberties Union*, 521 U.S. 844, 117 S.Ct. 2329, 138 L.Ed.2d 874, http://laws.findlaw.com/us/521/844.html (1997).

[46]Pub. L. No. 105-119, Tit. II, §209(e), 111 Stat. 2440, 2482 (1997). See *Utah v. Evans*, 536 U.S. 452, 122 S.Ct. 2191, 153 L.Ed.2d 453, http://laws.findlaw.com/us/000/01-714.html (2002).

[47]Pub. L. No. 107-155, §403, 116 Stat. 81 (2002). See *McConnell v. Federal Election Commission*, 251 F. Supp. 2d 176 (D.D.C. 2003) http://www.dcd.uscourts.gov/mcconnell-2002-ruling.html. The Supreme Court obliged Congress by scheduling a four-hour oral argument for September 8, 2003, during its usual summer recess, and decided the case on December 10, 2003. *McConnell v. Federal Election Commission*, 540 U.S. 93, 124 S.Ct. 619, 157 L.Ed.2d 491, (2003) http://laws.findlaw.com/us/000/02-1674.html. See in particular the district court opinion of Judge Karen LeCraft Henderson in this case for an evaluation of how useful the McCain-Feingold provision for expedited judicial review was, especially in light of the fact that the statute that it amended, the Federal Election Campaign Act, already provides for a form of expedited review. See 2 U.S.C. §437h.

[48]Pub. L. No. 104-130, 110 Stat. 1200 (1996), 2 U.S.C. 692. See *Raines v. Byrd*, 521 U.S. 811, 117 S.Ct. 2312, 138 L.Ed.2d 849, http://laws.findlaw.com/us/521/811.html (1997), and *Clinton v. City of New York*, 524 U.S. 417, 118 S.Ct. 2091, 141 L.Ed.2d 393, http://laws.findlaw.com/us/524/417.html (1998).

[49]The Flag Protection Act of 1989, 18 U.S.C. 700(d), similarly makes it the duty of the Supreme Court to advance and expedite the case.

actual dispute between the parties. The federal courts will not render an advisory opinion on the abstract question of whether a law is constitutional.

We have all heard, however, of instances in which a new statute—relating to abortion or flag burning or the like—is challenged in court immediately upon enactment, sometimes even before the date on which the law goes into effect. Can there be a justiciable controversy before the effective date of the law? Can a party have standing to sue at that time? Can the case be ripe for judicial resolution?

The answers to these questions are "Yes," "Yes," and "Yes—perhaps." The 1934 Declaratory Judgment Act provides some guidance here. The Act steps carefully through the fire swamp of justiciability to avoid the problems of case-or-controversy, standing to sue, and ripeness.[50] The statute takes these issues boldly by the horns by stating, in pertinent part, "In a case of actual controversy within its jurisdiction, except with respect to [certain named classes of cases] . . . any court of the United States, upon the filing of an appropriate pleading, may declare the rights and other legal relations of any interested party seeking such declaration, whether or not further relief is or could be sought." There must be an "actual controversy," a real and not merely hypothetical or speculative conflict posed by the statute in question and the existing legal rights of the plaintiff. The plaintiff, to have standing, must be an "interested party"—one whose legally recognized interests or rights conflict with, or are placed in imminent danger by, the new, challenged statute. The conflict, however, need not have reached the point of harming or causing legal damage to the plaintiff— the Act says the courts may declare the rights and legal relations of an interested party "whether or not further relief . . . could be sought." In other words, the plaintiff need not yet have sustained legally remediable damages before bringing an action based upon Declaratory Judgment Act jurisdiction.

We might also note here that for the past few decades, cases alleging that a statute adversely affects, or "chills," the plaintiff's exercise of First Amendment rights have also been entertained by federal courts even though the statutes in question have not yet been used by the government or anyone else to bring legal actions, civil or criminal, against the plaintiff.[51]

The Declaratory Judgment Act and the First Amendment cases stand for the principle that federal courts will consider a statute or government action before any remediable harm has been done and that the court's consideration may include the statute's or action's constitutionality. Clearly the Act and the First Amendment cases push the outer edge of the envelope in the three areas of justiciability that we

---

[50]28 U.S.C. Section 2201. The constitutionality of the statute was established in the case of *Aetna Life Insurance Company v. Haworth*, 300 U.S. 227, 57 S.Ct. 461, 81 L.Ed. 617, http://laws.findlaw.com/us/300/227.html (1937).

[51]See for example *NAACP v. Button*, 371 U.S. 415, 83 S.Ct. 328, 9 L.Ed.2d 405, http://laws.findlaw.com/us/371/415.html (1963), and *Secretary of State v. Munson*, 467 U.S. 947, 104 S.Ct. 2839, 81 L.Ed.2d 786, http://laws.findlaw.com/us/467/947.html (1984). See Wright, Miller, Cooper, and Freer, *Federal Practice and Procedure: Jurisdiction 2d*, §§3531 & 3532 (2003), and Nowak and Rotunda, *Constitutional Law*, 6th ed., §16.8 (2000). Nowak and Rotunda warn against confusing standing and First Amendment issues. In First Amendment overbreadth cases, the plaintiffs have (or may have) standing because the challenged statute has already affected or "chilled" their behavior when they bring suit.

discussed. The federal courts, however, have made it equally clear that the courts, not Congress, will make the final determinations of whether the requirements of justiciability are met in cases brought under the Act by dismissing a number of Declaratory Judgment Act cases on grounds of nonjusticiability.[52]

A good example of this judicial independence is found in the 1996 Line Item Veto Act and the initial challenge to the Act presented in the case of *Raines v. Byrd*. The Act provided that "[a]ny Member of Congress or any individual adversely affected by [the Act] may bring an action, in the United States District Court for the District of Columbia, for declaratory judgment and injunctive relief on the ground that any provision of this part violates the Constitution."[53] Relying on this provision, Senator Robert Byrd and other members of Congress filed suit promptly after enactment of the law, but the Supreme Court held that the "members of Congress do not have a sufficient 'personal stake' in this dispute and have not alleged a sufficiently concrete injury to have established Article III standing," and that the case must be dismissed.[54]

---

## *Microsoft v. United States*

The recent antitrust action by the United States government against Microsoft is also an example of the use—or attempted use—of expedited review, though the case did not present a constitutional issue and the statute relied upon was not a recent one. The case was brought in the United States District Court for the District of Columbia. When the court rendered its judgment, the opinion included language to the effect that it would be prudent for the Supreme Court to review the case directly without intermediate review by the United States court of appeals. This language was included to conform to the requirements of an old statute, the Expediting Act of 1903, 15 U.S.C. §29(b), that provides for direct review to the Supreme Court if "the district judge who adjudicated the case enters an order stating that immediate consideration of the appeal by the Supreme Court is of general public importance in the administration of justice." The appellate jurisdiction of the Supreme Court is discretionary, however, not mandatory; the Court denied the appeal and remanded the case to the United States Court of Appeals for initial review. *Microsoft v. United States*, 530 U.S. 1301, 122 S.Ct. 350, 147 L.Ed.2d 1048 (2000). The Supreme Court has, in fact, repeatedly indicated its preference over the years for initial appellate review by the Courts of Appeals whenever possible.

---

[52]See Charles Alan Wright, Arthur R. Miller, and Mary Kay Kane, *Federal Practice and Procedure: Civil*, §§2751 *et seq* (1998), for cases. Wright, Miller, and Kane indicate that the federal courts are not keen on considering constitutional issues on the basis of Declaratory Judgment Act actions, but on occasion they have. See, for example *Powell v. McCormack*, 395 U.S. 486, 89 S.Ct. 1944, 23 L.Ed.2d 491, http://laws.findlaw.com/us/395/486.html (1969).

[53]Section 692(a)(1) of the Act, Pub. L. No. 104-130, 130 Stat. 1200 (1996). *Raines v. Byrd*, 521 U.S. 811, 815-816, 117 S.Ct. 2312, 2316, 138 L.Ed.2d 849, 856, http://laws.findlaw.com/us/521/811.html (1997).

[54]521 U.S. at 830, 117 S.Ct. at 2322-2323, 138 L.Ed.2d at 864.

# CONCLUSION

To new students and to most practicing attorneys, the litigation process is dauntingly complex, and the practice of litigation is stressful even to seasoned practitioners. We have examined the process here in order to (1) get a better understanding of the principal judicial function that common law courts are intended to perform—deciding cases; and (2) to better understand the main points in the litigation process that serve to originate appellate proceedings—the judicial rulings.

Since early in the development of the common law, the litigation process has aimed at the identification of the precise points of disagreement—factual, legal, or both—between the parties in order to provide an efficient means of resolving them. Pretrial procedure defines these issues: if the issues are factual, a trial will resolve them; if the issues are legal, a judge will resolve them. Although the foundation of the litigation process is no longer the royal writs, it is still based upon specific theories of liability, called "causes of action" in civil cases and "charges" or "offenses" in criminal cases, many of which have their roots in the old writs. Trials are designed to be efficient, fair, and "rational," and the losers in court today are almost always guaranteed a right to appellate review.

Appellate opinions guide the judges and the attorneys at each stage of the litigation process, but as we now know, the cases reviewed by appellate courts have not all been to trial; in other words, a litigant can be a loser without having lost in trial. Today, trial court rulings on motions for summary judgment and motions to dismiss account for a huge number of the cases that are appealed. Most appeals are of "final judgments," but judicial rulings that prevent plaintiffs or defendants from continuing the litigation—rulings that "throw the litigant out of court"—are final judgments even though they may have occurred before a trial was held. This procedural aspect of the case is often important if we are to understand the decision of the appellate court. For example, an appellate court owes a trial court less deference for its rulings on legal issues than for its rulings on matters of fact.

If we turn our focus away from the technical procedure that our trial courts and appellate courts enforce over litigation, we become aware that our carefully constructed legal systems owe any success that they might have to the fact that very few cases are ever appealed and even fewer ever go to trial. As explained in Appendix E, the overwhelming majority of civil cases that are filed in United States courts are settled by the parties—some, it is true, during or after trial; some even after appeal; but most before trial—and the court systems of this country would collapse under the sheer weight of the volume of cases if this were not so. It is true that criminal cases go to trial more often than civil cases, but if plea bargains did not occur in over 80 percent of the cases, the presently existing court systems would be flooded out by the criminal cases alone. It is ironic that our litigation methods have been so meticulously created only to have most litigants voluntarily leave the system without ever using its principal icons—the public trial and the appellate court argument. As we turn to a survey of the main courts in the federal and state systems, keep in mind that one of their principal objectives today—if not *the* principal objective—is to encourage the parties before them to settle their differences, go home, and not make further use of the facilities.

# Chapter 4

# Federal and State Courts

## Chapter Outline

# FEDERAL COURTS—THE POWERS OF CONGRESS

> The judicial Power of the United States, shall be vested in one supreme Court, and in such inferior Courts as the Congress may from time to time ordain and establish. The Judges, both of the supreme and inferior Courts, shall hold their Offices during good Behaviour, and shall, at stated Times, receive for their Services, a Compensation, which shall not be diminished during their Continuance in Office.
>
> —U.S. Const. Art. III, § 1.

The first sentence in Article III of the Constitution expressly authorizes Congress to create courts. We saw in Chapter 1 that the brief reference to possible "inferior" courts—courts subordinate to the "supreme Court"—was the result of a compromise in the Philadelphia deliberations. This chapter presents a sketch of the present-day federal and state court systems and brief accounts of the principal courts in those systems. An appendix includes descriptions of several other important federal courts.

Article III places two restrictions on Congress when Congress exercises this authority: (1) the judges of courts created pursuant to Article III shall have lifetime tenure and salaries that cannot be lowered during their time on the bench, and (2) the jurisdiction that Congress may confer on these courts is limited to that enumerated in Section 2.

But Congress may also create courts under authority granted expressly and implicitly by other sections of the Constitution. Article I, Section 8, Clause 9, enumerates the authority of Congress to "constitute Tribunals inferior to the supreme Court." Under the authority enumerated in Clauses 14 and 17 of Section 8, Congress has created courts for the military and for the District of Columbia, and under Article IV, Section 3, Clause 2, it has created courts for United States territories.[1]

Employing the Inferior Tribunals Clause of Article I, Congress has created additional federal tribunals in order to resolve certain kinds of legal disputes in addition to those indigenous to the territories, the District of Columbia, and the military. When Congress finds it necessary and proper to create such tribunals—and it has been doing so since at least 1866—Congress is not bound by the restrictions that Article III places upon courts exercising federal judicial power.[2] Thus, Congress may establish limited terms for the judges of these courts, may reduce judges' salaries while they are in office, and may give these courts jurisdiction and powers beyond the confines of Article III. Courts that are created under other constitutional authority, primarily Articles I and IV, are called **legislative courts.** Courts created under the authority of

---

[1]In fact, the distinction between "legislative" and "constitutional" courts was first made by Chief Justice John Marshall in *American Insurance Company v. 356 Bales of Cotton*, 26 U.S. (1 Pet.) 511, 7 L.Ed. 242, http://laws.findlaw.com/us/26/511.html (1828), a case that challenged the "wreckers court" that was created pursuant to congressional authorization in the territory of Florida.

[2]Indeed, Congress may vest in such courts functions, that is, judicial power, that may not be vested in courts created under Article III because of the limitations on federal judicial power discussed in Chapter 2. The 1866 date refers to the history of the United States Court of Federal Claims, which is described below.

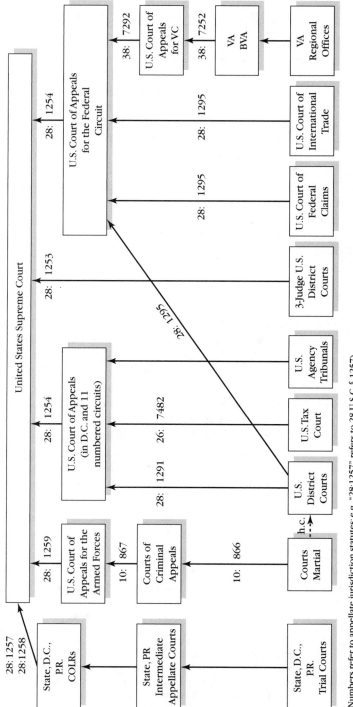

(Numbers refer to appellate jurisdiction statutes; e.g., "28:1257" refers to 28 U.S.C. § 1257)

**Figure 4.1** The Courts of the Federal Legal System

# Authority for Legislative Courts

The Congress shall have Power "to constitute Tribunals inferior to the supreme Court." **U.S. Const. Art. I, § 8, cl. 9.**

The Congress shall have Power "to make Rules for the Government and Regulation of the land and naval Forces." **U.S. Const. Art. I, § 8, cl. 14.**

The Congress shall have power "to exercise exclusive Legislation in all Cases whatsoever, over such District (not exceeding ten Miles square) as may, by Cession of particular States, and the Acceptance of Congress, become the Seat of the Government of the United States, and to exercise like Authority over all Places purchased by the Consent of the Legislature of the State in which the Same shall be, for the Erection of Forts, Magazines, Arsenals, dock-Yards, and other needful Buildings." **U.S. Const. Art. I, § 8, cl. 17.**

"The Congress shall have Power to dispose of and make all needful Rules and Regulations respecting the Territory or other Property belonging to the United States." **U.S. Const. Art. IV, § 3, cl. 2.**

---

Article III—the federal courts to which we have routinely referred in the previous chapters—are called **constitutional courts** or, not surprisingly, **Article III courts.**

The constitutional boundary between the two types of courts is difficult to discern and, in the words of Justice John Harlan, "has been productive of much confusion and controversy."[3] The general constitutional doctrine on this matter seems to be that the federal judicial power—that is, the exercise of the jurisdiction described in Article III, Section 2—must be vested in constitutional courts, but the doctrine recognizes three narrow exceptions: Article III judicial power may, on occasion, be vested (1) in territorial courts, (2) in military courts, and (3) in tribunals adjudicating "public rights" disputes.[4] The Supreme Court has also referred to the terms of the judges' tenure to distinguish between constitutional and legislative courts: if the judges sit for a term of years, then the court on which they sit is presumptively a

---

[3]*Glidden Co. v. Zdanok*, 370 U.S. 530, 534, 82 S.Ct. 1459, 8 L. Ed. 2d 671, http://laws.findlaw.com/us/370/530.html (1962) (plurality opinion by Justice John Harlan).

[4]**Public rights** cases are cases based squarely on federal statutes. Congress has vested the power to decide such disputes in many administrative agency tribunals as well as in federal courts. But even here, a sharp division between issues arising under federal statutes and those arising under state law, for example, has been impossible to maintain. See *Commodity Futures Trading Commission v. Schor*, 478 U.S. 833, 106 S.Ct. 3245, 92 L.Ed.2d 675, http://laws.findlaw.com/us/478/833.html (1986).

We say that it only "seems" to be the general rule because in a recent case addressing this distinction, *Northern Pipeline Construction Co. v. Marathon Pipe Line Co.*, 458 U.S. 50, 102 S.Ct. 2858, 73 L. Ed. 2d 598, http://laws.findlaw.com/us/458/50.html (1982), the judgment was again announced by a plurality of the court rather than a majority, just as the earlier judgment in *Glidden Co. v. Zdanok, supra*, had been announced. See particularly the probing dissent of Justice Byron White in the *Northern Pipeline* case.

legislative court; if they sit during good behavior, that is, if they have lifetime tenure, the court is presumptively a constitutional court.

What this distinction between constitutional and legislative courts makes clear is that not all federal courts are the same in terms of their status under the Constitution and of the power they may exercise. Though the precise constitutional distinction between the two sets of courts is not as clear, we might hazard the following generalizations. The judicial power of Article III courts is limited to deciding concrete cases and controversies as enumerated in Article III, Section 2. Legislative courts generally may not perform these essential functions of Article III courts, but may perform functions that are not permitted to Article III courts.[5] The principal exception to this latter rule is the legislative courts that Congress sets up in United States territories to act as both local courts of general jurisdiction and as Article III courts. These territorial courts, such as the United States district courts of Guam, the Northern Marianas, and the Virgin Islands, may perform functions that constitutional courts also perform and also functions that state courts of general jurisdiction may perform but that other Article III courts may not.[6]

In this chapter, we shall first describe the major constitutional courts and then turn to descriptions of several legislative courts of the federal system. Finally, we will present an overview of the state judicial systems of the United States.

## Constitutional or Article III Courts

*Original Jurisdiction—The United States District Courts*
*http://www.uscourts.gov/allinks.html*

The Judicial Districts and the Judges

Several different federal courts, including the United States Supreme Court, are courts of original jurisdiction, but the principal trial courts in the federal system are the United States district courts. Congress has divided the country into 94 judicial districts and has created an Article III federal court, called a "United States district court," for each district.[7] Although each state includes at least one judicial district, states may be divided into more than one district depending on their size and the

---

[5] *Northern Pipeline Construction Co. v. Marathon Pipe Line Co., supra,* note 4.

[6] A recent case that exemplifies the constitutional distinction between constitutional courts and legislative courts is *Nguyen v. United States,* 539 U.S. 69, 123 S.Ct. 2130, 156 L.Ed.2d 64, http://laws.findlaw.com/us/ 000/1-10873.html (2003). The petitioners were convicted of federal drug offenses in the United States District Court of Guam, an Article IV territorial court. The Supreme Court vacated the judgment of a three-judge panel of the United States Court of Appeals for the Ninth Circuit, which affirmed the convictions, holding that the panel did not have the authority to affirm the district court's judgment because the panel included the Chief Judge of the District Court for the Northern Mariana Islands, an Article IV court. The judgment of the court of appeals panel was therefore invalid because it did not proceed from a valid Article III appellate court.

[7] In addition to the 89 judicial districts in the 50 states, Congress has created districts for Puerto Rico, the Virgin Islands, Guam, the Northern Mariana Islands, and the District of Columbia. The old district of the Canal Zone in Panama was eliminated by law in 1982.

amount of federal litigation they attract. Thus, New York, Texas, and California each contains four districts while 26 states contain only one.[8] (See Fig. 4.2.)

For each of these 94 United States district courts, Congress allocates a certain number of judgeships, which is determined, theoretically at least, on the basis of need; again, the extent of the territory of the district and the amount of litigation are key factors. As of 2003, a total of 680 permanent judgeships for the district courts have been authorized by law. A dwindling few districts have only one judge assigned to them, but some have many more.[9] For example, the United States District Court for the Southern District of New York, one of the busiest courts in the nation, presently has 28 authorized judgeships; the central district of California has 27; and the eastern district of Pennsylvania and northern district of Illinois have 22 each.[10]

## Jurisdiction

The number and the type of cases over which the federal district courts have been given jurisdiction reflect the broad scope of the federal judicial system. In the year ending September 30, 2003, 323,604 cases were filed in United States district courts. Of these, 70,642 (22 percent) were criminal cases, and the rest (252,962, or 78 percent) were civil.[11] District court civil cases fall into three main categories. (See Fig. 4.3.)

Over half of the civil cases are brought on the basis of **federal question jurisdiction**—the jurisdiction that authorizes the district courts to decide cases "arising under the Constitution, laws, or treaties of the United States." From these three sources of federal question cases, most of the cases by far arise under federal law rather than under the Constitution or United States treaties. One might think that if federal courts were to handle any kind of legal issues at all, they should certainly handle these "federal question" issues, yet Congress did not assign complete federal question jurisdiction to federal trial courts until 1875.[12]

---

[8]Twelve states contain two districts, and nine states contain three.

[9]At present, only three districts—the eastern district of Oklahoma, the district of Guam, and the district of the Northern Mariana Islands—have but one authorized judgeship specifically assigned to them. See 28 U.S.C. §133, 48 U.S.C. § 1424b (Guam) and 48 U.S.C. § 1821 (Northern Marianas). The latter two courts, and the District Court of the Virgin Islands (48 U.S.C. §§ 1611-1617), are combination United States district courts and territorial courts; their judges serve for a term of years, and hence the courts are legislative courts and not Article III courts even though they are "United States district courts."

[10]Of course, a number of the federal judgeships are vacant at any given time. Also, federal judges may assume "senior status" and hear only a few cases each year. The assumption of senior status by a federal judge opens a vacancy in the authorized number of judgeships.

[11]The district courts have exclusive original jurisdiction over federal crimes under 18 U.S.C. § 3231. The major sources of civil jurisdiction are discussed in the following text.

[12]Students of constitutional law should recall that up until 1976, challenges to the constitutionality of federal statutes required the convening of three-judge district courts under 28 U.S.C. 2284. The judgments of these three-judge courts could be appealed directly to the Supreme Court. See the discussion of "Expedited Consideration of Constitutional Issues" at pages 80-81, *supra*.

## Geographic Boundaries
of United States Courts of Appeals and United States District Courts

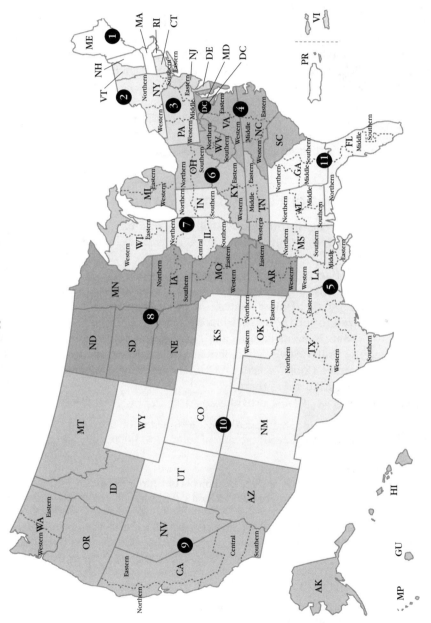

**Figure 4.2**
*Source:* Adapted from the Office of Public Affairs, Administrative Office of the United States Courts.

The second significant set of cases before the district courts—**United States Party** cases or simply **U.S. Cases**—is made up of cases that are based simply on the fact that the federal government or one of its agencies is a party to the suit. The federal government and its agencies may also be sued in state courts, but the federal **removal statute** (28 U.S.C. § 1441) allows these defendants to transfer the case to an appropriate United States district court. Cases in which the United States government is a plaintiff include a wide variety of disputes, such as contract and real estate disputes; cases in which the United States is a defendant include automobile liability issues, medical malpractice issues, and many more.

The third major category of district court cases is the so-called **diversity** or **diversity of citizenship** cases.[13] The "diversity" that is referred to here is the diversity of the state (or national) citizenship of the parties in the case. Simply put, if none of the defendants is a citizen of any of the states of which the plaintiffs are citizens,

---

## Types of Federal Court Jurisdiction

**Federal Question:** "The district courts shall have original jurisdiction of all civil actions arising under the Constitution, laws, or treaties of the United States." 28 U.S.C. § 1331.

**United States Party:** "Except as otherwise provided by Act of Congress, the district courts shall have original jurisdiction of all civil actions, suits or proceedings commenced by the United States, or by any agency or officer thereof expressly authorized to sue by Act of Congress." 28 U.S.C. § 1345.

28 U.S.C. § 1346 is more complicated. It allocates jurisdiction over certain cases in which the United States is a defendant to the district courts concurrently with the United States Court of Federal Claims and expressly denies the district court original jurisdiction over others.

**Diversity:** 28 U.S.C. § 1332 provides, in part:

(a) The district courts shall have original jurisdiction of all civil actions where the matter in controversy exceeds the sum or value of $75,000, exclusive of interest and costs, and is between—
(1) citizens of different States;
(2) citizens of a State and citizens or subjects of a foreign state;
(3) citizens of different States and in which citizens or subjects of a foreign state are additional parties; and
(4) a foreign state, defined in section 1603(a) of this title, as plaintiff and citizens of a State or of different States.

---

[13]In addition to these three categories, which amount to 99.9 percent of the caseload, 15 local jurisdiction cases were brought in 2003 in district courts, such as those of Guam and the Virgin Islands, that also operate to some degree as courts of local jurisdiction. These included contract, real property, and tort actions between private parties.

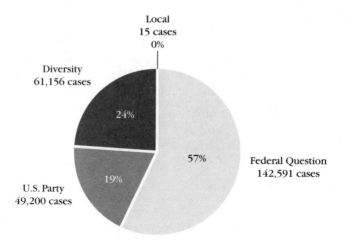

**Figure 4.3**  Cases Filed in United State District Courts, 2003

and if the amount of money in question, called the "jurisdictional amount," exceeds the statutory minimum, then the plaintiffs may bring suit in federal district court regardless of the subject matter of the case. This means that the federal courts, under their diversity jurisdiction, may decide product liability (exploding toasters) and personal injury (skiing accidents) cases as well as cases based upon violations of contracts between private individuals, as long as the amount in question is more than $75,000, which is the current statutory jurisdictional amount. In these cases, the federal courts require the parties to observe the federal procedural rules, but the courts must apply the substantive laws and legal rules of the relevant states; in short, the federal courts basically sit as state courts in diversity cases. All of these cases, of course, could also be brought in state courts, and many critics of diversity jurisdiction believe they should be, but there are politically powerful forces arrayed against the critics, and the elimination of diversity jurisdiction is not a short-term probability. As long as diversity jurisdiction exists, it will be the basis for a substantial portion of the federal caseload.

What these facts and figures show is that the United States district courts do a lot more than decide constitutional law cases or even federal law cases. In diversity cases and in many United States party cases, the cases and controversies are exactly the same as those decided every day in state courts, and the jurisdiction of the federal and the state courts in most of these cases is concurrent. Moreover, even in the federal question cases, the United States district court jurisdiction is not exclusive; state courts routinely decide cases "arising under the Constitution, laws, or treaties of the United States," too. The cases in federal courts are not necessarily more important than the cases that state courts decide, nor do they necessarily involve more money than lawsuits in state courts. Rather, the jurisdiction of the United States district courts largely overlaps the jurisdiction of the state courts of this country, and the district courts are best seen as another set of trial courts handling routine litigation.

## *Bankruptcy and Magistrate Courts*

Strictly speaking, these two sets of federal courts are not separate Article III institutions at all. For one thing, bankruptcy judges and magistrate judges are selected by federal judges, serve a set term of years, and may be removed from office for good cause.[14] For another, the statutes that establish these courts indicate that these courts are adjuncts of the federal district courts.[15] Yet in the year ending September 30, 2003, more than 2.5 million cases were filed with or disposed of by bankruptcy and magistrate judges. Courts handling a caseload of this magnitude must be recognized in any survey of the federal judiciary.

## United States Bankruptcy Courts
http://www.ncbj.org

Ever since the liberalization of bankruptcy laws for individuals and farmers, the number of bankruptcy cases filed in federal courts has soared. In 1981, a total of 360,329 cases were filed in federal courts. About 13 percent of those cases were filed by businesses. In 1991, as a result of new bankruptcy laws, 880,399 cases were filed, of which only 7 percent were business cases. In 2003, over 1.6 million cases were filed, of which only 2.2 percent were business cases.

It is misleading to call these bankruptcy proceedings "cases," if we understand cases to be adversarial lawsuits. The overwhelming majority of bankruptcy cases are filed voluntarily by the individuals or businesses who are in financial difficulty—the usual test being that the debts of the party outweigh the assets and the party cannot pay the debts as they come due—and who may also file a plan to pay off their creditors according to the priorities and procedures established by law. The bankruptcy judges review and authorize these plans. The judges also decide the validity of claims by creditors against the bankrupt party and of counterclaims by the bankrupt party, also called the "bankrupt."[16]

Not all bankruptcy proceedings are instituted voluntarily or proceed consensually, however, and many produce disputes between the creditors and the troubled parties. In 2003, about 97,000 of the bankruptcy cases involved adversarial proceedings of one type or another, the most in 20 years. In the course of handling these adversarial proceedings, legal controversies must be addressed and resolved by the

---

[14]For bankruptcy judges, see 28 U.S.C. § 152(a)(1) (bankruptcy judges are appointed by the United States court of appeals and serve 14-year terms) and (e) (bankruptcy judges are removable "only for incompetence, misconduct, neglect of duty, or physical or mental disability"). For magistrate judges, appointment is governed by 28 U.S.C. § 631(a) and (e) (appointment by district court judges for 8-year terms) and removal by § 631(i) (removable for the same reasons as bankruptcy judges or if the judicial conference determines that "the services performed by his office are no longer needed"). In 2003 there were 324 authorized bankruptcy judgeships.

[15]"In each judicial district, the bankruptcy judges in regular service shall constitute a unit of the district court to be known as the bankruptcy court for that district." 28 U.S.C. § 151.

[16]See *Bankruptcy Basics* on the Administrative Office of the United States Courts Web site at http://www.uscourts.gov/bankbasic.pdf.

courts. It was the vesting of too much judicial power in non–Article III bankruptcy judges that led the Supreme Court to invalidate the offending provisions of the 1978 Bankruptcy Act in the case of *Northern Pipeline Construction v. Marathon Pipe Line Co.*[17] Subsequently, Congress enacted revised legislation in 1984, which is presently in effect.[18]

Under the 1984 law, the responsibilities of bankruptcy judges fall into two categories: "core" and "noncore." Core matters are those relating directly to the administration of the bankrupt's estate. The bankruptcy judge has jurisdiction over these matters, subject to an appeal to the United States district courts.[19] Noncore matters are less directly related to the administration of the estate. Regarding these noncore matters, the bankruptcy judges may submit proposed findings of fact and conclusions of law to the district courts, but it is the district court judges who ultimately enter the orders.[20]

## United States Magistrate Judges
http://www.fedjudge.org/index.asp

Like the bankruptcy judges, United States magistrate judges, originally known as "commissioners" and then as "magistrates" before their title was changed to "magistrate judges" in 1990, exercise judicial power both independently and as subordinates to the district courts.

In 2003, the more than 500 full-time and part-time magistrate judges disposed of 948,570 matters, almost twice the number that they disposed of in 1993. Disposing of a "matter" in this context does not generally mean exercising original jurisdiction over a case from filing to judgment. Rather, more than 90 percent of the matters in question are preliminary and pretrial proceedings in criminal and civil cases, such as issuing warrants, holding detention and evidentiary hearings, hearing and deciding motions, and presiding over pretrial conferences—all vital and time-consuming proceedings that would otherwise have to be handled by the district court judges. In all of these matters, the litigants may ask the district court judges to review the magistrate judges' decisions.

---

[17]*Northern Pipeline Construction Co. v. Marathon Pipeline Co., supra,* note 4. The 1978 Act established United States "bankruptcy courts" in every judicial district and gave them jurisdiction over "all civil proceedings arising under title 11 [of the bankruptcy code] or arising in or related to cases under title 11." 28 U.S.C. § 1471(b) (1976 ed., Supp. IV). Bankruptcy judges, under the 1978 Act, were appointed for 14-year terms and were removable by the judicial council of the judicial circuit for cause. Their salaries were set by statute and subject to diminution. The 1984 Act continued these provisions (28 U.S.C. §§ 151–153), but attempted to avoid the problem of *Northern Pipeline* by providing that Article III district court judges have appellate jurisdiction over all bankruptcy judge rulings (28 U.S.C. § 158) and have original jurisdiction over all Article III (noncore) issues (28 U.S.C. § 157(c)). At present there are about 300 bankruptcy judges.

[18]Pub.L. 98-353, July 10, 1984; 28 U.S.C. §§ 151–158.

[19]28 U.S.C. § 157(b)(2). In 2002, about 2,500 appeals were taken to the district courts under this statute.

[20]28 U.S.C. § 157(c).

In addition to these duties, however, the magistrate judges also exercised original jurisdiction, including conducting jury and nonjury trials, in almost 100,000 cases— over 83,000 federal misdemeanor and petty offense cases and more than 13,000 civil cases in which the parties consented to have a magistrate judge try the case.

District court judges have also been referring so-called "prisoner litigation" cases to magistrate judges for evidentiary hearings, proposed findings, and recommended rulings. These civil cases, consisting in 2003 of over 13,000 habeas corpus applications by state and federal prisoners as well as almost 11,000 cases in which prisoners alleged civil rights violations, constitute a significant fraction of the total of cases filed in the United States district courts each year.

In fact, in 2003 almost 55,000 habeas corpus, civil rights, and other actions were filed in the United States district courts by state and federal prisoners. This amounted to over 20 percent of all the civil cases filed in the district courts. As we shall see in the next section, prisoner actions account for a major portion of the federal appellate court caseload as well.

## Appellate Jurisdiction—The United States Courts of Appeals
*http://www.uscourts.gov/allinks.html*

### The Circuits and the Judges

In establishing the federal appellate court system, Congress divided the territory of the United States into 12 geographical regions or "circuits" and established a United States court of appeals for each (Fig. 4.1).[21] The District of Columbia constitutes one of the circuits—the United States Court of Appeals for the District of Columbia Circuit, or USCA-DC. The other 11 are identified by the number of the circuit each serves—thus, the United States Court of Appeals for the First Circuit, or USCA-1, and so on. Currently, 167 judgeships are authorized for the regional appellate courts; the allotment of judges ranges from 6 judges for the First Circuit to 28 judges for the Ninth.[22] In addition to these 12, Congress has also established a nonregional Article III court of appeals for the Federal Circuit, a court with highly specialized jurisdiction, and two Article I appellate courts—the United States Court of Appeals for the Armed Forces and the United States Court of Appeals for Veterans Claims. In this section, we shall look at the 12 regional courts of appeals.

### Jurisdiction

The United States courts of appeals are the principal courts of appellate jurisdiction in the federal system. As such, they perform two important functions. First, because the appellate jurisdiction of the courts of appeals is entirely mandatory, unsuccessful litigants in all federal trial courts, whether constitutional or legislative courts, are guaranteed an opportunity for appellate review before the courts of appeals. Second,

---

[21]28 U.S.C. § 41.

[22]28 U.S.C. § 44.

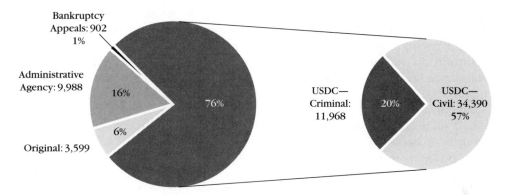

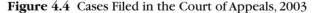

**Figure 4.4**  Cases Filed in the Court of Appeals, 2003

the courts of appeals are obligated to apply Supreme Court precedents to the thousands of cases that they must review each year whenever such precedents are available, and in this way the courts of appeals supervise the district courts and provide the cohesion that binds the federal courts into a legal system. Although it is the ultimate judicial authority in the federal court system, the Supreme Court, with its discretionary appellate jurisdiction and limited resources, simply cannot supervise the federal courts as closely as the courts of appeals can. Where there are no clear precedents—that is, where the cases before the courts of appeals are **cases of first impression**—the courts must decide the appeals as best they can upon the available precedent, but they need not follow the precedents of the other coequal courts of appeals. Disagreements among the circuits about the appropriate legal rules and principles to follow often lead the Supreme Court to review a case with the purpose of resolving the inconsistent appellate court rulings.

In the year ending September 30, 2003, almost 61,000 cases were filed in the regional courts of appeals, and of these cases over 46,000 were direct appeals from the United States district courts.[23] (See Fig. 4.4.) A quarter of these were criminal case appeals, and the rest were civil. The courts of appeals also heard appeals from the federal bankruptcy courts and from administrative agencies. Of the 22,000 cases that the courts of appeals decided on the merits, *most were decided solely on the basis of the written briefs submitted by counsel, not after oral arguments.* If oral arguments are heard, the courts of appeals almost always hear them by sitting in panels of three judges, not *en banc.*

Convicted criminals provided most of the caseload of the courts of appeals. In addition to the more than 11,000 direct appeals in federal criminal cases in 2003, state and federal prisoners also filed almost 18,000 prisoner litigation cases—requests from state and federal prisoners who want either collateral review of their convictions or direct review of their failed claims that their federal civil rights have been

---

[23]28 U.S.C. § 1291.

violated. Additionally, most of the matters classified as "original proceedings" on the dockets of the courts of appeals are motions generated by prisoners.

The fate of most of the prisoner litigation is significantly different from the fate of the direct criminal appeals and the nonprisoner civil cases. Generally, in any given year, almost as many appeals are thrown out on procedural grounds—because the appellants did not properly follow the appellate procedural rules—as are decided on the merits. When we look at appeals of prisoner petitions, however, we find that almost three-quarters of these appeals are thrown out on procedural grounds. This result is probably due to the lack of technical legal proficiency of the petitioners since prisoners usually proceed **pro se**—that is, they represent themselves and are not represented by attorneys. Only about 25 percent of the direct criminal appeals and less than half of the non-prisoner civil appeals, cases in which most appellants are represented by counsel, are thrown out for procedural defects. When considering the caseload statistics of the federal courts, it is important to keep in mind the huge portion of their workload that is made up of prisoner litigation.

## Legislative Courts

*Original Jurisdiction—The United States Court of Federal Claims*
*http://www.uscfc.uscourts.gov/*

### History

In 1855, Congress created the Court of Claims as an agency to investigate and certify claims against the federal government. Congress in 1863 amended the law to give the Court of Claims the authority to render final judgments in claims matters. These judgments were appealable in some instances to the United States Supreme Court, but the Supreme Court decisions were then subject to subsequent certification by the Secretary of the Treasury and appropriation by Congress. The Supreme Court, in *Gordon v. United States,* decided that the ultimate authority of the Secretary of the Treasury to revise the judgments of the Court of Claims (and the judgments of the Supreme Court itself) meant that the power exercised by the Court of Claims was not true federal (Article III) judicial power at all and thus that the Supreme Court could not be constitutionally empowered to participate in such a nonjudicial claims certification function exercised by the Court of Claims.[24] In 1866, in response to the *Gordon* decision, Congress amended the authorization statute to remove the certification authority of the Secretary of the Treasury; thereafter, the judicial nature of the Court of Claims was upheld.

Once the judicial nature of the Court of Claims was established, the question of its status as either a legislative or a constitutional court did not seem to occur until 1929, and then only as *dictum* in a case that challenged the constitutional status of the United States Court of Customs Appeals.[25] In the *Bakelite* case, the Supreme

---

[24]*Gordon v. United States*, 69 (2 Wall.) U.S. 561, 17 L. Ed. 921, http://laws.findlaw.com/us/69/561.html (1865).

Court held that the Court of Customs Appeals was an Article I court and opined that the Court of Claims was one, too. This opinion was confirmed in *Williams v. United States,* a 1933 case that squarely presented the issue of the constitutional status of the Court of Claims.[26]

Twenty years later, Congress formally amended Court of Claims authorization statute, declaring, "Such court is hereby declared to be a court established under article III of the Constitution of the United States."[27] In the case of *Glidden v. Zdanok,* decided nine years later, the Supreme Court confirmed that the Court of Claims is indeed an Article III court, and federal court expert Professor Charles Wright was moved to say in 1976, "The Court of Claims and the Court of Customs and Patent Appeals are now definitely 'constitutional' courts."

In 1982, however, Congress apparently had second (third?) thoughts and again amended the authorization statute, renaming the court the "United States Claims Court" and stating, "The court is declared to be a court established under article I of the Constitution of the United States," leading one to recall the old legal maxim, "Always check the pocket parts." The 1982 declaration has not yet been challenged in a case before the Supreme Court, but Congress, apparently still unable to keep its hands off the court, decided in 1992 to change its name again: it is now the United States Court of Federal Claims.[28]

Today, the United States Court of Federal Claims is located in Washington, D.C., and consists of 16 judges serving 15-year terms.[29]

## Jurisdiction

In general, the United States Court of Federal Claims is the place to sue the federal government for damages resulting from contractual dealings with the government. The court has original jurisdiction over nontort claims against the United States arising under the Constitution, the laws, or the administrative regulations of the United States government.[30] The court is authorized to order equitable remedies and to issue declaratory judgments as necessary to afford complete remedies to successful claimants.[31]

---

[25]*Ex parte Bakelite Corp.*, 279 U.S. 438, 49 S.Ct. 411, 73 L.Ed. 789, http://laws.findlaw.com/us/279/438.html (1929). The old Court of Customs Appeals became the Court of Customs and Patent Appeals in 1958, but was superseded in 1982 by the United States Court of Appeals for the Federal Circuit. See former 28 U.S.C. § 211, repealed by Pub.L. 97-164.

[26]See *Williams v. United States*, 289 U.S. 553, 53 S.Ct. 751, 77 L.Ed. 1372, http://laws.findlaw.com/us/289/553.html (1933).

[27]28 U.S.C. § 171, as amended by the Act of July 28, 1953.

[28]28 U.S.C. § 171, Pub.L. 102-572, Title IX, Section 902(a)(1), October 29, 1992, 106 Stat. 4516.

[29]28 U.S.C. § 171–173.

[30]28 U.S.C. § 1491 (a)(1).

[31]28 U.S.C. § 1491 (a)(2). Jurisdiction to render declaratory judgments in certain income tax cases is granted in 28 U.S.C. § 1507.

The court of federal claims also has jurisdiction over several specific subjects, such as claims "by any person unjustly convicted of an offense against the United States and imprisoned"[32] and claims "for damages to oyster growers on private or leased lands or bottoms arising from dredging operations or use of other machinery and equipment making river and harbor improvements authorized by Act of Congress"[33] as well as over other equally specific types of claims.[34] In 2003, 3,123 cases were filed with the court.

Although the court of federal claims, like all federal courts, is a court of limited jurisdiction and as such has only that jurisdiction that Congress affirmatively gives it, several statutes expressly—and perhaps unnecessarily—deny certain jurisdiction to the court of federal claims.[35]

The jurisdiction that would seem to take the court of federal claims out of the realm of Article III and mandate its status as an Article I court is the authorization found in 28 U.S.C. § 1492 to issue advisory reports or opinions: "Any bill, except a bill for a pension, may be referred by either House of Congress to the chief judge of the United States Claims Court for a report."[36]

An earlier statute providing authority for the court (then still the Court of Claims) to issue legal advice to executive department heads was repealed by the same 1953 statute that declared the Court of Claims to be an Article III court, and thus a court that could not, consistent with the "case-or-controversy" doctrine of justiciability, issue advisory opinions.[37] Section 1492, however, which traces its roots to the 1887 Tucker Act, was not repealed in 1953 and, in fact, was affirmed in a 1955 Court of Claims decision.[38]

### *Appellate Jurisdiction—The United States Court of Appeals for the Armed Forces*
*http://www.armfor.uscourts.gov/*

The United States Court of Appeals for the Armed Forces is the highest military court in the United States.[39] It is composed of five civilian judges, nominated by the president and confirmed by the Senate. They each serve 15-year terms and may be removed for cause. The court was created by Congress in 1950 under the name of the Court of Military Appeals to represent the principle of civilian control of the

---

[32]28 U.S.C. § 1495.

[33]28 U.S.C. § 1497.

[34]See 28 U.S.C. §§ 1494, 1496, 1498, 1499, and 1505.

[35]See 28 U.S.C. §§ 1501 (pension cases), 1502 (treaty cases), and 1509 (tax shelter and tax understatement cases).

[36]28 U.S.C. § 1492. The statute stipulates that the report must conform to the requirements of 28 U.S.C. § 2509, which spells out the procedure in bill reference cases.

[37]See Justice John Harlan's opinion in *Glidden v. Zdanok, supra,* note 3.

[38]*Gay Street Corp. of Baltimore, Maryland v. United States,* 127 F. Supp. 585 (1955).

[39]See 10 U.S.C. §§ 941–944.

armed forces: the court was to be "completely removed from all military influence of persuasion."[40]

The United States Court of Appeals for the Armed Forces exercises appellate jurisdiction, both discretionary and mandatory, over criminal cases coming to it from the four military courts of criminal appeals—one each for the army, the air force, the navy and marines, and the coast guard—which are themselves appellate courts reviewing decisions of courts-martial in their respective branches of the military.[41]

The jurisdiction of the court of appeals for the armed forces is primarily discretionary: only in cases in which the death penalty has been imposed or in cases certified to the court by the judge advocate general (JAG) must the court review the case, and there have not been many of these cases in recent years.[42] In 2002 and 2003, for example, no mandatory appeals were filed; in 2001 only 3 were filed, and all were JAG certifications. On the other hand, 694 petitions for review were filed in 2003. The court granted about 16 percent of the petitions that it considered in 2003, heard 56 oral arguments, and disposed of 114 cases on the merits.[43]

The four courts of criminal appeals, which in 2002 reviewed over 3,300 cases, were originally created in 1920 as "boards of review." (The boards of review became "courts of military review" in 1968 and "courts of criminal appeals" in 1994.) Before 1920, the only review of court-martial convictions possible was review by the president of the United States, and that was available only in two instances: (1) in cases involving a general officer or a cadet and (2) in cases in peacetime where an officer was dismissed and where a death sentence was handed down. The jurisdiction of the new boards covered most of these cases. After an expansion of their jurisdiction again in 1948, the 1950 Uniform Code of Military

---

[40]Quoted from the court's Web site. The Court of Military Appeals was renamed the United States Court of Military Appeals in 1968 and the United States Court of Appeals for the Armed Forces in 1994.

[41]The jurisdiction of the courts of criminal appeals is found at 10 U.S.C. § 866 and in Rule 2 following that section.

The Coast Guard in peacetime is administratively part of the Department of Homeland Security. The constitutionality of the appointment process of the Coast Guard Court of Criminal Appeals judges was recently addressed by the Supreme Court in *Ryder v. United States*, 515 U.S. 177, 115 S.Ct. 2031, 132 L.Ed.2d 136, http://laws.findlaw.com/us/515/177.html (1995), and *Edmond v. United States*, 520 U.S. 651, 117 S.Ct. 1573, 137 L.Ed.2d 917, http://laws.findlaw.com/us/520/651.html (1997). That of the Navy Marine Corps Court of Criminal Appeals was challenged in *Weiss v. United States*, 510 U.S. 163, 114 S.Ct. 752, 127 L.Ed.2d 1, http://laws.findlaw.com/us/510/163.html (1994).

[42]The jurisdiction is stated at 10 U.S.C. § 867 and again in Rules 4, 18, and 23 of the "Rules of Practice and Procedure" of the court. The court has mandatory appellate jurisdiction over "all cases in which the sentence, as affirmed by a Court of Criminal Appeals, extends to death" and "all cases reviewed by a Court of Criminal Appeals which the Judge Advocate General orders sent to the Court of Appeals for the Armed Forces for review." 10 U.S.C. § 867(a)(1) and (2). Petitions by convicted defendants fall under the court's discretionary appellate jurisdiction. 10 U.S.C. § 867(a)(3).

Collateral review of military court convictions is also available through petitions for writs of habeas corpus in the U.S. District Courts.

[43]*Annual Report of the Code Committee on Military Justice* for the period from October 1, 2002, to September 30, 2003, available on the USCA-AF Web site. All statistics are from this and previous reports.

Justice authorized the creation of one or more boards of review in each service, each consisting of a panel of three lawyers who were usually senior judge advocates from their respective services.

## *Administrative Agency Tribunals*
## *http://www.faljc.org*

All of the tribunals that have been described so far have been called "courts" of one kind or another, but litigation and adjudication are also conducted by the executive administrative agencies of the federal government.[44] Although the adjudicative tribunals of the federal administrative agencies are not usually thought of as legislative courts, they are established by federal statute, they have limited jurisdiction, and their proceedings are recognizably "court-like." Hearings are held, witnesses testify, lawyers argue motions and points of law, and presiding officers find facts and make legal judgments, but the authority of each of these administrative agency tribunals is quite narrowly focused. Litigants usually have a right of appeal to a United States court of appeals.[45] At some agencies, the judges are authorized to make final decisions, subject only to appellate review by the court of appeals. At other agencies, the judges submit proposed findings and rulings to their agency heads for final determination. These proceedings are usually conducted by a corps of some 1,300 administrative law judges, formerly called "hearings examiners," who are members of the federal civil service and who are located throughout the United States.[46] Treated in some respects as Article I judges, these judges do not serve for a term of years, but rather serve simply as employees of the federal government and are eligible for reassignment, retirement, and so on under the rules applicable to other federal employees.

According to the Federal Administrative Law Judges Conference (FALJC), more than 30 federal agencies regularly employ administrative law judges. The Social Security Administration has the largest contingent—over 1,100 judges who conduct hearings regarding Social Security benefits—followed by the National Labor Relations Board (60) and the Department of Labor (50). Some agencies, such as the Departments of Agriculture and Housing and Urban Development, the Environmental Protection Agency, and the Federal Communications Commission, use just a few judges to conduct a limited number of hearings. The Social Security judges, however, are quite busy, often holding several half-hour hearings each day. Overall, FALJC estimates

---

[44]Agencies of state governments perform similar functions at the state level.

[45]These proceedings are governed by the Administrative Procedure Act, 5 U.S.C. § 500 et seq., which prescribes the procedure for dispute resolution by the agencies as well as the procedure for promulgating new regulations by the agencies. Each of the agencies also has its own rules and procedures.

[46]5 U.S.C. § 3105 states, "Each agency shall appoint as many administrative law judges as are necessary for proceedings required to be conducted in accordance with sections 556 and 557 of this title. Administrative law judges shall be assigned to cases in rotation so far as practicable, and may not perform duties inconsistent with their duties and responsibilities as administrative law judges."

that hundreds of thousands of hearings are conducted by administrative law judges each year. Decisions of administrative agency tribunals are generally appealable to the heads of the agencies and then to either United States district courts or United States courts of appeals.

## STATE COURTS

In the year ending September 30, 2003, over 320,000 civil and criminal cases were filed in the United States District Courts, over 1.5 million new bankruptcy cases were filed in the United States Bankruptcy Courts, and nearly 100,000 cases were filed directly with United States Magistrate Courts. Adding to this total the cases filed in the federal courts that handle much lower volumes of cases, we may safely say that over 2 million cases were filed in the federal courts.

This considerable number pales, however, when we turn to the court systems of the 50 states and find that in 2002 alone, about *96 million cases were filed in state trial courts*! (Fig. 4.5.) Clearly, no discussion of the American courts would be complete without a description of the courts that are the sites of the bulk of the litigation activity in this country.

The state courts generally reflect the same common law institutional tradition as the federal courts. We have seen that Article III of the Constitution gives Congress wide latitude in fashioning a federal court system, restricting Congress only in matters of judicial tenure, jurisdiction, and judicial power. The states, however, are even freer to experiment with different structures of court systems, for Article III does not apply directly to the states and the states need not observe Article III principles of

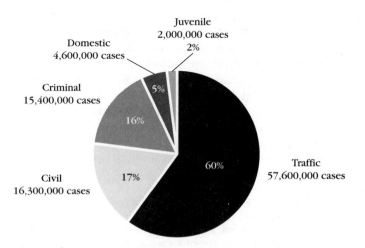

**Figure 4.5** Cases Filed in the State Trial Courts, 2002

judicial appointment and tenure, jurisdiction, and judicial power that govern the federal system.[47]

The result is a broad variety of organizational structures in the 50 state court systems.[48] Beyond the commonplace observations that each state system is composed of at least one trial court and one appellate court, generalization is difficult.

The prototypical structure of state court systems includes trial courts of general and limited jurisdiction, an intermediate appellate court (IAC), and a high appellate court, or "court of last resort" (COLR). (See Fig. 4.6.)

Roughly a dozen of the states have systems closely matching the prototype. Virginia (Fig. 4.7), for example, has courts of limited jurisdiction (district courts), courts of general jurisdiction (circuit courts), an intermediate court of appeals (the court of appeals), and a court of last resort (the supreme court).

The simplest state court systems are those of South Dakota and the District of Columbia, which have only a trial court of general jurisdiction and a court of last resort. The most complex appears to be that of New York (Fig. 4.8).

Population alone does not determine the complexity of a state court system, however. The large states of New York and Texas, indeed, have intricately structured systems, but the systems of the most populous state in the union, California (Fig. 4.9), and the state of Illinois are quite simple, reflecting the results of the twentieth-century court unification movement discussed in Chapter 1.

The simplicity of the California and the Virginia systems should be contrasted with the Georgia system (Fig. 4.10), which is more characteristic of state systems before the state court reform movement.

## Courts of Original Jurisdiction

All federal trial courts, except those few that also serve as territorial courts, are courts of limited or special jurisdiction. State trial courts, on the other hand, may be courts of either general or limited jurisdiction. As we saw above in Chapter 2, the concept of general jurisdiction can only be understood in light of the history of the English and American courts, but for the following discussion, a simpler, more practical distinction between courts of general and limited jurisdiction is generally followed: a court of *general* jurisdiction is presumed to have jurisdiction over every justiciable legal dispute within its territorial authority except those that the legislature has expressly excluded from it, whereas a court of *limited* jurisdiction is presumed to have jurisdiction over only those matters expressly assigned to it by legislation.

In state systems, limited jurisdiction courts are often created either to decide a particular *limited* category of cases, such as juvenile or domestic relations cases, or,

---

[47]Thus, state judges ascend to the bench by appointment, election, or some combination of the two, and they generally serve for a statutory term of years rather than for life. Of the U.S. Constitution, only Article IV, Sections 1 (full faith and credit) and 2 (jurisdiction over treason, felonies, and crimes), and Article VI (the supremacy clause) directly apply to state courts and state judges. Discussions of state court jurisdiction and judicial power follow.

[48]Fifty-two if we include the District of Columbia and Puerto Rico.

State Court Structure Prototype, 2002

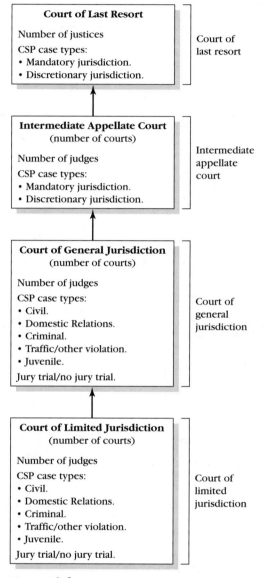

**Figure 4.6** State Court Structure Prototype
*Source:* B. Ostrom, N. Kauder, and R. LaFountain, *Examining the Work of State Courts, 2003: A National Perspective from the Court Statistics Project* (National Center for State Courts 2004).

**Virginia Court Structure, 2002**

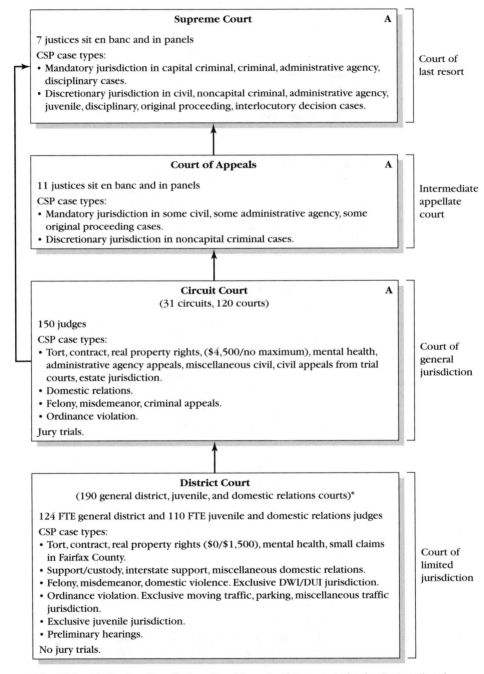

**Figure 4.7** Virginia Court Structure
*Source:* B. Ostrom, N. Kauder, and R. LaFountain, *Examining the Work of State Courts, 2003: A National Perspective from the Court Statistics Project* (National Center for State Courts 2004).

**New York Court Structure, 2002***

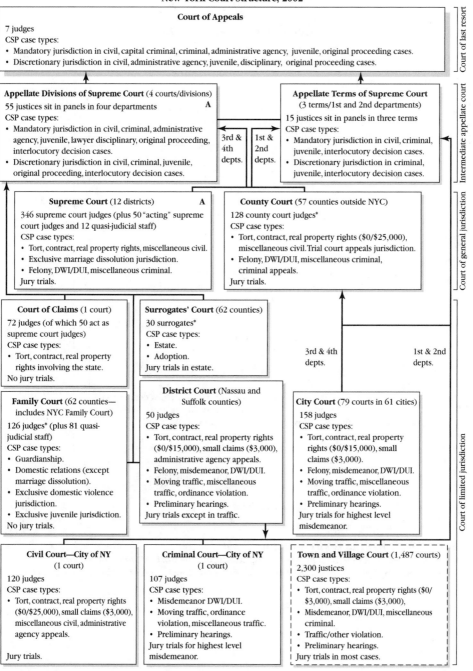

**Court of Appeals**

7 judges
CSP case types:
- Mandatory jurisdiction in civil, capital criminal, criminal, administrative agency, juvenile, original proceeding cases.
- Discretionary jurisdiction in civil, administrative agency, juvenile, disciplinary, original proceeding cases.

*Court of last resort*

**Appellate Divisions of Supreme Court** (4 courts/divisions)

55 justices sit in panels in four departments    A
CSP case types:
- Mandatory jurisdiction in civil, criminal, administrative agency, juvenile, lawyer disciplinary, original proceeding, interlocutory decision cases.
- Discretionary jurisdiction in civil, criminal, juvenile, original proceeding, interlocutory decision cases.

3rd & 4th depts.    1st & 2nd depts.

**Appellate Terms of Supreme Court**
(3 terms/1st and 2nd departments)

15 justices sit in panels in three terms
CSP case types:
- Mandatory jurisdiction in civil, criminal, juvenile, interlocutory decision cases.
- Discretionary jurisdiction in criminal, juvenile, interlocutory decision cases.

*Intermediate appellate court*

**Supreme Court** (12 districts)    A

346 supreme court judges (plus 50 "acting" supreme court judges and 12 quasi-judicial staff)
CSP case types:
- Tort, contract, real property rights, miscellaneous civil.
- Exclusive marriage dissolution jurisdiction.
- Felony, DWI/DUI, miscellaneous criminal.
Jury trials.

**County Court** (57 counties outside NYC)

128 county court judges*
CSP case types:
- Tort, contract, real property rights ($0/$25,000), miscellaneous civil. Trial court appeals jurisdiction.
- Felony, DWI/DUI, miscellaneous criminal, criminal appeals.
Jury trials.

*Court of general jurisdiction*

**Court of Claims** (1 court)

72 judges (of which 50 act as supreme court judges)
CSP case types:
- Tort, contract, real property rights involving the state.
No jury trials.

**Surrogates' Court** (62 counties)

30 surrogates*
CSP case types:
- Estate.
- Adoption.
Jury trials in estate.

3rd & 4th depts.    1st & 2nd depts.

**Family Court** (62 counties—includes NYC Family Court)

126 judges* (plus 81 quasi-judicial staff)
CSP case types:
- Guardianship.
- Domestic relations (except marriage dissolution).
- Exclusive domestic violence jurisdiction.
- Exclusive juvenile jurisdiction.
No jury trials.

**District Court** (Nassau and Suffolk counties)

50 judges
CSP case types:
- Tort, contract, real property rights ($0/$15,000), small claims ($3,000), administrative agency appeals.
- Felony, misdemeanor, DWI/DUI.
- Moving traffic, miscellaneous traffic, ordinance violation.
- Preliminary hearings.
Jury trials except in traffic.

**City Court** (79 courts in 61 cities)

158 judges
CSP case types:
- Tort, contract, real property rights ($0/$15,000), small claims ($3,000).
- Felony, misdemeanor, DWI/DUI.
- Moving traffic, miscellaneous traffic, ordinance violation.
- Preliminary hearings.
Jury trials for highest level misdemeanor.

**Civil Court—City of NY**
(1 court)

120 judges
CSP case types:
- Tort, contract, real property rights ($0/$25,000), small claims ($3,000), miscellaneous civil, administrative agency appeals.
Jury trials.

**Criminal Court—City of NY**
(1 court)

107 judges
CSP case types:
- Misdemeanor DWI/DUI.
- Moving traffic, ordinance violation, miscellaneous traffic.
- Preliminary hearings.
Jury trials for highest level misdemeanor.

**Town and Village Court** (1,487 courts)

2,300 justices
CSP case types:
- Tort, contract, real property rights ($0/$3,000), small claims ($3,000),
- Misdemeanor, DWI/DUI, miscellaneous criminal.
- Traffic/other violation.
- Preliminary hearings.
Jury trials in most cases.

*Court of limited jurisdiction*

*Unless otherwise noted, numbers reflect statutory authorization. Many judges sit in more than one court so the number of judgeships indicated in this chart does not reflect the actual number of judges in the system. Fifty County Court judges also serve Surrogates' Court and six County Court judges also serve Family Court.

**Figure 4.8** New York Court Structure
*Source:* B. Ostrom, N. Kauder, and R. LaFountain, *Examining the Work of State Courts, 2003: A National Perspective from the Court Statistics Project* (National Center for State Courts 2004).

**California Court Structure, 2002**

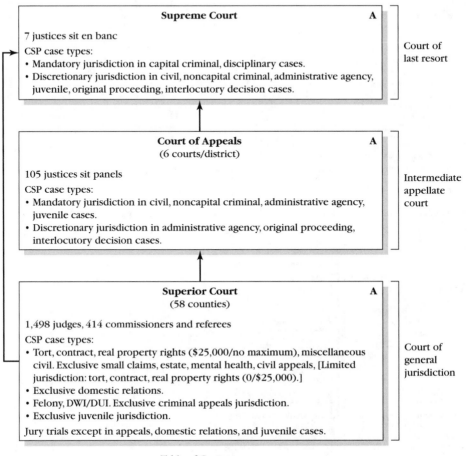

| Supreme Court | A |
|---|---|
| 7 justices sit en banc | Court of last resort |

CSP case types:
• Mandatory jurisdiction in capital criminal, disciplinary cases.
• Discretionary jurisdiction in civil, noncapital criminal, administrative agency, juvenile, original proceeding, interlocutory decision cases.

**Court of Appeals**     A
(6 courts/district)

105 justices sit panels

CSP case types:
• Mandatory jurisdiction in civil, noncapital criminal, administrative agency, juvenile cases.
• Discretionary jurisdiction in administrative agency, original proceeding, interlocutory decision cases.

Intermediate appellate court

**Superior Court**     A
(58 counties)

1,498 judges, 414 commissioners and referees

CSP case types:
• Tort, contract, real property rights ($25,000/no maximum), miscellaneous civil. Exclusive small claims, estate, mental health, civil appeals, [Limited jurisdiction: tort, contract, real property rights (0/$25,000).]
• Exclusive domestic relations.
• Felony, DWI/DUI. Exclusive criminal appeals jurisdiction.
• Exclusive juvenile jurisdiction.
Jury trials except in appeals, domestic relations, and juvenile cases.

Court of general jurisdiction

Table of Contents

Note: All trial courts were unified as of 7/1/00.

**Figure 4.9**  California Court Structure
*Source:* B. Ostrom, N. Kauder, and R. LaFountain, *Examining the Work of State Courts, 2003: A National Perspective from the Court Statistics Project* (National Center for State Courts 2004).

## Georgia Court Structure, 2002

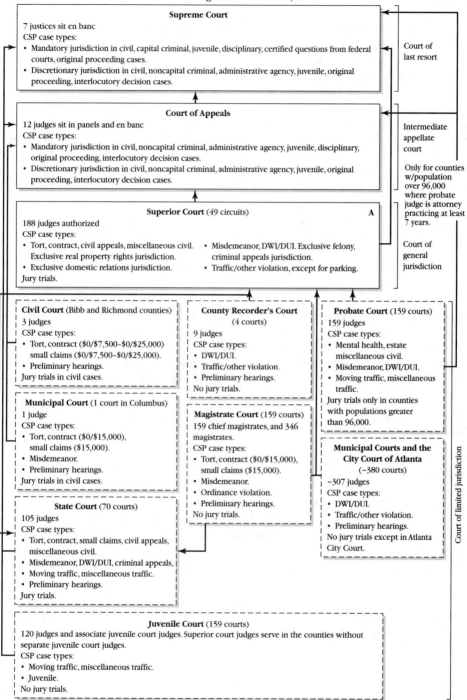

**Supreme Court**

7 justices sit en banc
CSP case types:
- Mandatory jurisdiction in civil, capital criminal, juvenile, disciplinary, certified questions from federal courts, original proceeding cases.
- Discretionary jurisdiction in civil, noncapital criminal, administrative agency, juvenile, original proceeding, interlocutory decision cases.

Court of last resort

**Court of Appeals**

12 judges sit in panels and en banc
CSP case types:
- Mandatory jurisdiction in civil, noncapital criminal, administrative agency, juvenile, disciplinary, original proceeding, interlocutory decision cases.
- Discretionary jurisdiction in civil, noncapital criminal, administrative agency, juvenile, original proceeding, interlocutory decision cases.

Intermediate appellate court

Only for counties w/population over 96,000 where probate judge is attorney practicing at least 7 years.

**Superior Court** (49 circuits)                                                              A

188 judges authorized
CSP case types:
- Tort, contract, civil appeals, miscellaneous civil. Exclusive real property rights jurisdiction.
- Exclusive domestic relations jurisdiction.
Jury trials.
- Misdemeanor, DWI/DUI. Exclusive felony, criminal appeals jurisdiction.
- Traffic/other violation, except for parking.

Court of general jurisdiction

**Civil Court** (Bibb and Richmond counties)
3 judges
CSP case types:
- Tort, contract ($0/$7,500–$0/$25,000) small claims ($0/$7,500–$0/$25,000).
- Preliminary hearings.
Jury trials in civil cases.

**County Recorder's Court**
(4 courts)
9 judges
CSP case types:
- DWI/DUI.
- Traffic/other violation.
- Preliminary hearings.
No jury trials.

**Probate Court** (159 courts)
159 judges
CSP case types:
- Mental health, estate miscellaneous civil.
- Misdemeanor, DWI/DUI.
- Moving traffic, miscellaneous traffic.
Jury trials only in counties with populations greater than 96,000.

**Municipal Court** (1 court in Columbus)
1 judge
CSP case types:
- Tort, contract ($0/$15,000), small claims ($15,000).
- Misdemeanor.
- Preliminary hearings.
Jury trials in civil cases.

**Magistrate Court** (159 courts)
159 chief magistrates, and 346 magistrates.
CSP case types:
- Tort, contract ($0/$15,000), small claims ($15,000).
- Misdemeanor.
- Ordinance violation.
- Preliminary hearings.
No jury trials.

**Municipal Courts and the City Court of Atlanta**
(~380 courts)
~307 judges
CSP case types:
- DWI/DUI.
- Traffic/other violation.
- Preliminary hearings.
No jury trials except in Atlanta City Court.

**State Court** (70 courts)
105 judges
CSP case types:
- Tort, contract, small claims, civil appeals, miscellaneous civil.
- Misdemeanor, DWI/DUI, criminal appeals.
- Moving traffic, miscellaneous traffic.
- Preliminary hearings.
Jury trials.

Court of limited jurisdiction

**Juvenile Court** (159 courts)
120 judges and associate juvenile court judges. Superior court judges serve in the counties without separate juvenile court judges.
CSP case types:
- Moving traffic, miscellaneous traffic.
- Juvenile.
No jury trials.

**Figure 4.10** Georgia Court Structure
*Source:* B. Ostrom, N. Kauder, and R. LaFountain, *Examining the Work of State Courts, 2003: A National Perspective from the Court Statistics Project* (National Center for State Courts 2004).

like general jurisdiction courts, to decide a wide variety of types of cases, but only so long as the civil cases are worth a *limited* amount of money and the criminal cases involve misdemeanors and not felonies. An example of this second purpose is the familiar "small claims court" that may decide any case, whether based on contract, tort, or real estate, that prays for a judgment of up to $5,000, $30,000, or some other maximum amount. Sometimes states have both kinds of these courts of limited jurisdiction. Thus, the limited jurisdiction probate courts of Michigan have exclusive jurisdiction over adoption proceedings and juvenile matters, while the limited jurisdiction Michigan District Courts have exclusive jurisdiction over contract, tort, and real property cases up to $25,000. Michigan's general jurisdiction circuit courts have exclusive jurisdiction over contract, tort, and real property cases worth more than $25,000 and over divorce, custody, and support cases.

Courts of general jurisdiction have no upper limits on the amount at issue in civil cases, and they may try felony cases and impose a wide range of criminal sentences, including the death penalty. Often, courts of limited jurisdiction may not hold jury trials; courts of general jurisdiction, of course, not only may but must employ trial by jury in some cases.

Most states have created court systems consisting of both courts of limited jurisdiction and those of general jurisdiction that variously possess exclusive or concurrent jurisdiction over the full range of cases—common law, statutory, and constitutional—that are recognized by common law courts. Remember that if the jurisdiction over a particular kind of case has not been specifically assigned to or excluded from state courts by statute, the courts of general jurisdiction are presumed to possess it.

## Limited Jurisdiction

The state courts of limited jurisdiction handled about 64 million cases in 2002, leading to the conclusion of the National Center for State Courts that "the bulk of the nation's disputes are handled in these courts of limited jurisdiction."

Over 13,000 limited jurisdiction courts with approximately 18,000 judges exist in the states that have established such courts. About two-thirds of their caseload in 2001 consisted of traffic cases; the other third is primarily misdemeanor criminal and small claims civil cases, but also includes over 2 million domestic relations and juvenile cases. The huge volume of traffic cases often leads people to identify limited jurisdiction courts as simply "traffic courts," but the approximately 20 million criminal, civil, and domestic relations cases handled annually by these courts reveal a much broader range of judicial business performed by these courts. If Americans find that "going to court" is on their schedule, chances are the court they are going to is a court of limited jurisdiction.

## General Jurisdiction

Each state has at least one court of general jurisdiction. Throughout the 50 states, plus Puerto Rico and the District of Columbia, there are over 2,000 courts of general jurisdiction presided over by more than 11,000 judges.

In 2002, almost 32 million cases were filed in the states' courts of general jurisdiction. Again, traffic cases were the largest single category, but civil, criminal, domestic relations, and juvenile cases constituted over half of the caseload of these courts.

By far the largest single type of civil case filed in courts of general jurisdiction was domestic relations cases, followed by the core of the traditional common law civil actions (torts, contracts, and real property cases, including small claims in some states) and personal estate cases. The criminal cases in courts of general jurisdiction are usually felony cases.

General jurisdiction courts often have appellate jurisdiction over the decisions of the courts of limited jurisdiction. The most common type of review exercised by courts of general jurisdiction, an appeal *de novo,* is not really appellate jurisdiction in the usual sense of reviewing decisions of the courts of limited jurisdiction and rendering a decision, with accompanying opinion, to affirm, reverse, and so on the judgment of the lower court. An appeal *de novo* is simply a request, after the case has been heard by a court of limited jurisdiction, for a new trial in a court of general jurisdiction. The case begins *de novo*—from the beginning, with no reference to the prior adjudication in the other court. Some courts of general jurisdiction also possess the more routine appellate jurisdiction power to review the rulings and the record of some of the proceedings initiated in courts of limited jurisdiction.

## Court Names

The names of limited jurisdiction courts, like the names of the other categories of state courts—the courts of general jurisdiction, the intermediate courts of appeals, and the courts of last resort—are not consistent throughout the nation. In addition to several limited jurisdiction "district courts" and "county courts" are various "city" or "municipal courts," "justice of the peace courts," "probate courts," "magistrate courts," "alderman's courts," "mayor's courts," "orphans' courts," and "family courts," to name just a few.

In most states the courts of general jurisdiction are called "superior courts" or "circuit courts," but in Wyoming the "circuit courts" are courts of *limited* jurisdiction, and in Colorado the "district courts" are courts of *general* jurisdiction! Pennsylvania calls its principal general jurisdiction courts the "courts of common pleas," and New York calls them either "county courts" or "supreme courts." On the other hand, the "courts of common pleas" in Delaware and the "county courts" of Florida are limited jurisdiction courts. In Pennsylvania, the superior court is an appellate court, and New York's supreme courts have an appellate division to go along with their trial division. In short, there is no systematic order to the names of the state courts of general jurisdiction.

At the appellate level, not all courts of last resort are called "supreme courts"; some, such as New York's and Maryland's, are called "courts of appeals." And the intermediate courts of appeals have a similar range of names, from Pennsylvania's "commonwealth court" and "superior court" to Maryland's "court of special appeals."

## Courts of Appellate Jurisdiction

By "state courts of appellate jurisdiction," we mean courts with the power to review judgments of other "lower" courts and affirm or change those judgments: we do not mean the state courts of general jurisdiction that possess the power of *de novo* consideration as we just discussed. Generally, litigants in any state trial court have the opportunity to seek appellate review from another court in the state system. In roughly half of the states, litigants in certain courts of limited jurisdiction have the opportunity to appeal to a court of appellate jurisdiction as an alternative to asking a court of general jurisdiction for a trial *de novo*. In the others, litigants who are dissatisfied with the decision of a court of limited jurisdiction are limited to an appeal to a court of general jurisdiction for review or for *de novo* consideration.

Again, the variety of organizational schemes in the states precludes all but the most banal generalities, so we turn directly to considerations of the intermediate appellate courts and the courts of last resort. We shall focus on the formal organizational structures and on whether the jurisdiction is mandatory or discretionary.

### Intermediate Appellate Courts

Although each state has, almost by definition, a court of last resort with the power to review most or all of the judicial and administrative decisions of the other trial and appellate courts within the state, 11 states and the District of Columbia do not have any intermediate appellate courts. Appeals from the trial courts in these states must be taken directly to the courts of last resort.

Of the 39 states and Puerto Rico that do have IACs, 5 have more than one.[49] In 5 of the states, the IAC docket consists entirely of cases assigned to these courts by the courts of last resort.[50]

The caseload of these courts has held remarkably steady over the past decade. In 1992 just over 183,000 cases were filed in the state IACs; ten years later, the total was about 187,000. Eighty-five percent of these appeals to IACs were brought under the courts' mandatory appellate jurisdiction: in 12 of the states, the jurisdiction of the IAC is all mandatory, and in 13 it is predominantly mandatory. Similar to the federal appellate courts is the jurisdiction possessed by most of these state courts to entertain original proceedings, which are typically applications for extraordinary writs or for extraordinary action in cases pending in a lower trial court. Also like the federal appellate courts, the state intermediate courts of appeals bear the brunt of appellate review in the states and therefore also the supervision of the state trial courts.

### Courts of Last Resort

All states have courts of last resort, usually, but not always, called "supreme courts." Two states—Texas and Oklahoma—have two courts of last resort, one of which reviews criminal appeals while the other reviews all other appeals. There are more

---

[49]Alabama, Indiana, New York, Pennsylvania, and Tennessee.

[50]Hawaii, Idaho, Iowa, Mississippi, and Oklahoma.

than 350 judgeships for these courts, and in 2002 about 90,000 cases were filed in them. Over two-thirds of these cases were brought under the discretionary appellate jurisdiction of the COLRs, reflecting the trend toward discretionary jurisdiction over the last century that is also seen in the United States Supreme Court, although only four courts of last resort have entirely discretionary appellate jurisdiction.

The high courts of the states are distinct in some important respects from the United States Supreme Court and, indeed, from all federal appellate courts. Thirteen of the courts (including Puerto Rico) have the power to issue advisory opinions to the executive branch, the legislative branch, or both branches of state government. This power is usually mandatory.[51] All but four of these courts also have jurisdiction over disciplinary matters involving state lawyers, judges, or both.[52] Both of these functions are outside of the legitimate judicial power of the federal courts.

## CONCLUSION

This chapter has surveyed several of the courts in the federal system, including those tribunals that handle the most litigation, and has provided a summary of the general characteristics of the state court systems. (Accounts of additional federal courts are found in Appendix D.) Two general points can be made about this material. The first is that the courts in these systems and in any common law system can be understood in terms of the kinds of jurisdiction that they possess—general or limited, original or appellate, and exclusive and concurrent. You can now see that these concepts, which were discussed in Chapter 2, both indicate the basic functions and litigation procedures that the courts will exercise and outline the relationships between and among the courts in the American legal systems. From this perspective we can see that the federal and the state systems are constructed in similar hierarchical fashion.

The second point is more important. In the United States, neither the federal nor the state court system is "more important" than the other. Although it is true that the effect of a federal court ruling can be nationwide, whereas the effect of a state court decision is essentially limited to one state, the subject matter of the cases in all these systems is mostly the same. Federal courts handle state law issues, and state courts decide federal law issues. Nor are the systems distinguished on the basis of the "size" of the case. Cases before the federal courts are not necessarily worth more than those before the state courts; in fact, the largest single judgment that I am aware of to date—the $157 billion award in the *Engle v. Liggett Group* case (reversed on appeal)—was awarded by a Florida state court. Moreover, the volume of cases in the state courts (including those of the District of Columbia and Puerto Rico) dwarfs the

---

[51]Colorado, Delaware, Florida, Maine, Massachusetts, Oklahoma, and Rhode Island courts have mandatory jurisdiction here; Alabama, Michigan, New Hampshire, North Carolina, Puerto Rico and South Dakota courts of last resort have discretionary jurisdiction.

[52]Missouri, Tennessee, Texas, and Vermont do not.

caseload of federal courts. Most attorneys who litigate do so in state courts (of course, most attorneys who practice law rarely if ever enter a courtroom), but it is also true that litigating attorneys often practice before both state and federal courts, often treating them as alternative forums, each with their immediate advantages and disadvantages to the litigator. Even as we turn to the United States Supreme Court, we shall see that in most technical respects it is not much different from the courts we have just reviewed. Its influence on lawyers and judges, however, is unique and deserves special treatment.

# Chapter 5

# The Supreme Court

## Chapter Outline

There are a number of excellent texts on the United States Supreme Court that discuss everything from a comprehensive history of the Court to the process of nominating justices. The present brief account focuses only on the court's structure, its jurisdiction, its litigation procedure, and the preparation and the effect of its decisions and opinions. The account includes, as it must, frequent reference to Court history.

## THE STRUCTURE OF THE SUPREME COURT

The judicial Power of the United States, shall be vested in one supreme Court, and in such inferior Courts as the Congress may from time to time ordain and establish. The Judges, both of the supreme and inferior Courts, shall hold their Offices during good

Behaviour, and shall, at stated Times, receive for their Services, a Compensation, which shall not be diminished during their Continuance in Office. U.S. Const. Art. III, § 1.

As we noted in our earlier discussion of the lower federal courts, the Framers of the Constitution gave Congress remarkably little guidance for creating a federal judiciary. The lack of specific instructions regarding the inferior federal courts is understandable, given the refusal of the 1787 Convention to mandate such courts. The Framers gave Congress the authority to create inferior federal courts if Congress saw fit; there is no evidence that the Framers wished to limit congressional discretion to a particular set of courts or a particular legal system.

The Framers did, however, mandate a "supreme Court." If Congress were constitutionally obligated to create the court, we might well expect a blueprint, or at least some detailed directions, for the design of this third branch of our national government, but we get only the bare command that "the judicial Power of the United States, shall be vested in one supreme Court." The constitutional provision makes no reference to the number of justices to sit on the court, to their qualifications, or to the procedures or techniques to be used by the Court for performing its judicial functions.

We might ask what the mandate to create the Court really meant. What if Congress decided not to create the Supreme Court at all? To whom would Congress be accountable? The Court is the only one of the three primary institutions of our national government that was not established directly by the Constitution itself. Congress did not have to legislate a presidency, though by statute Congress has since created almost all of the other agencies and offices in the executive branch. By statute Congress has also created all of the judicial branch institutions subordinate to the Supreme Court. The Supreme Court itself, however, though mandated by the Constitution, would presumably not exist if Congress did not create it. What if Congress had decided not to?

In this instance, the question is moot. As evidenced by its prompt development of the first Judiciary Act in 1789, Congress, following the initiative of the Senate, was not long delayed by a lack of direction for creating a high court. It created a "Supreme Court" of six justices, five associates and a chief. That total would have been reduced by one in the famous "Midnight Judges Act" of 1801 (the Judiciary Act of 1801), but the 1801 Act was repealed before it could take effect.[1] Thereafter, the number of justices was increased by one for each new judicial circuit that was added to our growing country, until a maximum of ten justices was reached in 1863. The Republican Congress of 1866 sought to deprive President Johnson of any influence over further court appointments by statutorily reducing, through attrition, the number of justices

---

[1] The response of the Jefferson administration to the Midnight Judges Act provides an interesting footnote to the question of the role of Congress in creating the Supreme Court. A month after repealing the Judiciary Act of 1801, the new Congress canceled the Supreme Court's 1802 term, thus effectively eliminating the Court for one year. See 1 Stat. 156, §1. No legal action was brought to contest the validity of the legislation, though the constitutionality of the statute was questioned, particularly by Federalists. Charles Warren, *The Supreme Court in United States History,* vol. 1 (Boston: Little, Brown, and Company, 1947), 222–224.

to seven. In 1869, with President Johnson safely out of office, Congress raised by statute the total to nine justices.[2] There it has remained to this day, though from time to time there have been proposals, notably President Roosevelt's "court-packing" plan of 1937, to raise that total.

Regarding the qualifications of the justices, the Framers did discuss property qualifications for federal office holders, including federal judges, but ultimately decided against placing such criteria in the text of the Constitution, preferring instead to rely upon the good judgment of those voters, legislators, and executive officers who are responsible for electing or appointing the officials.[3] The account in Madison's *Notes* does not reveal any substantial discussion of establishing age and citizenship qualifications for judges similar to those for members of Congress and for the president and vice president.

The lack of constitutional regulation of the procedures and methods to be used by the federal courts in performing their constitutional functions can be explained, perhaps, by the familiarity that most of the convention delegates had with the institutional practices of common law courts. Still, the first Judiciary Act imposed a number of directives and regulations on the federal courts even while it authorized the courts to develop their own rules.[4]

# THE JURISDICTION OF THE SUPREME COURT

In all Cases affecting Ambassadors, other public Ministers and Consuls, and those in which a State shall be Party, the supreme Court shall have original Jurisdiction. In all other Cases before mentioned, the supreme Court shall have appellate Jurisdiction, both as to Law and Fact, with such Exceptions, and under such Regulations as the Congress shall make. U.S. Const. Art. III, § 2, cl. 2.[5]

The United States Supreme Court is a court of both original and appellate jurisdiction. This jurisdiction is mandated by Article III, but Congress also expressly grants the jurisdiction by statute.[6] This raises several questions. In light of the constitutional mandate, what authority does Congress have over the jurisdiction of the Supreme Court?

---

[2]The Judiciary Acts that affected the number of justices are as follows: the Judiciary Act of 1789, 1 Stat. 73, 1789 (six justices); the Judiciary Act of 1801, 2 Stat. 89, 1801 (five); the repeal of the 1801 Act, 2 Stat. 132, 1802 (six); the addition of the Seventh Circuit, 2 Stat. 420, 1807 (seven); the addition of the Eighth and Ninth Circuits, 5 Stat. 176, 1837 (nine); the creation of the Tenth Circuit, 12 Stat. 794, 1863 (ten); the Republican anti-Johnson legislation, 14 Stat. 209, 1866 (seven); and the post-Johnson legislation, 16 Stat. 44, 1869 (nine).

[3]See Madison's *Notes* of June 13, July 21, and July 26.

[4]1 Stat. 73, §17.

[5]The phrase "all other Cases before mentioned" refers to the enumeration of all potential federal court jurisdiction in the first paragraph of Article III, Section 2.

[6]The original jurisdiction is set forth in 28 U.S.C. §1251; the appellate jurisdiction is described in 28 U.S.C. §§1253, 1254, 1257, 1258, and 1259.

Why does Congress grant the Court by statute jurisdiction that the Constitution already extends to the Court? What is the true source of the jurisdiction of the Court? In this section we will review the Court's jurisdiction and consider these questions.

## Original Jurisdiction

The Court's original jurisdiction is set out in 28 U.S.C. §1251.

Subsection (a) of the statute gives the Court original and exclusive jurisdiction over cases between states of the Union. At present, this is the Court's only exclusive original jurisdiction. We shall examine the Original Docket and the procedures that the Court follows in original cases below, but we note here that only one or two original cases, if any, are filed under this subsection each term.

Subsection (b) grants the Court original but not exclusive jurisdiction over three other categories of cases: (1) cases in which foreign diplomats are parties, (2) cases between a state and the federal government, and (3) cases brought by a state against aliens or against citizens of other states. Jurisdiction over these cases is concurrent with other federal and state courts. As a result, and with the tacit encouragement of the Court, the plaintiffs in these categories of cases regularly file such cases in other courts that are better prepared to conduct trial proceedings and that also generally provide at least one level of appellate review.

The issue of the extent of congressional authority over the Court's original jurisdiction has arisen in several cases before the Court. In *California v. Arizona,* an original suit between two states was brought before the Court even though a federal statute gave the United States District Courts exclusive original jurisdiction over the matter.[7] The Court avoided a constitutional issue by construing the statute to mean that Congress made the district court jurisdiction exclusive of the *state* courts but concurrent with the Supreme Court. In the course of its opinion, the Court said,

---

## 28 U.S.C. §1251:

(a) The Supreme Court shall have original and exclusive jurisdiction of all controversies between two or more States.

(b) The Supreme Court shall have original but not exclusive jurisdiction of:

(1) All actions or proceedings to which ambassadors, other public ministers, consuls, or vice-consuls of foreign states are parties;

(2) All controversies between the United States and a State;

(3) All actions or proceedings by a State against the citizens of another State or against aliens.

---

[7]440 U.S. 59, 99 S.Ct. 919, 59 L.Ed.2d 144, http://laws.findlaw.com/us/440/59.html (1979). The statute in question was 28 U.S.C. §1346f.

"The original jurisdiction of the Supreme Court is conferred not by the Congress but by the Constitution itself. This jurisdiction is self-executing, and needs no legislative implementation. . . . It is similarly clear that the original jurisdiction of this Court is not constitutionally exclusive—that other courts can be awarded concurrent jurisdiction by statute."[8] By this reading, then, the statute enacted by Congress— Section 1251—does not grant the Court its original jurisdiction; Section 1251 simply exercises the power of Congress to delineate the Court's *exclusive* and *concurrent* original jurisdiction.[9]

A second original jurisdiction issue—whether Congress can add to the constitutional grant of original jurisdiction to the Supreme Court—was presented, of course, in *Marbury v. Madison.*[10] In *Marbury* the constitutional issue was whether Congress could give the Supreme Court original jurisdiction to issue writs of mandamus, as it had done in Section 13 of the 1789 Judiciary Act. The Court held that the original jurisdiction of the Court is strictly limited to the cases adduced in the second paragraph of Article III, Section 2. Since the original jurisdiction to issue writs of mandamus cannot be found there, the Supreme Court does not and *may not* have it, and Section 13 was repugnant to the Constitution and void.

Counsel for William Marbury had argued that the Court should construe the original jurisdiction set forth in Article III to be the irreducible minimum that the Court must possess, but that Congress may add to it. The Court rejected this position:

> If congress remains at liberty to give this court appellate jurisdiction, where the constitution has declared their jurisdiction shall be original; and original jurisdiction where the constitution has declared it shall be appellate; the distribution of jurisdiction, made in the constitution, is form without substance.
>
> Affirmative words are often, in their operation, negative of other objects than those affirmed; and in this case, a negative or exclusive sense must be given to them, or they have no operation at all.[11]

A third issue is whether Congress has the authority to delete any of the original jurisdiction set out in Article III. The precedent here is less clear, probably because Congress has not attempted to delete the Court's original jurisdiction. The *California* opinion only expressed doubt that Congress possesses that power.[12]

---

[8]440 U.S. at 65, 99 S.Ct. at 923, 59 L.Ed.2d at 150.

[9]A recent example of this discretionary authority can be found in the 1978 amendments to Section 1251. Before Congress changed the law in 1978, the Supreme Court had exclusive original jurisdiction over all cases brought "*against* ambassadors and other public ministers of foreign states" and their servants; it had concurrent but not exclusive original jurisdiction over all cases brought "*by* ambassadors or other public ministers of foreign states or to which consuls or vice-consuls of foreign states are parties." (emphasis added) The 1978 change made all this original jurisdiction concurrent with other courts. See Pub. L. No. 95-393, 92 Stat. 808, § 8(b)(1) and (2).

[10]5 U.S. (1 Cranch) 137, 2 L.Ed. 60, http://laws.findlaw.com/us/5/137.html (1803).

[11]5 U.S. (1 Cranch) at 174, 2 L.Ed. at 73.

[12]"[I]t is far from clear that [Congress] can withdraw the constitutional jurisdiction over such suits." 440 U.S. at 65, 99 S.Ct. at 923, 59 L.Ed.2d at 150.

## Appellate Jurisdiction

The Supreme Court's appellate jurisdiction over cases from the United States courts of appeals is set forth in 28 U.S.C. §1254, and the jurisdiction over cases coming from state courts is set forth in 28 U.S.C. §1257. Since 1988, all of this appellate jurisdiction is discretionary. [13]

How much authority does Congress have over the Court's appellate jurisdiction? The Court considered this question in two nineteenth-century cases. In *Ex parte McCardle,* the Court addressed the question of whether Congress could take away the Supreme Court's appellate jurisdiction over habeas corpus cases that were filed in the federal courts. [14] The Court agreed with the petitioner "that the appellate jurisdiction of this court is not derived from acts of Congress. It is, strictly speaking, conferred by the Constitution. But it is conferred 'with such exceptions and under such regulations as Congress shall make.'" [15] Citing the earlier case of *Durousseau v. The United States,* [16] the Court observed:

> [T]he judicial act was an exercise of the power given by the Constitution to Congress "of making exceptions to the appellate jurisdiction of the Supreme Court." "They have described affirmatively . . . its jurisdiction, and this affirmative description has been understood to imply a negation of the exercise of such appellate power as is not comprehended within it." [17]

This, the Court continued, is "the principle that the affirmation of appellate jurisdiction implies a negation of all such jurisdiction not affirmed." In other words, like the statute describing the Court's original jurisdiction (28 U.S.C. §1251), these Acts of Congress only *appear* to be authoritative grants of jurisdiction: they actually are affirmations of constitutionally granted appellate jurisdiction that has not been "excepted" or "regulated."

Thus, the question of what jurisdiction the Court would have if Congress had not legislated on the matter is the counterpart to the question we considered above about the role of Congress in creating the court that was mandated by the Constitution.

---

[13]We may note here that the Supreme Court also has appellate jurisdiction over cases from three-judge district courts (28 U.S.C. §1253), from the Supreme Court of Puerto Rico (28 U.S.C. §1258), and from the United States Court of Appeals for the Armed Forces (28 U.S.C. §1259). The latter two statutes provide for discretionary appellate jurisdiction, but parties wishing review of the decisions of three judge courts have an appeal as of right, the last general category of mandatory appellate jurisdiction remaining to the Court. See pages 80–83, *supra.*

[14]74 U.S. (7 Wall.) 506, 19 L.Ed. 264, http://laws.findlaw.com/us/74/506.html (1869).

[15]74 U.S. (7 Wall.) at 512-13, 19 L.Ed. at 265.

[16]10 U.S. (6 Cranch) 307, 3 L.Ed. 232, http://laws.findlaw.com/us/10/307.html (1810). The Court in *McCardle* said that *Durosseau* "held, that while 'the appellate powers of this court are not given by the judicial act, but are given by the Constitution,' they are, nevertheless, 'limited and regulated by that act, and by such other acts as have been passed on the subject.'" 74 U.S. (7 Wall) 513, 19 L.Ed. at 265. But see the comments of Robert Clinton in the articles cited in note 34 on page 31, *supra.*

[17]Id. Recall the similar rule in *Marbury* construing the Constitution. 5 U.S. (1 Cranch) at 174, 2 L.Ed. at 73.

# Principal Appellate Jurisdiction of the Supreme Court

28 U.S.C. §1254 reads:

Cases in the courts of appeals may be reviewed by the Supreme Court by the following methods:

(1) By writ of certiorari granted upon the petition of any party to any civil or criminal case, before or after rendition of judgment or decree;

(2) By certification at any time by a court of appeals of any question of law in any civil or criminal case as to which instructions are desired, and upon such certification the Supreme Court may give binding instructions or require the entire record to be sent up for decision of the entire matter in controversy.[18]

28 U.S.C. §1257 reads:

(a) Final judgments or decrees rendered by the highest court of a State in which a decision could be had, may be reviewed by the Supreme Court by writ of certiorari where the validity of a treaty or statute of the United States is drawn in question or where the validity of a statute of any State is drawn in question on the ground of its being repugnant to the Constitution, treaties, or laws of the United States, or where any title, right, privilege, or immunity is specially set up or claimed under the Constitution or the treaties or statutes of, or any commission held or authority exercised under, the United States.

(b) For the purposes of this section, the term "highest court of a State" includes the District of Columbia Court of Appeals.

The Court in *Ex parte McCardle* points to the mootness of both issues in light of historical events:

> It is unnecessary to consider whether, if Congress had made no exceptions and no regulations, this court might not have exercised general appellate jurisdiction under rules prescribed by itself. For among the earliest acts of the first Congress, at its first session, was the act of September 24th, 1789, to establish the judicial courts of the

---

[18]Subsection (2) refers to the procedure of U.S. Courts of Appeals certifying a question to the Supreme Court for instruction, waiting until the Supreme Court responds, and then proceeding as instructed. It amounts to an interlocutory appeal, and like interlocutory appeals, the practice is not encouraged. According to David Siegel:

> The practice was . . . discouraged by the Court in *Wisniewski v. U.S,* 353 U.S. 901, 77 S.Ct. 633, 1 L.Ed.2d 658 (1957), in which the Court said that the certification device must be reserved for only "exceptional" cases, such as where a case before the Supreme Court involves a conflict and the court of appeals has before it a case involving the same issues; that it's the "task" of the court of appeals "to decide all properly presented cases coming before it." The courts of appeals have apparently taken this statement to heart; it amounts to a subtle suggestion that a court of appeals invoking the certification statute is just passing the buck.

See the note by David Siegel entitled "Commentary on 1988 Revision," which follows 28 U.S.C.A. §1254 in *United States Code Annotated*.

United States. The act provided for the organization of this court, and prescribed regulations for the exercise of its jurisdiction.[19]

In short, the Court says that even if this is a good question, it need not be answered because from the beginning of our federal court system, Congress has prescribed the jurisdiction of the federal courts (and, we might add, had established the institution of the Supreme Court).

The question of the true foundation of the jurisdiction of the Supreme Court still emerges periodically. In the 1980s, there were several serious attempts in Congress to withdraw appellate jurisdiction from the Supreme Court as well as from the inferior federal courts. The idea was that all of the appellate jurisdiction could be constitutionally withdrawn ("excepted") from the Supreme Court because Article III does not limit the power of Congress to regulate and make exceptions to its appellate jurisdiction. Some argued that the Court has certain appellate "core functions" to perform, such as the supervision of the federal courts and the resolution of conflicts between the circuits, and that attempts to remove the appellate jurisdiction needed to accomplish these tasks would be unconstitutional.[20]

On the separate question of whether the Court's appellate jurisdiction is mandatory or discretionary, the trend throughout the last century has been toward the statutory replacement of the Court's mandatory jurisdiction with discretionary jurisdiction. Until recently, the Supreme Court had mandatory appellate jurisdiction over several important classes of cases, including all cases from United States courts of appeals involving decisions that held state laws repugnant to the Constitution, treaties, or federal laws[21] and all cases from state courts in which either (1) a federal treaty or statute was held to be invalid or (2) a state statute was upheld after its validity was challenged on grounds that it was unconstitutional or repugnant to treaties or federal statutes.[22] Statutory changes in 1988 to this jurisdiction of the Supreme Court eliminated all mandatory appellate review except appeals from decisions of three-judge United States district courts.[23]

---

[19]Id. Still, it is easier to understand how the Court would address questions about the constitutional validity of congressional attempts to allocate federal court jurisdiction than about the question of a congressional elimination of the Supreme Court itself. After all, the Court has already decided cases presenting the issue of jurisdictional statutes (see *Marbury*, *McCardle*, and *California v. Arizona*); how would a court that has been legislated out of existence address the question of the very legislation that terminated it?

[20]See, for example, the symposium on congressional power to restrict federal court jurisdiction in 27 Villanova Law Review (1982). See also Nowak and Rotunda, *Constitutional Law*, 6th ed., §§ 2.9 and 2.10. Robert Clinton, *supra*, argues that the Framers of the Constitution intended that all of the jurisdiction set out in Article III, Section 2, be vested in the federal court system. Clinton concludes that *Ex parte McCardle* mistakenly construes the power of Congress over the jurisdiction of federal courts. See note 34 on page 31, *supra*.

[21]Formerly Subsection (2) of 28 U.S.C. §1254.

[22]Formerly Subsections (1) and (2) of 28 U.S.C. §1257.

[23]Appellate jurisdiction over three-judge district courts is granted in 28 U.S.C. §1253. The broad jurisdictional changes of 1988 are found in the Supreme Court Case Selection Act, Pub.L. 100-352, 102 Stat. 662. See Bennett Boskey and Eugene Gressman, "The Supreme Court Bids Farewell to Mandatory Appeals,"

# SUPREME COURT PROCEDURE

The Supreme Court sits during an annual term commencing on the first Monday in October. The Court recesses the following year sometime during the last week of June or the first week of July.[24] This summer recess continues until the Court convenes for the new term on the first October Monday, unless the Court decides to meet during the summer to consider emergency matters. Each term of the Court is named after the month and year in which it begins. Thus, we speak of the "October 2000 Term" or the "October 2004 Term." The Court designates certain days during the nine months following that first Monday on which it will be in formal session. On these days, it engages in two principal functions: handing down orders in cases filed with the court, and hearing oral arguments in cases that it has accepted for review.

As an appellate tribunal, the procedure of the Supreme Court is quite similar to that required by other courts of appeals, both federal and state, that exercise discretionary jurisdiction.[25] As a court of original jurisdiction, its procedure is quite different from most other trial courts.

## The Dockets

Cases are constantly being **docketed**—that is, filed—with the Court, during the summer recess as well as throughout the rest of the year. Cases filed in the Supreme Court are divided into three different **dockets,** or lists of cases pending before the Court: (1) the Appellate Docket or "paid case" docket, (2) the Miscellaneous or 5000 Series Docket, consisting of *in forma pauperis* cases; and (3) the Original Docket.[26] The first two dockets are cases seeking appellate review, and the third contains cases brought on the basis of the Court's original jurisdiction. (See Fig. 5.1)

The term **paid case** refers to the fact that the parties are able to pay all of the usual expenses of bringing a case to the Supreme Court: the $300 filing fee and the costs of printing the pleadings. The cases are numbered sequentially by the clerk of the Court, beginning with the first case filed after the summer recess begins. Thus, the first paid cases filed after the October Term of 2003 recessed on June 29, 2004,

---

109 S.Ct. 109 (1989). This article is an excellent survey of the history and present status of Supreme Court jurisdiction.

[24]Congress established the first Monday in October starting date, 28 U.S.C. § 2, which the Supreme Court follows in Rule 3 of the rules of the Court. The late June recess time has been established by tradition. The rules of the Supreme Court are available via the Court's Web site at http://www.supreme courtus.gov.

[25]Although most United States courts of appeals have no discretionary jurisdiction, intermediate appellate courts and courts of last resort of at least 48 states have discretionary jurisdiction over part of their docket.

[26]There is also a category of cases called the Special Docket that includes applications for stays of execution and motions for filing cases out of time, or after the deadline.

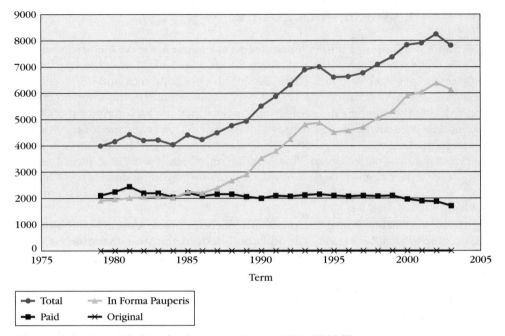

**Figure 5.1** Cases Filed in the Supreme Court, 1979–2003 Terms

were numbered 04-1, 04-2, and so on.[27] All cases not disposed of during the term in which they are filed are carried over to the next term for disposition.

In recent years, about 2,000 paid cases have been filed each term, a number that has remained remarkably constant over the past 25 years.[28]

The real increase in the Court's caseload over the past 25 years has been in the number of *in forma pauperis* or unpaid cases placed on the Miscellaneous Docket. In the October 2003 Term, 6,092 *in forma pauperis* cases were filed. This is over three times as many *in forma pauperis* cases as were filed during the 1979 Term.[29] *In forma pauperis* cases are filed by petitioners, often prisoners, who allege to the Court that they are unable to pay the usual court and printing costs and who

---

[27]Note that the new docket number sequences begins when the Court begins its summer recess, not when the new October Term begins. In 2004, for example, the new numbering began on June 29, 2004, but the October 2004 Term began October 4, 2004.

[28]During the October 2003 Term, 1,722 paid cases were filed. Since the 1979 Term, in which 2,084 paid cases were filed, only twice, in 1980 and 1981, did the number of paid cases filed with the court exceed 2,200.

[29]The October 2003 Term total of 6,092 *in forma pauperis* cases represents more than a 200 percent increase over the 1,899 filed in the October 1979 Term. The total number of cases filed in the October 2003 Term was also about double that of 1979: 7,814 cases in 2003 and 3,985 cases in 1979.

ask the court to waive those requirements.[30] Often the petitions are handwritten or personally typed by the petitioners themselves without the help of counsel, and many of these cases present questions of the constitutionality of some aspect of criminal law and procedure.

As with the paid cases, each unpaid case is numbered sequentially, but the numbering begins with the number 5001 and the cases are often referred to as the "5000 Series." Thus, the first unpaid case filed after the beginning of the summer recess of the October 2003 Term was numbered 04-5001.

The final docket is the **Original Case** Docket. These cases are usually filed by one state against another under 28 U.S.C. §1251(a), which gives the court original and exclusive jurisdiction over disputes between the states. These cases often involve boundary disputes, disputes over water rights, and challenges by one state against a law of another state.

The Original Docket is by far the smallest of the three. In the 25 terms from 1979 through and including 2003, only 48 original cases were filed. They, too, are numbered sequentially, but since the 1920s their docket numbers have been carried over from term to term. Thus, the current "No. 1, Orig." was filed in the October Term 1921; "No. 130, Orig." was filed in the October Term 1999.

## Procedure in Original Jurisdiction Cases

> This Court is . . . structured to perform as an appellate tribunal, ill-equipped for the task of factfinding and so forced, in original cases, awkwardly to play the role of factfinder without actually presiding over the introduction of evidence.[31]

Given the awkwardness described by the Court in *Ohio v. Wyandotte Chemicals*, what procedure does the Court employ in deciding original cases? To begin with, the Court exercises discretionary jurisdiction over original cases even though courts of original jurisdiction generally do not possess such discretion. In *Wyandotte*, the Court conceded that "precedent leads almost ineluctably to the conclusion that we are empowered to resolve this dispute in the first instance," but still refused to take the case:

> Ordinarily, the foregoing would suffice to settle the issue presently under consideration: whether Ohio should be granted leave to file its complaint. For it is a time-honored maxim of the Anglo-American common-law tradition that a court possessed

---

[30]The Court has lately been cracking down on litigants who abuse this procedure. See, for example, *Martin v. District of Columbia Court of Appeals et al.*, 506 U.S. 1, 113 S.Ct. 397, 121 L.Ed.2d 305, http://laws. findlaw.com/us/506/1.html (1992), where the Court said in part:

> [Petitioner] is a notorious abuser of this Court's certiorari process. We first invoked Rule 39.8 to deny [petitioner] *in forma pauperis* status last November. . . . At that time, we noted that [petitioner] had filed 45 petitions in the past 10 years, and 15 in the preceding 2 years alone. . . . Since we first denied him *in forma pauperis* status last year, he has filed nine petitions for certiorari with this Court.

[31]*Ohio v. Wyandotte Chemicals Corp.*, 401 U.S. 493, 498, 91 S.Ct. 1005, 28 L.Ed.2d 256, http://laws.find law.com/us/401/493.html (1971).

of jurisdiction generally must exercise it. . . . Nevertheless, although it may initially have been contemplated that this Court would always exercise its original jurisdiction when properly called upon to do so, it seems evident to us that changes in the American legal system and the development of American society have rendered untenable, as a practical matter, the view that this Court must stand willing to adjudicate all or most legal disputes that may arise between one State and a citizen or citizens of another, even though the dispute may be one over which this Court does have original jurisdiction.[32]

A party wishing to file an original case with the Court must first file a "motion for leave to file," which must be granted before the Court will address the merits. As a result, almost all cases filed under the Court's *concurrent* original jurisdiction will be rejected; the parties must go to another court, usually a United States district court, that shares jurisdiction.

For the one or two original cases, usually controversies between states over boundaries or water rights, that the Court receives each term under its *exclusive* original jurisdiction, Rule 17 of the Court's Rules permits the Court to use "as guides" the Federal Rules of Civil Procedure and the Federal Rules of Evidence that govern the district courts. Consequently, although the Court did preside over several full-blown jury trials in its earliest years, it has for more than a century appointed a "special master" to gather evidence and prepare a report that includes a review of the evidence and findings of fact for the Supreme Court.[33] After the report is filed with the Court, the parties have the opportunity to file, and perhaps to argue orally, exceptions to the report. After consideration of the proposed exceptions, the Court files a final decree. The decree is, of course, not appealable; there is no higher court to appeal to.

## Appeals as of Right

Initially, all appellate jurisdiction of the Supreme Court was mandatory, which in principle required the Court to review and decide on the merits each properly appealed case. Given the Court's relatively light caseload during its first 60 years, this requirement provided no great burden.[34] But after 1850, the annual filings increased

---

[32]401 U.S. at 496-97, 91 S.Ct. at 1008-09, 28 L.Ed.2d at 261-62. Keep in mind that the Supreme Court had original jurisdiction over this case concurrently with the district courts; Ohio initially could have brought its action in a United States district court.

[33]See *Mississippi v. Arkansas*, 415 U.S. 289, 296n1, 94 S.Ct. 1046, 39 L.Ed.2d 333, http://laws.findlaw.com /us/415/289.html (1974)(Douglas, J., dissenting). The use of special masters in boundary disputes is common even in the district courts.

It should also be recalled that in *Marbury v. Madison*, which was an application for a writ of mandamus, the Court, acting as a trial court, heard the testimony of witnesses, including the attorney general of the United States, Levi Lincoln.

[34]According to former Justice Strong, only ten cases were filed with the Court in 1801. The annual number grew slowly over the following decades until by 1850 an average of 71 cases was filed each year, a number that the justices could dispose of during their annual three-month term. William Strong, *The Needs of the Supreme Court*, 132 North American Review 437, 438 (May 1881).

significantly. By 1880, almost 400 cases were docketed each year and the justices could no longer keep up. The cases they failed to reach each year were held over from year to year until, according to former Justice William Strong, "the number of cases set down for argument at the October sessions of 1880 was eleven hundred and fifty-two. . . . The consequences of this are obvious. Cases cannot be heard within less than from two and a half to three years after they have been brought into the court."[35] Apart from reciting the familiar maxim "justice delayed is justice denied," Justice Strong declared the state of affairs an embarrassment and pleaded for congressional action.

The situation was ultimately addressed both legislatively and judicially. In 1891, Congress passed the Evarts Act, which established a system of federal circuit courts of appeals that immediately siphoned off some of the cases that would have been directly appealable to the Supreme Court before 1891.[36] The Act also authorized the Court to exercise discretionary appellate jurisdiction via the writ of certiorari over some kinds of cases decided by the circuit courts of appeals.

The restructuring of the federal judiciary and the establishment of a new tier of federal appellate courts provided immediate, if temporary, relief to the Court, but the inexorable increase in federal cases made further action necessary.[37] By 1925, about 20 percent of the appellate cases brought to the Court were based on its discretionary appellate jurisdiction and 80 percent on its mandatory appellate jurisdiction.[38] The "Judges' Bill" (also sometimes referred to as the "Certiorari Act") of 1925 basically reversed that ratio.[39] Until the legislation of 1988 made practically all of the Supreme Court's appellate jurisdiction discretionary, approximately 20 percent of the appellate cases filed with the Court each term were still filed as appeals as of right under the Court's mandatory appellate jurisdiction.[40]

Filing an appeal as of right did not guarantee that the Supreme Court would consider the merits of the case, however. Already in the nineteenth century, the Court had dismissed several appeals without hearing them on the grounds that they did not present a "substantial federal question." In the early twentieth century, the Court

---

[35]Id. at 439. See also William Strong, *Relief for the Supreme Court,* 151 North American Review 567–576 (November 1890).

[36]Act of March 3, 1891, ch. 517, 26 Stat. 826, §§ 2, 6. The new circuit courts of appeals were granted final appellate jurisdiction over several categories of cases from the district courts and the circuit courts (§ 6), but the Supreme Court was granted discretionary appellate jurisdiction over the judgments of the Circuit Courts of Appeals in these cases. The Supreme Court retained mandatory appellate jurisdiction over some direct appeals from the district courts and the existing circuit courts (§ 5) and over some appeals from the new circuit courts of appeals (§ 6).

[37]According to Chief Justice Fred Vinson, by 1925 the delay between docketing and hearing or otherwise disposing of the cases was back up to one and a half to two years. See the address he gave to the American Bar Association in 1949, entitled "Work of the Supreme Court," 69 S.Ct. *v.*

[38]Congress had extended the Court's discretionary appellate jurisdiction to additional kinds of cases in 1914. Act of Dec. 23, 1914, ch. 2, 38 Stat. 790.

[39]Act of Feb. 13, 1925, ch. 229, 43 Stat. 936.

[40]The 1988 Act is Pub. L. No. 100-352, 102 Stat. 662.

refined that doctrine. In 1928, the Court amended its own rules to require parties filing appeals as of right to file a "jurisdictional statement" describing "the basis on which it is contended this court has jurisdiction on appeal." These jurisdictional statements came to be treated practically as petitions for certiorari, and most appeals as of right were disposed of without argument.[41]

This judicial response was not free from problems, however. A disposition of an appeal as of right is presumptively a disposition on the merits; thus each dismissal "for want of a substantial federal question" was a judgment on the merits and was difficult, at best, to distinguish from an affirmance of the lower court judgment. The discretionary denial of a petition for a writ of certiorari, on the other hand, was never presumed to pass judgment on the merits, so the legislative replacement of most of the Court's mandatory jurisdiction with the discretionary writ of certiorari procedure in 1988 was a doctrinally neater method of giving the Court control over its dockets.[42]

Since the 1988 legislation, only a few appeals as of right are filed with the Court each term. Most of these cases concern issues arising under the Voting Rights Act of 1965 and its amendments.

## Petitions for Writs of Certiorari and Briefs in Opposition

As you may recall, discretionary appellate jurisdiction requires the party seeking review (the "petitioner") to first persuade the court that the case in question is a good one to review. Then, after the court decides to review the case, the petitioner and the party opposing review (the "respondent") must apprise the court of the questions at issue ("the merits") in written briefs and, perhaps, oral arguments.

In the Supreme Court, the petitioner's request for review takes the form of a petition for a writ of certiorari, and to say that a case is filed or docketed in the Supreme Court almost always means that a petitioner has filed a petition for a writ of certiorari. The petition contains the reasons why the petitioner believes that the Court should review the case. If the case is accepted for review, the Court "grants the writ of certiorari"; if it is not accepted, the Court "denies the writ."

The petition must be filed within 90 days of the entry of the lower court's final judgment. Once the Supreme Court receives the petition and the other parties to the case have been served, those other parties have several options.[43] Parties who agree with the petitioner's request that the Court review certain rulings or who, perhaps,

---

[41]The Court also developed and sharpened the justiciability doctrines to permit it to avoid deciding appeals that were otherwise within its jurisdiction. See the excellent account of this entire subject in Wright, Miller, and Cooper, *Federal Practice and Procedure*, §§ 4014 & 4015 (1996).

[42]It is also true that however similarly the Court treated jurisdictional statements to petitions for writs of certiorari in the years prior to 1988, the formal change to discretionary jurisdiction was accompanied immediately by a decrease in the number of cases accepted for oral argument. See Figure 5.3.

[43]Cases sometimes have several parties with significantly different interests in the dispute. See Chayes, *The Role of the Judge in Public Law Litigation*, 89 Harvard Law Review 1281 (1976).

want the Court to review different rulings in the case may, within 30 days, **cross-petition** the court for a writ of certiorari.

Much more common, however, is the desire of the respondents, who have won the case thus far and presumably are happy with the decision of the appellate court that issued the favorable ruling, to persuade the Court to leave the lower court ruling alone. The respondents may, again within 30 days, file a **brief in opposition** to the petition urging the court to deny review to the petitioners and, perhaps, pointing out errors in the petition. The petitioner may then file a **reply brief** in response to the brief in opposition. Either party may thereafter file supplemental briefs, and even nonparties may ask leave to file *amicus curiae* briefs in support of one party or another in the case.[44]

Understandably, with thousands of new cases being filed with the court each term, the Court has imposed regulations upon the parties to promote an orderly processing of these documents. We have already noted the deadlines applicable to the various filings. Time limits of this kind are part of the official rules of procedure of all courts.

What is perhaps surprising is the specificity of format that the Supreme Court imposes on the different documents to be submitted by the parties.[45] In addition to requiring that the documents be printed rather than merely typed (unless the printing requirement is waived for a particular litigant), the Court prescribes the size of the type, the margins and spacing, the kind of paper, and the kind of binding. The Court has established an elaborate color coding system for the covers of the papers that are filed by the parties and has set maximum page lengths for the various briefs and petitions. The purpose of all of this is obviously to enable the Court to handle a huge amount of paper expeditiously.

The content of the documents is also closely regulated. Rule 14 is an object lesson in the root meaning—brevity—of the legal term "briefs": short, succinct statements of legal arguments. The rule prescribes several necessary components of a petition for certiorari:

(1) the questions presented for review, expressed *concisely* in relation to the circumstances of the case, without unnecessary detail. The questions should be *short* and should not be argumentative or repetitive;

(2) a list of all the parties in the case;

(3) a table of contents and a table of legal authorities cited in the petition;

(4) citations to all previous opinions in the case:

(5) "a *concise* statement" of the basis of the Court's jurisdiction;

(6) the constitutional provisions, treaties, etc. involved in the case, or mere citations if the provisions are lengthy;

(7) "a *concise* statement of the case" and the material facts;

---

[44] *Amicus curiae* ("friend of the court") briefs, often referred to simply as *amicus* briefs, may also be requested by the Court. Rule 37.

[45] See Supreme Court Rule 33 for the following requirements. Additional printing requirements are listed in Rule 34.

(8) "a direct and *concise* argument amplifying the reasons relied on for allowance of the writ"; and,

(9) an appendix containing the texts of all the opinions in the case.[46]

The rule concludes with two reminders: "A petition for a writ of certiorari should be stated *briefly* and in plain terms and may not exceed the page limitations specified in Rule 33." And just in case the lawyers missed the point: "The failure of a petitioner to present with accuracy, *brevity,* and clarity whatever is essential to ready and adequate understanding of the points requiring consideration is a sufficient reason for denying the petition" (emphasis added).

## Court Consideration of Petitions and Opposition Briefs

Assuming that the Court has received a proper petition and opposing brief, what is next? During the summer, when the Court is in recess, no formal action is taken on any but emergency petitions, but the justices, or rather the justices' law clerks, are indeed keeping up with the filings, and the Court disposes of hundreds of them during the first Monday session of the new October Term.[47]

The dispositions of the petitions are announced in the "orders list" handed down at the Monday sessions during the term, but the actual deliberations begin when each justice receives copies of each of the documents in each case. Typically, the law clerks for each justice review the petitions and prepare memoranda summarizing the case and making a recommendation. In recent years, several members of the Court have been pooling their clerks on this job to facilitate consideration of the constant flow of petitions. It is important to note, however, that once the clerks have finished their preliminary assessments of the petitions and their memo preparation, the consideration of petitions is entirely up to the justices. At the Court's conferences, only the justices attend: unlike most meetings in the legislative and executive branches, no clerks or other aides are in the room.

Chief Justice William Rehnquist has described how the justices consider the petitions. Before each **Friday conference,** the chief justice prepares a list of the petitions that he thinks merit serious consideration, a list that he estimates to include 15 to 30 percent of all the petitions up for review that day. This so-called "discuss list" is distributed, and any of the other eight justices may add cases to the list. If a petition is not on this list, it is "dead listed" and presumably is not discussed before being denied. The chief justice defends the practice against criticism that the conference does not give each petition the collegial consideration it deserves:

> For the sixty years since the enactment of the Certiorari Act of 1925, there have been significant ideological divisions on the Court, such that one group of justices might be inclined to review one kind of case, and another group of justices inclined

---

[46]Rule 14 (emphasis added). Rule 15, which regulates the briefs in opposition, reply briefs, and other supplemental briefs, maintains this emphasis on brevity.

[47]At the opening of the October 2004 Term, for example, the Court disposed of more than 1,600 petitions. 73 U.S.L.W. 3177.

to review another kind of case. When one realizes that any one of nine justices, differing among themselves as they usually do about which cases are important and how cases should be decided, may ask that a petition for certiorari be discussed, the fate of a case that is "dead listed" . . . is a fate well deserved. It simply means that no one of the nine justices thought the case was worth discussing at conference with a view to trying to persuade four members of the Court to grant certiorari. It would be a totally sterile exercise to discuss such a case at conference since no justice would be a proponent of granting it and it would end up being denied in less time than it takes to write this paragraph.[48]

The petitions, the briefs in opposition, and any other documents at this stage of the process address the question of whether the Court should exercise its discretionary jurisdiction and decide to review a particular case. The decision to grant review is formally the decision to grant the writ of certiorari for which the petitioner prayed. This decision is usually referred to as granting certiorari or simply as **granting cert** in a particular case.

For each petition, the justices basically have three options: (1) to deny cert, (2) to grant cert and put the case on track for oral argument at a later date, or (3) to grant cert and decide the case summarily—that is, without oral argument. Cert will be granted in any case if four of the justices wish to review it. This practice, begun after the passage of the 1925 "Judges' Bill," is known as the **Rule of Four.** Cert is denied in the overwhelming majority of cases: out of the 1,622 petitions disposed of at the opening of the October 2004 Term, only 8 petitions were granted. The Court granted certiorari and set for oral argument only 5 paid cases and 3 *in forma pauperis* cases. On that day, it denied certiorari in 307 paid and 1,301 *in forma pauperis* cases.[49]

The rules of the Supreme Court set forth the principal criteria for deciding whether to accept a case for review. **Rule 10** makes clear that "a petition for a writ of certiorari will be granted only for compelling reasons." The rule then adduces three such basic reasons: (1) to resolve conflicting decisions on important, usually federal, questions between courts; (2) to supervise as necessary the judicial proceedings of lower federal courts; and (3) to review decisions on important questions of federal law that have not yet been, but should be, addressed by the Supreme Court.

Note that Rule 10 does not include anything like "rectification of egregious injustice" as one of the criteria for selecting a case for review. In the memorable words of Chief Justice Fred Vinson,

> *The Supreme Court is not, and never has been, primarily concerned with the correction of errors in lower court decisions.* In almost all cases within

---

[48]William Rehnquist, *The Supreme Court: How It Was, How It Is* (New York: William Morrow, 1987), 266–267. See also Justice Byron White, *The Work of the Supreme Court: A Nuts and Bolts Description,* 54 New York State Bar Journal 346 (1982); and for an earlier account, Justice William Brennan, *How the Supreme Court Arrives at Decisions,* New York Times, October 12, 1962.

[49]Another 1 paid case and 5 *in forma pauperis* cases were summarily decided. 73 U.S.L.W. 3177. During the complete October 2003 Term, a total of 7,814 appellate cases were filed, and only 137 cases—111 paid and 26 unpaid—were granted cert. These numbers represent 6.4 percent of the paid but only 0.4 percent of the *in forma pauperis* cases filed. 73 U.S.L.W. 3044.

# Rule 10. Considerations Governing Review on Writ of Certiorari

Review on a writ of certiorari is not a matter of right, but of judicial discretion. A petition for a writ of certiorari will be granted only for compelling reasons. The following, although neither controlling nor fully measuring the Court's discretion, indicate the character of the reasons the Court considers:

(a) United States court of appeals has entered a decision in conflict with the decision of another United States court of appeals on the same important matter; has decided an important federal question in a way that conflicts with a decision by a state court of last resort; or has so far departed from the accepted and usual course of judicial proceedings, or sanctioned such a departure by a lower court, as to call for an exercise of this Court's supervisory power;

(b) a state court of last resort has decided an important federal question in a way that conflicts with the decision of another state court of last resort or of a United States court of appeals;

(c) a state court or a United States court of appeals has decided an important question of federal law that has not been, but should be, settled by the Court or has decided an important federal question in a way that conflicts with relevant decision of this Court.

A petition for a writ of certiorari is rarely granted when the asserted error consists of erroneous factual findings or the misapplication of a properly stated rule of law.

the Court's appellate jurisdiction, the petitioner has already received one appellate review of his case. The debates in the Constitutional Convention make clear that the purpose of the establishment of one supreme national tribunal was, in the words of John Rutledge of South Carolina, "to secure the national rights & uniformity of Judgmts." The function of the Supreme Court is, therefore, to resolve conflicts of opinion on federal questions that have arisen among lower courts, to pass upon questions of wide import under the Constitution, laws, and treaties of the United States, and to exercise supervisory power over the lower federal courts.[50]

The fact that one, four, or even all members of the Court believe that the decision set forth in one of the petitions is a bad or mistaken decision—a decision, perhaps,

---

[50]Chief Justice Fred M. Vinson, "Work of the Supreme Court," Address to the American Bar Association, *supra,* note 37 (emphasis added).

resting on "erroneous factual findings" or on a "misapplication of a . . . rule of law"—does not automatically mean that the Court will grant cert in that case. The mistake, if you will, must be "compelling." The Court must consider the extent of the consequences of reviewing a particular legal issue. Keep in mind also that in many of the cases granted cert (in the 2000 Term almost a third), the Court affirms the lower court decision. If the motivation for granting cert in most cases was simply to correct injustices, it would be difficult to explain why the Court affirms—sometimes unanimously—as many cases as it does.

A second point is important to note about the Court's disposition of petitions. Many times the news media will report that "the Court has approved this or that lower court ruling today." This implies that the Court handed down a decision that affirmed a lower court's ruling on the merits in the case. But a quick review of the text of the Court's Orders List indicates that the Court had rendered no formal decisions at all on the day of the news story. What really happened? Almost always, the reporter or editor took the denial of cert in a newsworthy case to be a decision on the merits—an affirmation. But this, as you now know, is not correct. By denying cert, the Court was simply saying that the issues presented were not "compelling" enough to take up the Court's precious time.

A third point concerns the nature of the cases that the Court chooses to consider. Odd as it may seem, less than half of the cases that the Court set for oral argument and decided by written opinion over the past decade turned on issues of constitutional law; most addressed questions relating to federal statutes and the federal rules of judicial procedure.

## Granting Certiorari—Summary Disposition

If the Court grants the writ of certiorari, two main consequences may follow. The familiar course is for the Court to set the case for oral argument. This will be examined below. The Court may also, however, summarily dispose of the case on the merits by affirming, reversing, vacating, and so on the case in the same statement that grants cert.[51] In these cases, the Court has determined that the information presented in the petition and accompanying documents is sufficient to allow the Court to dispense with further proceedings, though in some of these cases individual members of the Court would prefer to hear oral argument.[52] The number of cases disposed of on the merits by summary disposition occasionally exceeds the number decided after oral argument. In the October 2000 Term, for example, the Court

---

[51]Rule 16.1. The most common use of summary dispositions is to vacate lower court judgments that conflict with a Supreme Court decision that was rendered after the lower court made its ruling but before the petition was reviewed by the Supreme Court.

[52]See, for example, the dissenting opinion of Justice Antonin Scalia in *Mireles v. Waco*, 502 U.S. 9, 15, 112 S.Ct. 286, 116 L.Ed.2d 9, http://laws.findlaw.com/us/502/9.html (1991): "I frankly am unsure whether the Court's disposition or Justice [John Paul] Stevens' favored disposition is correct; but I am sure that, if we are to decide this case, we should not do so without briefing and argument."

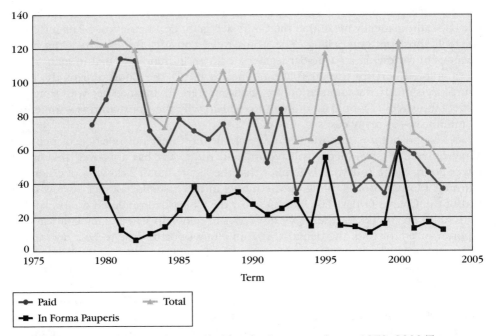

**Figure 5.2** Cases Summarily Decided by the Supreme Court, 1979–2003 Terms

decided 124 cases by summary judgment and disposed of only 86 cases after oral argument. (See Fig. 5.2.)

## Granting Certiorari—Oral Argument

When the Court sets a case for oral argument, it proceeds much like any other court of appeals exercising discretionary review. The granting of cert is followed by the lower court sending up a copy of the record.[53] By Rule 25, the parties to the case must file 40 copies of their briefs on the merits within certain prescribed times: the petitioner within 45 days of the order granting cert, and the respondent within 30 days of receiving the petitioner's brief.

At the time the Court grants cert, or later, it may also request individuals or institutions to submit briefs *amicus curiae*. In particular, the Court may invite the solicitor general of the United States, who represents the United States government in litigation before the Supreme Court, to submit briefs in cases that present a federal question or clearly involve the interests of the government. The solicitor general may

---

[53]Rule 16.2 provides that even though cert is granted, the clerk of the Supreme Court "requests" the clerk of the lower court to certify and transmit the record. "A formal writ will not issue unless specially directed." In other words, when the Court grants the petition for a writ of certiorari, in practice it does not actually issue a writ of certiorari!

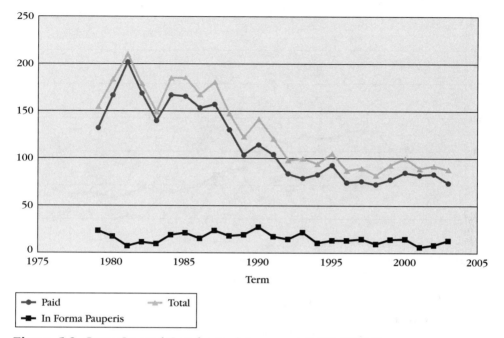

**Figure 5.3** Cases Granted Cert for Oral Argument, 1979–2003 Terms

also be invited to participate in oral argument, even though the United States is not a party to the case.[54]

Except for the enhanced stature of participating in the big show, attorneys making oral arguments proceed very much as they would before any appellate court. One difference between oral argument before the Supreme Court and argument before United States courts of appeals is that the Supreme Court hears every case *en banc,* that is, before all members of the Court. Federal appeals courts usually hear cases in panels of three judges, although *en banc* argument is possible, usually on those rare occasions when rehearing has been granted. Sometimes members of the Supreme Court remove or **recuse** themselves from participating in the decision of the case because of personal interests or previous participation in the litigation. Of course, illness also sometimes prevents a justice from participating.

Oral argument before the Court must be witnessed to be appreciated. Often, argument is not like the moot court exercises and competitions of law schools, but

---

[54]In the recent case of *Dickerson v. United States,* 530 U.S. 428, 120 S.Ct. 2326, 147 L.Ed.2d 405, http://laws.findlaw.com/us/530/428.html (2000), in which the validity of a statutory replacement for the *Miranda* rights requirement was at issue, the United States government refused to argue for the validity of the federal statute, an unusual but not unprecedented position for the government to take. The Court therefore invited an *amicus curiae* to argue the case and to defend the validity of the statute, 18 U.S.C. §3501, against the arguments of the petitioner.

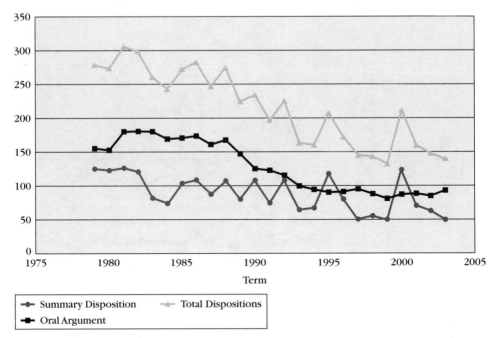

**Figure 5.4** Cases Decided on the Merits by the Supreme Court, 1979–2003 Terms

more like the "collaborative articulation of shared purposes" described by Lon Fuller. Each attorney clearly represents the legal interests of his client, but attorneys generally do not get very far if they adamantly and even unreasonably stress only the strengths of their own case and the weaknesses of their opponents'. Rather, the justices, as do the judges of state and federal appellate courts, generally want oral argument to function as an aid to their analysis of the issues and to their assessment of the parties arguments. "We treat lawyers as a resource rather than as orators who should be heard out according to their own desires," said Justice Byron White.[55] The attorneys are most effective when they help the justices to clarify their thinking about the case and the issues. Even so, however, some oral arguments take on the appearance of skirmishes or even battles between counsel and the justices, and not a few justices enjoy the battle of wit and intellect to which oral argument lends itself.

## DECIDING CASES AND PREPARING OPINIONS

In recent years, the Court has been scheduling oral arguments on the first three days of the week during about 14 weeks of each term. Immediately after coming off the bench on Wednesday afternoons of argument weeks, the justices meet in a

---

[55]Justice Byron White, *The Work of the Supreme Court, supra,* note 48, 383

**Wednesday conference** to discuss and take a preliminary vote on the cases that were heard on the Monday two days prior. The cases argued on Tuesday and Wednesday are discussed during the regular Friday conference. As described by Chief Justice Rehnquist, the Chief Justice proceeds first, recapping the facts and the legal issues of the case and indicating his opinion of how the Court should rule. He is followed by each of the other justices, proceeding in the order of seniority, until each justice has spoken.[56] Their votes are then informally recorded in order to identify the majority.

To decide a case—and by "decide," I mean here to dispose of a case by affirming, reversing, or vacating the judgment of the lower court—a majority of the participating justices must agree. Since all nine justices almost always participate, the votes of five or more justices determine how to decide the case. If one justice does not participate and the remaining eight justices split four-to-four, the case is affirmed: there must be a majority of participants to reverse or vacate a lower court decision. If only seven justices participate, at least four justices must agree on a decision, and so on.

If the chief justice is in the majority, he assigns the writing of the opinion to one of his fellow majority members; if he is not, then the senior member of the majority performs the task of assignment. In some cases, consensus reigns on the questions of both the judgment—yet another term for the decision—and the rationale for the judgment. In those cases, the opinions often come quickly and are handed down within weeks of oral argument. But in many cases, consensus is difficult to obtain, not only within the Court as a whole, but also within the majority identified at conference. In such cases, the task of writing an opinion can be a daunting one.

Remember that many cases before the Court present multiple legal issues and that each issue requires a response and a holding. The purpose of the opinion is to present a public rationale for the Court's judgment and, more particularly, for the Court's holdings or responses to each of the issues presented in the case. It is the task of the opinion writer to forge a rationale acceptable to at least five members of the Court for each holding. When five or more members join the opinion, the result is an **opinion of the Court** and each of the holdings constituting the opinion has precedential value.

When no more than four justices can agree on a rationale for the judgment or on a rationale for any of the constituent holdings, their opinion is a **plurality opinion** regarding the judgment or regarding one or more of the holdings. Plurality opinions do not constitute legal precedents because the Court as an institution has not indicated *its* position on the legal questions at issue. Indeed, the Court in such opinions does not exist as an "it," a unified institution. Of course, the Court has decided the case: "it" has

---

[56]Chief Justice Rehnquist writes:

> [M]y sixteen years on the Court have convinced me that the true purpose of the conference discussion of argued cases is not to persuade one's colleagues through impassioned advocacy to alter their views, but instead by hearing each justice express his own views to determine therefrom the view of the majority of the Court. This is not to say that minds are never changed in conference; they certainly are. But it is very much the exception, and not the rule, and if one gives some thought to the matter this should come as no surprise. Rehnquist, *supra*, note 48, 295.

rendered a judgment to affirm, reverse, or vacate the lower court judgment, but the wider and more enduring influence of Court decisions rests on the opinions, not the individual decisions. The opinions tell one and all how the Court approaches particular issues and allow judges, attorneys, and other individuals and organizations to adjust their behavior and policies to the norms indicated by the Court's reasoning.

In a few cases each term, the designated opinion writer may have great difficulty articulating a rationale that a majority of the justices can accept even if the justices indicated in conference their agreement on the judgment. Usually, the writer circulates a draft of a proposed majority opinion as soon as possible and solicits comments and criticism from the other justices, including those in the minority. In these difficult cases, three situations may develop. First, the opinion writer may attempt to compromise with other members of the majority who have difficulty with the draft opinion. This may pose the danger, however, that the agreement reached with some members of the initial majority may prove unacceptable to other members. If this problem can be avoided, a majority opinion will eventually be formed.[57]

Second, the opinion writer may not be able to find common ground on each issue with all of the other justices in the majority. In such cases, if the opinion can garner the support of at least five justices, it is still an opinion of the Court. Other justices who agree with the Court's judgment but not its rationale will likely issue separate opinions "concurring in the judgment," meaning that they agree with the Court's disposition of the case but not with the majority's rationale.

If the opinion cannot attract majority support for a rationale on any or all of the issues presented, then the opinion writer simply "announces the judgment of the Court and an opinion in which Justices So-and-so and So-and-so join." This is a plurality opinion and has no precedent value, although it does, together with the other separate opinions of the justices, indicate the various approaches to the legal issues in question taken by the various justices.[58]

---

[57]Again, Chief Justice Rehnquist:

> The willingness to accommodate on the part of the author of the opinion is often directly proportional to the number of votes supporting the majority result at conference; if there were only five justices at conference voting to affirm the decision of the lower court, and one of those five wishes significant changes to be made in the draft, the opinion writer is under considerable pressure to work out something that will satisfy the critic, in order to obtain five votes for the opinion. Chief Justice [Charles Evans] Hughes once said that he tried to write his opinions clearly and logically, but if he needed the fifth vote of a colleague who insisted on putting in a paragraph that did not "belong," in it went, and let the law reviews figure out what it meant.
>
> But if the result at conference was reached by a unanimous or a lopsided vote, a critic who wishes substantial changes in the opinion has less leverage. Ibid., 302.

[58]On rarer occasions, the members of the Court apparently cannot even agree sufficiently to formulate a plurality opinion and the court simply renders its decision in a *per curiam* opinion. Noteworthy is the case of *Furman v. Georgia*, 408 U.S. 238, 92 S.Ct. 2726, 33 L.Ed.2d 346, http://laws.findlaw.com/us/408/238.html (1972), where the Court announced the reversal of the three related cases before it in a *per curiam* statement; each of the nine justices then proceeded to issue separate opinions—five concurring in the judgments, four dissenting.

Third, and most rare, the opinion writer may not only not be able to attract a majority, but may actually lose the majority as one or more justices think over the issues and rationale more carefully. Sometimes this shifting of majority and minority occurs early in the deliberations, and sometimes it occurs later, perhaps after the wavering justice has had the opportunity to read the dissenting opinion that has been circulated, if one has been circulated. In either case, it is usually a blow to the pride of the designated opinion writer, whose opinion now becomes a dissenting opinion.

Dissenters are under no such pressure for consensus. Dissenting justices—those who disagree with the majority's disposition of the case—may join in a single dissenting opinion, write their own individual dissents, or join the opinions of other individual dissenters. Nor must a dissenter disagree with all of the majority opinion. In cases in which the disposition rests on several holdings, a justice may write an opinion "concurring in part and dissenting in part"—that is, the writer agrees with at least one majority holding but disagrees with the other(s) or with parts of the other. Sometimes careful analysis and "nose-counting" (see the next sidebar) is necessary to determine which parts of a Supreme Court opinion have majority support and precedential value and which parts do not.

When the members have finally decided on and written the opinions—majority, concurring, concurring in the judgment, dissenting, and concurring in part and dissenting in part—to be handed down in the case, the Court decides at a Friday conference which opinions are ready, and those opinions are announced in the form of a "bench opinion" at the beginning of one of the sessions the following week. Printed copies of each set of opinions, called "slip opinions," are distributed by the Court's press officer at that time and are also published the same day on the Court's web site. Still later the opinions in several cases are printed in a paperbound version of several hundred pages; these are called the "preliminary prints." Each of these paperbound copies amounts to part of a complete volume of the *United States Reports* that will be published in a hardbound copy a year or more after the cases are first handed down. (This process is also followed by the publishers of the *Supreme Court Reporter* and the *Lawyers' Edition*.)

Through its opinions, the Court exercises considerable control over all of the nation's courts, and through them the influence extends to all the nation. Although the Court can decide only the issue or conflict between the parties before it, the opinion indicates how the Court is likely to resolve similar disputes in the future.

# THE EFFECT OF APPELLATE DECISIONS AND OPINIONS

What is the effect of a Supreme Court decision? Its principal effect is the resolution of one or more legal disagreements between the parties. The decision does not necessarily "decide the case" in the sense of determining which party will eventually

---

# "Nose Counting"

In recent decades, most Supreme Court opinions—especially those that address more than one issue—are divided into sections, each of which is headed by a roman numeral. Usually, the first section presents the necessary facts and procedural history of the case, each middle section discusses one of the issues, and the last section restates the Court's holdings and consequent judgment. The sections that address the issues may be further subdivided depending on the complexity of the issues being addressed.

For example, the following excerpt is taken from the headnote of the complex case of *Buckley v. Valeo*, 424 U.S. 1 (1976), in which various provisions of the Federal Election Campaign Act were challenged. Which parts of the *per curiam* opinion have precedential value?[59]

"*Per curiam* opinion, in the "case or controversy" part of which all participating Members joined; and as to all other Parts of which BRENNAN, STEWART, and POWELL, JJ., joined; MARSHALL, J., joined in all but Part I-C-2; BLACKMUN, J., joined in all but Part I-B; REHNQUIST, J., joined in all but Part III-B-1; BURGER, C. J., joined in Parts I-C and IV (except insofar as it accords de facto validity for the Commission's past acts); and WHITE, J., joined in Part III. BURGER, C. J., WHITE, J., MARSHALL, J., BLACKMUN, J., and REHNQUIST, J., filed opinions concurring in part and dissenting in part. STEVENS, J., took no part in the consideration or decision of the cases."

---

walk out of the courtroom the winner, because many cases are remanded to the lower courts for further proceedings in light of the Supreme Court's decision and opinion. The decision simply determines the contended legal relationships between the parties in the litigation immediately before the Court. In the narrower sense of a "case" as a set of contended legal issues—usually referred to as the "merits"—that the parties want the Court to resolve, the Court decides concrete cases and controversies and does not render advisory or speculative opinions on matters not necessary for those decisions. As we have seen, this reflects the nature of the judicial power exercised by common law courts.

If the extent of the Court's legal and political influence was the decision of a few hundred separate lawsuits and criminal cases per year, it would be difficult to understand the Supreme Court, or any appellate court or court of last resort, as a signifi-

---

[59]If you have been able to decipher the voting and the holdings of *Buckley v. Valeo*, you may want to try your hand at these more recent cases: *Miller v. Albright*, 523 U.S. 420, 118 S. Ct. 1428, 140 L. Ed. 2d 575, http://laws.findlaw.com/us/523/420.html (1998); *Williams v. Taylor*, 529 U.S. 362, 120 S. Ct. 1495, 146 L. Ed. 2d 389, http://laws.findlaw.com/us/529/362.html (2000); *Branch v. Smith*, 538 U.S. 254, 123 S. Ct. 1429, 155 L. Ed. 2d 407, http://laws.findlaw.com/us/000/01-1437.html (2003); *Demore v. Kim*, 538 U.S. 510, 123 S. Ct. 1708, 155 L. Ed. 2d 724, http://laws.findlaw.com/us/000/01-1491.html (2003); and *Pharmaceutical Research v. Walsh*, 538 U.S. 644, 123 S. Ct. 1855, 155 L. Ed. 2d 889, http://laws.findlaw.com/us/000/01-188.html (2003). There are more where these came from.

cant source of law and a powerful governmental institution.[60] It is true that the purpose of the Court's Rule 10 is to focus the Court's review on cases of "special and important" significance. But even if the Court resolves the legal issues between the parties in a hundred special and important cases a year, the **decisions** only affect those few hundred parties (and their employees, associates, and families, to be sure). We would miss the fundamental role played by the Supreme Court as a court of last resort.

What is the true nature of the legal and political—and even the social and economic—authority of the Court? The answer to this question focuses on the function of the Court's **opinions** in a legal system adhering to the principle of stare decisis. When the Supreme Court, and by like reasoning any court of last resort in a state system, renders an opinion on legal issues, the Court is proclaiming in that opinion that it will decide those legal issues the same way if they are ever presented to the Court again by other parties in other cases. This is vital information for judges, lawyers, and for persons whose business or pleasure is closely regulated by law, for it allows them to predict with reasonable accuracy what the courts will do and therefore to plan how to behave in light of that "prophecy."[61]

For judges in the legal system, such a pronouncement by the system's court of last resort means that if the judge resolves a legal issue in a way that does not conform to the precedent set by the court of last resort, *and the case is appealed to that high court,* the decision by the lower court will be reversed. Trial court and intermediate appellate court judges generally do not want to be reversed on appeal because they perceive reversals as rebukes. But even disregarding the personal attitudes of the judges, it is a principle of law that inferior courts in an American legal system are bound by the precedents set by the courts above them in the hierarchy.

For lawyers who are advising clients, this prophecy function of legal opinions is particularly important. In litigation, of course, the case law precedents largely determine the strength or weakness of a party's case, and hence the party's chances of winning or losing. Since clients generally want to avoid the risk, the expense, and the inconvenience of litigation—either as a plaintiff or a defendant—their attorneys' legal research provides an assessment of their chances of success, should they be involved in litigation, and thus allows counsel to make prudent suggestions. "In light of the case law," the attorneys might say, "structuring your employment policy this

---

[60]If the significance of the Supreme Court rested only on the deciding the ultimate winners of litigation, it would rest more on the thousands of cases denied certiorari than on the hundred or so that the court decides by written opinion. For in each case denied cert, the court has almost always effectively ended the litigative process in that case and has determined the winner by refusing to disturb the final judgment rendered by the lower court: the Supreme Court has "decided" the winner by not "deciding" the merits of the case! On the other hand, in many of the cases in which the Supreme Court grants certiorari, the Court ultimately remands the case back to the lower courts for further proceedings and thus does not directly decide the ultimate winner.

[61]Indeed, Oliver Wendell Holmes based his famous definition of "law" on this function of court opinions, judges, and lawyers: "The prophecies of what the courts will do in fact, and nothing more pretentious, are what I mean by the law." *The Path of the Law*, 10 Harv. L. Rev. 457, 461 (1897).

way may well make you liable to employee lawsuits; structuring the policy that way will avoid or lessen the likely liability." The legal advice, based on "prophecies of what the courts will do," if taken by the client, may result in company policies that affect thousands of people and millions of dollars.

You may have noted that the prophecy function for both judges and lawyers is significant only if a party enters—or is yanked by a prosecutor or a plaintiff—into the legal system. If there is no litigation, then "what the courts will do in fact" is irrelevant: they will not—they *cannot*—do anything if there is no case before them. Hamilton alluded to this in *Federalist* 78 when he said that in a governmental system of separated powers, the judiciary is the least dangerous department because "it may truly be said to have neither Force nor Will, but merely judgment; and must ultimately depend upon the aid of the executive arm even for the efficacy of its judgments."[62]

Trial judges in cases that are not likely to be appealed are not likely to be deterred from ruling as they want to rule despite strong appellate precedent to the contrary. Clients are not likely to be influenced by court rulings if there are strong disincentives at work to deter others from taking them to court or, perhaps, to deter the clients themselves from taking others to court to enforce policies or agreements. One very powerful reason for not appealing an adverse court ruling or for not going to court in the first place is money. As we note when discussing the funnel effect, the high cost of litigation and the toll in time, effort, and stress on parties and on potential parties mean both that meritorious lawsuits are often never filed in the first place and that meritorious appeals are often not pursued. Particularly in state courts, where the financial value of civil litigation may be in the neighborhood of a few hundred or a few thousand dollars, a losing party in the trial court often simply does not have the money to appeal a questionable decision by the local court. The state systems and federal system are not airtight: there is considerable inconsistency of legal decision making within each of these systems. The supervisory function of courts of last resort—the task of assuring litigants and potential litigants that the rules of law will be enforced uniformly by all of the courts that belong to a single legal system—is often thwarted.

Despite these limitations the greater part of courts' legal, political, economic, and social power is founded not on the specific decisions or judgments of the courts, but on the rationales for those decisions as articulated in the court opinions. In a legal system governed by the modern principle of stare decisis, court opinions serve to guide judges within the system and to advise individuals and organizations who have never been a party to a lawsuit and who hope they never will be. Through their opinions, the courts' authority extends far beyond their express function of exercising the judicial power by deciding the concrete cases and controversies before them.

---

[62]Although there are no "judiciary police" to go out and bring cases to the courts, law enforcement officers of the executive branch such as police, government regulators, and criminal prosecutors persistently use litigation and the threat of litigation to encourage behavior consistent with the rulings of the courts. Such devices as fee-shifting statutes and treble damage remedies also encourage litigation by private parties.

# Appendix A

# Finding and Citing Legal Sources

Legal sources—cases, statutes, and scholarly literature—usually conform to a notation system that is simple and efficient. Though there are some exceptions, the following summary will serve as a guide to help you find the most common materials cited in legal scholarship and to cite legal sources in your own work.

Different students will have different resources available to them. Some of you may have access to a university or government law library, which will include all of the materials cited below and more. Some may have access only to a college, university, or public library, which will probably have far fewer legal materials. Most all of us today have access to the Internet; but while making more and more free resources available for legal research, the Internet is still not sufficient to research thoroughly the kind of legal issues that might be the basis of an academic research paper. If you are fortunate enough to have access to the Internet subscription services of Westlaw and LEXIS-NEXIS, almost all of the materials cited below will be available online, but at a considerable price. It is very easy to do a couple of hours of legal research on Westlaw or LEXIS and run up a bill of several hundred dollars. If your school or employer is paying the bill and encouraging you to use the facilities—great! If you are paying the bill, you may want to learn more about the hard copy resources that are available. In the account that follows, I will make reference wherever possible to the Internet availability of the sources that are discussed, but will key the discussion to the hard copy materials.

## CASES—SUPREME COURT

Citations to court opinions have two general parts: (1) the italicized (underlined) name or "style" of the case followed by (2) the information necessary to find the opinion. The necessary information is presented in a pattern that is applicable to a great many legal sources: volume number, followed by the abbreviated name of the **reporter** (which is the series of books in which court opinions appear), followed by the number of the first page of the opinion, and concluded by the date of the opinion (in parentheses). It is a good practice to italicize or underline the case name in citations and in all other references to the case. The name of a case is treated the same as the title of a book. Thus, the case of "Baker versus Carr" is cited as follows:

> *Baker v. Carr,* 369 U.S. 186 (1962).

"Versus" is always abbreviated as "*v.*" in legal citations. "369" refers to the 369th volume of a set of books called *United States Reports,* abbreviated "U.S.," that is published by the United States Government. "186" refers to page 186 of volume 369 of *United States Reports,* and "(1962)" indicates that the opinion was handed down in 1962.

References to pages of the opinion other than the first page are cited by indicating the particular page number immediately after the number of the first page of the case. Thus a reference to page 199 of the *Baker v. Carr* opinion would be as follows:

> *Baker v. Carr,* 369 U.S. 186, 199 (1962)[1]

Two other sets of books publish all of the opinions of the United States Supreme Court: the *Supreme Court Reporter* and the *United States Supreme Court Reports— Lawyers' Edition,* referred to simply as the *Lawyers' Edition.*[2] In the *Supreme Court*

---

[1] Immediately subsequent footnote or endnote references may be cited as "*id.*" Thus, if you refer to a case several times with no intervening references to other sources, the subsequent reference would be listed as "*Id.* at 199." Where the subsequent reference follows intervening references to other sources, the reference would be "*Baker v. Carr,* 369 U.S. at 199."

[2] The coverage of the *Supreme Court Reporter,* published by West Publishing Company (now "West Group"), begins with the 1882 Term or volume 106 of the *United States Reports;* the *Lawyers' Edition,* now published by LEXIS Law Publishing, includes all of the published opinions since the Court's creation in 1789 and also includes accounts of the arguments presented. Since 1933 *United States Law Week,* published by the Bureau of National Affairs (BNA), has published Supreme Court slip opinions within a few days of their issuance. *Law Week* also includes summaries of each paid case docketed each year and valuable statistical data.

On the Internet, the Supreme Court now posts the slip opinions on its own web site, http://www.supremecourtus.gov, the same day that they are handed down, but only retains them on the Web for a couple of years until the final bound volume of the *United States Reports* is published. The Legal Information Institute of Cornell University posts this same information at http://supct.law.cornell.edu/supct/, but retains and indexes the cases for a longer period of time. Findlaw.com also posts and indexes Supreme Court opinions at http://www.findlaw.com, as does lexisONE at http://www.lexisone.com.

Supreme Court opinions are printed in four versions: (1) the initial "bench" opinion, which is distributed to the press at the time the opinion is announced by the Court; (2) the "slip" opinion, which is available later the same day on which the opinion is announced by the Court; (3) the "preliminary print," which is a paperbound edition published several months after the initial announcements of several opinions together; and (4) the final "bound version" of the *United States Reports.* Each successive version contains corrections—both minor corrections brought to the Court Reporter's attention by the public and, possibly, major corrections, including revisions to the opinion by the Court itself. Both the *Supreme Court Reporter* and the *Lawyers' Edition* publish the slip, preliminary print, and final bound versions successively. *Law Week* publishes only the slip opinions. The Supreme Court and the Legal Information

---

# Findlaw.com URL Citations

Findlaw.com is presently an excellent online source of Supreme Court opinions, because unlike the opinions posted by lexisONE, the opinions posted by Findlaw contain references to the *United States Reports* pagination (in green text) and thus allow you to cite specific pages of the opinions. If you know the *United States Reports* citation, you may go to the **Findlaw.com > US Laws: Cases & Codes > US Supreme Court—Opinions and Web Site > Citation Search,** and enter the volume number and page number in the proper boxes. Alternatively, you may go directly to the opinions without visiting the web site by plugging the volume number and the page number into the URL: http://laws.findlaw.com/us/VOL/PAGE.html. Thus, the URL citation for *Baker v. Carr* via Findlaw.com is http://laws.findlaw.com/us/369/186.html. Opinions since 1893 are also indexed by party name. Findlaw.com citations are attached to all Supreme Court opinions in this *Primer*.

---

*Reporter* (abbreviated "S.Ct."), the opinion in *Baker v. Carr* was published in volume 82 beginning on page 691; in the *Lawyers' Edition* (abbreviated "L.Ed." or "L.Ed.2d"), the opinion appears in volume 7 of the **second series** of *Lawyers' Edition* volumes ("L.Ed.2d") beginning on page 663. Thus, citations to the case in these books appear as follows:

> *Baker v. Carr,* 82 S.Ct. 691 (1962)
>
> and
>
> *Baker v. Carr,* 7 L.Ed.2d 663 (1962)

When citing United States Supreme Court opinions, customary practice calls for the inclusion of at least the *United States Reports* citation, followed by one or both of the other citations. This primer cites all three reporters when possible.

---

Institute web sites post the slip opinions; Findlaw.com posts the *United States Reports* final bound volume versions, complete with the *United States Reports* pagination, making it an excellent source for reference and research.

Originally, the volumes of Supreme Court decisions bore the names of the individual compilers. The first compiler, or official court reporter, was A. J. Dallas, and decisions contained in the volumes that he compiled were cited, for example, as 3 Dall. 171. Dallas (1790–1800) was succeeded by William Cranch (1801–1815); Henry Wheaton, abbreviated "Wheat." (1816–1827); Richard Peters, abbreviated "Pet." (1828–1842); Benjamin Howard, abbreviated "How." (1843–1860); Jeremiah Black (1861–1862); and John William Wallace, abbreviated "Wall." (1863–1874). Frequently, citations to opinions that first appeared in the compilations of these court reporters refer to both the *United States Reports* volume and the original volume: for example, *Marbury v. Madison*, 5 U.S. (1 Cranch) 137, 2 L.Ed. 60 (1803); and *McCulloch v. Maryland*, 17 U.S. (4 Wheat) 316, 4 L.Ed. 579 (1819).

# CASES—UNITED STATES DISTRICT COURTS AND COURTS OF APPEALS

The pattern that remains fairly constant in all case citations is as follows: (1) name of case, followed by the (2) volume number, (3) abbreviated name of reporter, (4) number of first page of opinion, and (5) date of opinion. The variable that poses the most difficulty to new students of the law is the name of the reporter, because there are many different sets of law reports being published.

The largest publisher of court opinions in the United States is the West Group of St. Paul, Minnesota. West publishes the *Supreme Court Reporter* and editions of court opinions of the United States courts of appeals, the United States district courts, other federal courts, state courts, and more. The two principal sets of federal court opinions with which all students should be familiar are the *Federal Reporter,* which includes written opinions of the United States courts of appeals, and the *Federal Supplement,* which prints United States district court opinions. Both of these sets have completed at least one "series" of numbers: the *Federal Reporter* is now in its third series, and the *Federal Supplement* is in its second.[3]

Here we encounter a slight change in the citation pattern. Because there are 13 different federal circuits and 94 different district courts, and because the identification of the particular circuit or district court issuing a ruling may be legally significant, lawyers identify the circuit or district in abbreviated form within the parentheses enclosing the date. For example:

> *National Treasury Employees Union v. United States,* 101 F.3d 1423 (D.C.Cir. 1996).

The citation tells us that the opinion can be found in the 101st volume of the third series of the *Federal Reporter* ("Fed third"), and the "D.C.Cir." in parentheses indicates that the opinion was issued by the United States Court of Appeals for the District of Columbia Circuit. If the opinion had been issued by another United States

---

[3]Federal court opinions from 1789 to 1880 were collected in a 30 volume set of books called *Federal Cases.* The first series of the *Federal Reporter,* which began in 1880, went from volume 1 to volume 300. The second series—referred to verbally as "Fed second" and abbreviated "F.2d"—began in 1925 and went from volume 1 to volume 999. Until the birth of the *Federal Supplement* series in 1932, the *Federal Reporter* series included federal district court opinions as well as appellate opinions. "Fed third" (abbreviated "F.3d") began in 1993 with volume 1 and will presumably give way to "Fed fourth" when it reaches 1,000 volumes. The *Federal Supplement,* or "Fed Supp" (abbreviated "F.Supp.") just completed its first series of 999 volumes and is now on its second series. Neither of these sets of opinions, incidentally, includes every single federal appeals court or district court opinions. In the last few years, many of the "unpublished opinions" of these courts can be found on the Internet at the Westlaw and Lexis sites, usually with court restrictions on their legal use and precedential value. But see *Anastasoff v. United States,* 223 F.3d 898 (8th Cir. 2000), in which a rule of the United States Court of Appeals for the Eighth Circuit that specified that unpublished opinions of the Eighth Circuit have no precedential effect was held unconstitutional by a panel of the Eighth Circuit Court of Appeals. The Eighth Circuit, acting *en banc,* later vacated the judgment as moot, thus leaving the status of unpublished opinions in the Eighth Circuit up in the air.

court of appeals—for example, by the eleventh circuit—the material in parentheses would be "11th Cir. 1996" instead of "D.C.Cir. 1996."

The *Federal Supplement* publishes opinions of United States District Courts and some other federal trial courts. The following sample citations are to district court opinions issued by (1) the United States District Court of the District of Columbia ("D.D.C."), (2) the Middle District of Pennsylvania ("M.D.Pa"), and (3) the Western District of New York ("W.D.N.Y."):

(1) *In re Grand Jury Proceedings*, 5 F. Supp.2d 21 (D.D.C. 1998)
(2) *Pansy v. Preate*, 870 F. Supp. 612 (M.D.Pa. 1994)
(3) *U.S. v. Occidental Chem. Corp.*, 965 F. Supp. 408 (W.D.N.Y. 1997)

Searchable databases of United States court of appeals and United States district court opinions are available via Findlaw.com and the circuit and district Web sites, but the databases go back only a few years. This is one area of Internet data that needs to be improved before adequate Internet research into federal district and appellate opinions can be conducted.

## CASES—STATE COURTS

Once we leave the law reports of the three principal federal courts, we face a myriad of state and local courts and law reports. A few general remarks and a few examples must suffice here. West Group publishes a series of regional state court law reporters that divide up the country by region as follows:

*Atlantic Reporter* (abbreviated A. for the first series and A.2d for the second[4]) includes state court opinions from Connecticut, Delaware, the District of Columbia, Maine, Maryland, New Hampshire, New Jersey, Pennsylvania, Rhode Island, and Vermont.

*North Eastern Reporter* (N.E. and N.E.2d) includes Illinois, Indiana, Massachusetts, New York, and Ohio.

*North Western Reporter* (N.W. and N.W.2d) includes Iowa, Michigan, Minnesota, Nebraska, North Dakota, South Dakota, and Wisconsin.

*South Eastern Reporter* (S.E. and S.E.2d) includes Georgia, North Carolina, South Carolina, Virginia, and West Virginia.

*South Western Reporter* (S.W., S.W.2d, and S.W.3d) includes Arkansas, Kentucky, Missouri, Tennessee, and Texas.

*Southern Reporter* (So. and So.2d) includes Alabama, Florida, Louisiana, and Mississippi.

*Pacific Reporter* (P., P.2d, and P.3d) includes Alaska, Arizona, California, Colorado, Hawaii, Idaho, Kansas, Montana, Nevada, New Mexico, Oklahoma, Oregon, Utah, Washington, and Wyoming.

---

[4]The first series of all of the regional reporters have long since been exhausted and the second series begun. Some regional reporters, notably the *Pacific Reporter* and the *South Western Reporter,* are already in the third series.

Each state also publishes its own court opinions separately, sometimes using publishing companies such as West. Thus, citations to state court opinions may include references to the state law reporter followed by reference to the regional reporter. The state law reporter generally indicates whether the ruling court was the court of last resort or an intermediate appellate court in the following manner: if the court issuing the opinion is the state's court of last resort, the state's abbreviation will appear by itself, as in the Washington state case of *DeFunis*, below. If the issuing court is an intermediate appellate court, the state abbreviation will be followed by the abbreviation "App." as in the Georgia state case of *KMart Corp.* that follows. If the state court is not indicated in the name of the reporter, such as when only the regional reporter is cited, the identification of the state court, whether a court of last resort or an intermediate appellate court, must be included with the date in the final parentheses.

For example, all of the following citations refer to the same court opinion:

(1)  *DeFunis v. Odegaard,* 84 Wash.2d 617, 529 P.2d 438 (1974)

or

(2)  *DeFunis v. Odegaard,* 84 Wash.2d 617 (1974)

or

(3)  *DeFunis v. Odegaard,* 529 P.2d 438 (Wash. 1974)

The reference in each of these citations to "Wash." (not "Wash.App.") indicates that the opinion was issued by the state's court of last resort, the Supreme Court of Washington, and the citation to "Wash.2d" is to the second series of a set of books reporting only the opinions of the Washington state supreme court. When citing the case as it appears only in the *Pacific Reporter*, as citation (3) does here, the reference to "Wash." must be included with the date in parentheses.

The following opinion is from Georgia's intermediate appellate court, as indicated by inclusion of "App." after the state name:

(1)  *KMart Corp. v. Jackson,* 239 Ga.App. 176, 521 S.E.2d 93 (1999)

or

(2)  *KMart Corp. v. Jackson,* 239 Ga.App. 176 (1999)

or

(3)  *KMart Corp. v. Jackson,* 521 S.E.2d 93 (Ga.App. 1999)

The first and second citations here do not require the "Ga.App." in the parentheses because it is clear from the name of the reporter, *Ga.App.,* an abbreviation of the set of *Georgia Appeals Reports,* that the opinion is from the Georgia intermediate appellate court. The citation to the *South Eastern Reporter* alone, however, requires the "Ga.App." identification to indicate the state court in question.

Some states, notably New York and California, have several different and overlapping reporters. For example, an opinion of the California Supreme Court may require three reporters to be listed:

*People v. Cortez,* 18 Cal.4th 1223, 77 Cal.Rptr.2d 733, 960 P.2d 537 (1998)

The first, "Cal.4th," refers to the set of official reports of the California Supreme Court. The second, "Cal.Rptr.2d," refers to West's *California Reporter,* which includes opinions from all levels of California courts. The last reference is to West's *Pacific Reporter,* which, if it were the only source cited, as it might well be if the cases were cited in legal documents filed in the courts of any of the other 49 states or in the federal courts, would require the "Cal." to be included in the parentheses with the date.

# DIGESTS

To research case law thoroughly, one must identify as many relevant cases as possible. To enable researchers to do this, several publishers, notably West Group, publish **digests** of court opinions organized by legal topics. Digests generally include a brief—usually one sentence—summary of the court's holding or statement on the topic in question. These summary statements allow the lawyer or legal researcher to review quickly a great number of potentially relevant court opinions and to select those that look particularly useful. The researcher then turns to the full court opinions of the selected cases for further study.

To research federal court opinions, West's *Federal Practice Digest,* now in its fourth series, includes United States district court and court of appeals decisions as well as Supreme Court opinions, all of which are organized on the basis of the "key number" system.

This same key number system is used to arrange West's regional and state digests. There is a regional digest for each regional reporter: the *Atlantic Digest* surveys and catalogs the cases in the *Atlantic Reporter,* the *North Eastern Digest* catalogs the cases in the *North Eastern Reporter,* and so on. Individual state digests are published for many states, as well, and these state digests include references to relevant federal court opinions interpreting the state's law.

---

## West's "Key Number" System

The most important system of classification of legal materials with cross-references to other publications is the "Key Number System" of West Publishing Company (now West Group or Thomson Legal Publishing). The key number system categorizes the entire body of law into an outline of thousands of topics. Each case that West publishes is analyzed in terms of these topics. The publications then allow someone who is interested in a particular key number topic to use one of the West Group digest publications to find a continually updated listing of all cases that contain material on the same topic. This kind of cross-referencing, digesting, and classification has long been an essential part of legal research, and the Westlaw Internet service makes it available in a format that, though quite expensive to use, speeds up the process considerably.

Digest research can also be done via computer using the Westlaw or LEXIS services. Westlaw, of course, utilizes the key number system, while LEXIS uses a comparable system. These electronic services also make possible "word searches" that allow the researcher to identify all cases in a selected database that contain the string of words or symbols specified by the researcher. Word searches can be enormously useful, and thus the service is priced accordingly by Westlaw and LEXIS.

No case law research is complete without checking to see if the cases you find have been overruled or expressly followed or criticized in later court opinions. This process is referred to as **Shepardizing** cases because of a series of publications, such as *Shepard's Federal Citations, Shepard's Atlantic Reporter Citations,* and so on, that provide this information for almost all court decisions in the United States. Cases can now be Shepardized on LEXIS or by using the periodical Shepard's booklets in law libraries and applying the coded apparatus explained in the booklets to the cases in question. Westlaw provides a similar service entitled "KeyCite."

# STATUTES

The enactments of the United States Congress are all gathered in a set of volumes called *United States Statutes at Large,* first published in 1845 and still published today.[5] During the century and a half of publication, the method of noting federal statutes, also called "session laws," has changed somewhat, however. In the first 150 years of the United States, laws were simply referred to by the date on which they were enacted and by a chapter ("ch.") number. The first law passed in the Sixty-first Congress, for example, was assigned "ch. 1," the second "ch. 2," and so on. Thus: Act of June 25, 1910, ch. 434, 36 Stat. 865. Some statutes have popular names and are cited by those names: White-Slave Traffic (Mann) Act, ch. 395, 36 Stat. 825 (1910).

By 1941, each enactment was also assigned a Public Law number based on the order in which it was enacted in a particular Congress, and since 1957, each law has been noted by this sequential number of the Congress and the number of the law: thus, Pub. L. 85-1 was the first public law enacted by the Eighty-fifth Congress.

No matter how the public law is cited, it appears in a certain volume and at a certain page of *United States Statutes at Large* (abbreviated "Stat."), and that fact allows one to readily find the law. The form of the citation to *United States Statutes at Large* is (1) volume number, (2) abbreviated name of the set of books ("Stat."), and (3) page number of first page of the law. The date of publication is omitted if it appears in the name of the Act. Thus, the original Voting Rights Act of 1965, which happens to be Pub. L. 89-110, is found at 79 Stat. 437 and may be cited as follows:

Voting Rights Act of 1965, Pub. L. No. 89-110, 79 Stat. 437.

---

[5] The first 18 volumes of the *Statutes at Large,* including enactments from 1789 to 1875, are available on the Web at http://Thomas.loc.gov. > **Historical Documents** > **A Century of Lawmaking . . .** > **Statutes at Large.**

Acts that do not have formal or popular titles are still cited by the date of their enactment: for example, Act of February 5, 1867, ch. 26, 14 Stat. 385.

*Statutes at Large* prints the complete texts of the laws as enacted by Congress; that is, the laws are not in their codified form. Many laws enacted by Congress contain bits and pieces relating to different topics. Since 1926, the laws of the United States have been organized—or **codified**—into one comprehensive code called the *United States Code,* which is divided by subject matter into 50 "titles" and many "sections" (usually indicated by the symbol "§") and "subsections" within each title. The code is published by two private publishing companies: West publishes the code under the name of *United States Code Annotated,* and LEXIS (succeeding Lawyers Cooperative) publishes it in the *United States Code Service.* It is also available on the Internet.[6] The codification itself is directed by the Law Revision Counsel of the House of Representatives.

Organization by subject matter requires that public laws, as enacted by Congress and as appearing in the *Statutes at Large,* be internally separated and classified into the code at the appropriate places. Often the references to federal laws will be references to sections of the code. For example, the Voting Rights Act of 1965, as passed by Congress in 1965, when codified, was placed in title 42 of the United States Code. The Voting Rights Act was subsequently amended at least nine times with additions and changes. One section of the original act is found in section 1971 of Title 42. This can be cited in three ways, depending upon the source in which it was found:

(1)  42 U.S.C. § 1971 (1965),

or

(2)  42 U.S.C.A. § 1971 (2003)(copyright of West publication),

or

(3)  42 U.S.C.S. § 1971 (2000)(copyright of Lexis publication).

The first is to the official government publication, the second cite is to the West publication, and the third is to the LEXIS publication.

A valuable source for guidance in interpreting the language and purpose of federal statutes is the *United States Code Congressional and Administrative News,* which publishes the texts of the public laws enacted each Congress along with excerpts from relevant "legislative history" (any House and Senate committee reports accompanying the bills), presidential signing statements, executive orders, proclamations, and the like.

All 50 states have comparable publications to the *Statutes at Large* and the *United States Code,* but many of the state codes follow different notation systems that require a bit of special familiarization. For example, statutes in Ohio are cited by

---

[6]In addition to the FindLaw site, http://www.findlaw.com, the code is also available on the United States House of Representatives site at http://uscode.house.gov/usc.htm and Cornell University's Legal Information Institute site, http://www.law.cornell.edu/.

section number, where the first digit or two indicate the title of the Ohio Code. Thus, Section 3323.04 is part of Title 33 of the Ohio Code. New York refers to the titles of its categories of statutes as "Laws"; hence, New York's "General Business Law §362" or "Highway Law §432." California refers to its categories of statutes as "Codes": for example, "Public Resources Code §1207" or "Streets and Highways Code §231." All of the sets of state law codes contain explanations of their particular citation system in the opening pages of each volume of the set. Many states are also publishing their codes on the Internet.[7]

## GOVERNMENT REGULATIONS

Laws that authorize the government, acting through its agencies, to do things usually authorize the agencies in question to promulgate **rules and regulations** for the implementation of the statutory objectives. Federal agency rules and regulations are subject to a series of procedural steps dictated by the Administrative Procedure Act, 5 U.S.C. 551 *et seq.*, which generally requires the agencies to publish their initial drafts of rules and regulations in the *Federal Register* in order to give interested parties a certain period of time to comment on the proposals and to suggest changes. Thereafter, the agencies consider the comments and publish the final versions in the *Federal Register* (abbreviated "FR" or "Fed.Reg."). These final versions are then periodically codified into the *Code of Federal Regulations* ("CFR" or "C.F.R.").[8]

References to the *Federal Register* and the *Code of Federal Regulations* follow the same "volume or title number/abbreviated name of publication/page number" pattern we used for cases and statutes. For example, in

63 Fed. Reg. 12345 (1998)

the first number refers to the volume number of the daily issue of the *Federal Register*, 63. The second number, 12345, refers to the page in that volume. The date is in parentheses.

The first number in references to the *Code of Federal Regulations* refers to the *subject matter title*, not volume number, into which the rule or regulation has been placed. The number after "C.F.R." is the number of the "Part" of the Title, followed by a decimal point and the number of the "Section" of the Part of the Title. Thus,

5 C.F.R. §831.402 (2002)

refers to Title 5, Part 831, Section 402 of the Code of Federal Regulations in its 2002 codification.

---

[7]See, for example, http://www.findlaw.com for links to many of these state, as well as federal, materials.

[8]*The Code of Federal Regulations* is available on the Internet at http://www.access.gpo.gov/nara/index.html, a publication of the National Archives and Record Administration.

# JOURNALS AND BOOKS

Most scholarly legal writing appears in **legal journals and law reviews**, many of which are sponsored and edited by law schools throughout the world. This fact makes these articles an essential resource for serious legal research. At least two comprehensive indexes of these periodicals exist: Wilson's *Index of Legal Periodicals* and the newer *Current Law Index*. These indexes are available via CD-ROM on many library computer terminals. The full texts of the articles, however, are generally not available on the Internet except via the Westlaw and LEXIS services, and even these services do not provide full texts of all law review articles from past years. Thus a major academic resource—law reviews and journals—is generally available only in law libraries, a condition that poses a major obstacle to legal researchers who do not have access to a comprehensive law library.[9]

This said, individual articles are cited as follows:

Robert A. Shapiro, *Polyphonic Federalism: State Constitutions in the Federal Courts*, 87 Cal. L. Rev. 1409 (1999).

David P. Currie, *Separating Judicial Power*, 61 Law & Contemp. Probs., Summer 1998, at 7.

Note the familiar pattern following the name of the article: Shapiro's article appears in the 87th volume of the *California* (University of California, Berkeley) *Law Review* and begins on page 1409 of that volume. The second article begins on page 7 of the Summer 1998 issue of volume 61 of *Law and Contemporary Problems*. Each legal periodical also indicates the abbreviation and citation format that it requests.

Multivolume **treatises** are another frequently used source in legal research. Some treatises are huge encyclopedias of legal topics. Neither the entries in these works nor the works themselves are attributed to specific authors: reference is made to the title of the article, perhaps to the section of the article, and to the volume number/treatise/page number facts of reference. One common general treatise or legal encyclopaedia is the *Corpus Juris Secundum* or "CJS." For example:

53 C.J.S. *Libel and Slander* § 6 (1987)

This refers to Section 6 of a multisection article on libel and slander in Volume 53 of CJS.

Another treatise is *American Jurisprudence*, or "Am.Jur." There have been several series of Am.Jur. over the years, and one must give care to identifying the particular series being used. This is also true of the *American Law Reports* or "A.L.R.," a publication with several series of volumes of selected cases and accompanying annotations and commentaries on the law in those cases.

---

[9]See, however, the University Law Review Project link on Findlaw.com and also the materials available via the Internet Legal Resource Guide, http://www.ilrg.com. Some journals have begun posting their issues online, but the numbers are still quite limited.

Single- and multivolume treatises by particular individuals are also used for research in particular areas of the law. For example, Alan Bromberg and Larry Ribstein's multivolume treatise, *Bromberg and Ribstein on Partnership*, published by Aspen Publishers, is cited:

> 1 Alan R. Bromberg and Larry E. Ribstein, *Bromberg and Ribstein on Partnership*, §2.05(b) (2003)

A valuable source for further research into much of the material in this primer is the well-known "Wright and Miller." For example,

> 1 Charles Alan Wright and Arthur R. Miller, *Federal Practice and Procedure: Civil 3d*, §1001 (2002)

Finally, books and monographs are also used in legal research, although often not to the extent that such sources are used in other fields of study. Legal notation eliminates the publisher and the city of publication from the usual facts of publication used in Chicago and MLA style references. For example,

> Christopher Howard, *The Hidden Welfare State: Tax Expenditures and Social Policy in the United States* (1997).

Citations to page numbers follow the name of the book and precede the date:

> Christopher Howard, *The Hidden Welfare State: Tax Expenditures and Social Policy in the United States,* 12–13 (1997).

## INTERNET SITES

In addition to the subscription services provided by Westlaw, LexisNexis, Commerce Clearing House, The Law.net, and many others, we have referred to several important free sites: Findlaw.com (http://www.findlaw.com), lexisONE (http://www.lexisone.com), the Legal Information Institute of Cornell University (http://www.law.cornell.edu/), and the Internet Legal Resource Guide (http://www.ilrg.com). In addition to these, we have referred throughout the text to many free government-sponsored sites, particularly those of state and federal courts. The present weakness of most of these law-related sites is the incompleteness of their historical materials. Older records, older cases, and older journal articles are still not available on the Web and will not be unless and until sufficient money and the commitment to posting the historical materials exist.

## OTHER TIPS

The bible of lawyers, judges, and other legal writers, along with this writer, for citing legal materials properly is *The Bluebook: A Uniform System of Citation,* now in its seventeenth edition and published by the editors of four Ivy League law reviews. This fat little book contains explanations and examples covering all imaginable legal sources and is a must for any practicing attorney or legal scholar. Another useful text is Darby Dickerson's *ALWD Citation Manual*. The account of citations found in this appendix uses the citation form set forth in *The Bluebook*. The *Primer* generally follows the *Bluebook* style for legal citations and law review articles, but uses the Chicago Style for books and textual conventions. The Chicago Style is often used in conjunction with *Bluebook* style in law reviews.

Almost every legal publication contains a section explaining how the publication is to be cited, how the material in the publication is indexed and organized, and how the publication relates to other publications, usually, but not always, by the same publisher. It should be noted that in this primer, where the publication's suggested citation style conflicts with the *Bluebook* form, I used the latter.

Finally, *"Always check the pocket parts!"* Many legal publications, such as statutory codes, treatises, and digests, attempt to keep up with the latest legal developments by issuing paperbound supplements that are designed to slip into a slot on the inside of the back cover of the bound volume. These are called **pocket parts,** and it is absolutely crucial for one doing research in hard copy materials to read them to make sure that the material in the main volume is still current. There is nothing worse than to learn that the holding, legal principle, or statute that you are relying upon in your argument has been amended—a catastrophe that might have been avoided if you had checked the pocket part.

# Appendix B

# Analyzing Opinions and Briefing Cases

## ANALYZING COURT OPINIONS

When doing legal research, lawyers treat court opinions in previously decided cases as potential sources of authoritative rules and principles for deciding current disputes. In common law systems, these rules in case law—called **precedents**—are as important as, if not more important than, statutes, regulations, and even clauses of the United States Constitution because these rules in case law provide the authoritative interpretations of the statutes, regulations, and clauses in question. How do we find these rules and principles in the cases? There is no single method of analysis that works every time, but the following tips on what to look for in court opinions may be helpful.

The function of courts is to resolve the controversies—the points of disagreement—between the parties to a case. At the trial court level, the controversies usually include disagreements about the facts—about what happened. Resolving the controversy in such cases will then require the trial court to resolve the disagreements about the facts. The purpose of the pretrial process is to determine the areas of agreement between the parties and to define precisely the remaining points of disagreement, which are usually called **issues of fact.** Trials then resolve the issues of fact—who did what, when, where, how, and why—that relate to the causes of action. Appellate courts accord great deference to these factual findings.

In addition to disagreements about facts, issues can also be disagreements about interpretations of law. Trial judges must also decide on interpretations or applications of the relevant legal rules in the case, but appellate courts are less deferential to the trial courts' legal interpretations and these interpretations are the principal subject of review by appellate courts.

Most of the opinions that we study in law courses are excerpts from appellate court opinions, not the written findings of fact and conclusions of law by trial court judges.[1] The appellants or petitioners in these cases asked the appeals court to reverse or vacate or modify the judgments of a lower court because of alleged errors in the rulings by the lower court judges. The appellees or respondents usually want the appellate court to affirm the judgment—that is, to leave the lower court decisions alone. After all, the appellees and respondents "won" the case below. Thus, the function of appellate courts, in deciding a case, is deciding what to do with the lower court judgment—to affirm it, reverse it, or vacate it—and to do this they must first decide whether the lower courts did indeed make erroneous rulings and, if so, whether the errors were serious enough to warrant reversal.

The issues—and most appellate cases present the court with several issues—before appellate courts are always framed as **issues of law** called "questions." For example, did the trial court (and by "trial court" in this context, we always mean the trial judge) err when it applied *this* rule of law as opposed to *that* rule of law to the facts? Or, did the trial court err in its interpretation or application of a particular rule to the facts?[2] The type of legal issue in the first question focuses on which rule should be applied; the type of legal issue in the second question focuses on whether the rule, assuming it to be the proper rule, was correctly applied.

The answers by the appellate court to such questions may be precedents if indeed the appellate court bases its ultimate decision to affirm or to reverse the judgment on its consideration of those particular questions and answers—which are called **holdings.** If the court considers a question that is not a necessary part of its decision to affirm or reverse the lower court judgment, the answer is not a holding but **dictum** or **obiter dictum.** Dictum, by definition, cannot serve as precedent, for it is not a rule that an appellate court relied upon to decide a case. Distinguishing holdings from dicta is not always easy, and many legal arguments revolve around the question of whether a particular pronouncement of an appellate court was a holding or dictum.

Returning to the two kinds of issues of law, in questions relating to the choice of which rule should be applied, one party might argue, for example, that the Fifth

---

[1]Appellate court determinations of the appropriate rules and the application of those rules are generally more authoritative precedents than trial court determinations, and the determinations of these issues by courts of last resort are more authoritative than determinations by intermediate appellate courts. In the absence of an appellate court determination, a trial court ruling may, of course, be the best precedent. Also, precedents are generally authoritative only in the legal system to which the court belongs. If an Ohio court addresses an issue on which no Ohio court has ever ruled—this is called a question or case of **first impression**—but on which the Michigan Supreme Court has ruled, the Ohio court does not have to follow the Michigan precedent. It may follow the Michigan ruling or may fashion its own different rule. Theoretically, all of the federal courts are part of the same legal system, but the different Courts of Appeals frequently refuse to follow the precedents of other circuits and fashion their own, often conflicting, rules. Sometimes, but certainly not always, the Supreme Court resolves such differences; the fact that many differences still remain is one reason that federal appellate case citations identify the particular circuit that rendered the opinion in question.

[2]Both types of questions are usually phrased in a standard form: "Whether the trial court erred when it applied this rule rather than that rule?" or "Whether the appellate court erred when it applied this rule in this way?"

Amendment should apply to the case while the opposing party might argue that not the Fifth but the Fourth Amendment should apply. This is a straightforward issue, but few legal disputes are so simple. More often, the disputes about which rule is the proper rule to apply are actually disputes about how to interpret a more general rule or principle in a particular case. For example, in a given case both parties may agree that the issue between them is governed by the Fifth Amendment, or by the Commerce Clause, or by Section 1983 of Title 28 of the United States Code, but they disagree about the appropriate interpretation of the Fifth Amendment or the Commerce Clause or Section 1983 in their case. The issue of whether the proper rule was applied by the lower court is actually the issue of whether the proper interpretation of one of these three laws was made. Disagreements of this type might require the court to fashion a new rule—a new interpretation—to resolve the dispute in the case before it.

The second type of questions relates to whether a rule, conceded to be the proper rule by both parties, was correctly applied to the facts by the lower court. Legal rules are often complex, having several parts or elements that must address corresponding facts. For example, rules defining burglary,[3] promissory estoppel,[4] or a Fourth Amendment search violation each have several distinct parts or elements.[5] Each of the elements of the applicable rule must be applied to and supported by the particular facts of the case. The question is, "Do the facts in the case before the court sufficiently establish or prove this or that particular element?" Appellate opinions addressing this type of question often involve questions of how the applicable rule should be interpreted in light of the particular facts of the case.

For example, to convict a defendant of common law burglary, the prosecutor must prove that the defendant is guilty of (1) breaking and entering (2) a dwelling house (3) of another (4) in the nighttime (5) with the intent to commit a felony therein. If any one of these elements is not proven beyond a reasonable doubt by the evidence at trial, the defendant cannot be convicted of common law burglary. He might still be guilty of theft or trespass or some other lesser included offense, but not of common law burglary as we have defined it.

Suppose the trial evidence shows that one evening, while the victim was eating dinner, the defendant walked into the victim's garage, saw a piece of equipment that

---

[3]The general definition of the common law crime of "burglary" is the (1) breaking and entering (2) of a dwelling house (3) of another (4) in the nighttime (5) with the intent to commit a felony therein.

[4]"A promise lacking mutual assent and not supported by consideration will be enforced:
    (1) Where a promisor makes a definite promise which he expects or reasonably should expect will induce action or forbearance of a substantial sort on the part of the promisee, and
    (2) Where the promise in fact induces such action or forbearance of a substantial character, and
    (3) Where injustice can be avoided only by enforcing the promise." *Restatement (Second) of Contracts,* Section 90.

[5]Search warrants may only be issued (1) by a neutral and detached magistrate (2) when they are based upon probable cause, (3) when they are supported by oath or affirmation, and (4) when they particularly describe the place to be searched and the items to be seized. The elements of the rules identified in the examples in these three footnotes are not definitive; each of these elements may be further broken down into smaller components.

he had never seen before, decided then and there to take it, and picked it up and left the garage. Does this constitute burglary? Has there been a "breaking and entering"? Must the defendant have "broken" something, such as a door or a window, to get in? Is opening a door or window and entering a house "breaking and entering"? Is entering a house through an already open door or window "breaking and entering"? Does "dwelling house" include one's garage? What if the garage is part of the house? What if the garage is totally detached from, but on the same city lot as, the house? What if the victim is the defendant's tenant? When does "nighttime" begin? Does "night" begin at some officially designated time of sunset or at "dusk"? And if the defendant simply broke in to look around and then, once in the house, decided to steal something, does this constitute "entering with the intent" to commit a felony therein? Is the value of the stolen object sufficient to establish felony theft or only misdemeanor theft? What method of evaluation should be applied?

All of these questions present issues that the court must resolve by interpreting the rule and its elements in light of the facts of a particular case. And once a court has answered one of these questions, other courts in later cases may use that answer and rationale as precedent to answer similar questions consistently with the earlier ruling.

The precedents that lawyers and judges seek in court opinions are (1) the holdings that resolve issues such as these and (2) the rationales that the courts offer for the holdings. The rationale for selecting or articulating the rule to be applied in a given case (the first type of questions described above) might involve consideration of other cases and opinions, consideration of the language and legislative history of a statute, philosophical speculation, or treatments of state, national, or world history. Any of these types and other types of reasoning may be used by a court to provide a reasonable basis for its determination of what the appropriate rule in cases such as the one before the court should be. The rationale for applying a given rule to the facts in the correct way (the second type of questions described above) will more likely include close attention to the factual details in the case before the court and a discriminating consideration of the facts in other cases that were cited by the attorneys for the parties in the appeal.

In all court opinions, one may assume that most, if not all, of the points discussed by the court were brought to its attention by the attorneys in their written briefs and oral arguments. Court opinions are primarily addressed to the attorneys in the case in order to explain why, in light of the attorneys' arguments, the court made the holdings that it did. Thus, when a court opinion says something like "It may be argued that" or when it discusses other cases and explains why they are not relevant to the case at hand, one may assume that the court is referring to arguments made by the attorneys and to cases cited by the attorneys in their briefs.

Court opinions, and most casebook excerpts, will contain (1) a discussion of the facts of the case, (2) a statement of the lower court judgment or disposition, (3) discussion of the issues or questions presented for review, (4) statements of the holdings resolving those issues, (5) discussion of the rationale for each separate holding, and (6) a statement of the court's own judgment or disposition of the case. As you read the opinions, keep in mind that practically every word you read is part of one of these six aspects of the opinion, usually, but not always, presented in a logical, well-organized fashion.

## BRIEFING CASES

A student's brief of a case requires the analysis we have just described to identify the true issues and holdings of the court and the rationales for those holdings.[6] It is also a useful device for helping the student remember the significant aspects of the opinion. Most court opinions address a number of different issues or questions, but since the opinions in casebooks are usually not complete opinions but excerpts selected by the casebook editor to focus on one or two particular issues, the briefs of casebook cases should be true to their name—*brief*—and be no more than one page long.

The opinions of the court are the explanations of the court's holdings, and the explanations are rationales or arguments articulating the court's reasoning in coming to its conclusions. The arguments almost always present the holding as a conclusion drawn logically from a more comprehensive legal principle or test or rule called the *ratio decidendi,* which, to repeat, is itself often another interpretation of yet

---

## Briefing Constitutuional Law Cases

In cases in constitutional law courses, the central issues in most cases can be stated as "Whether or not this statute or that action is constitutional?" Never be satisfied with such a general statement. Make the issue as precise as possible. This requires a precise identification of the aspect of law or constitutional doctrine that is relevant to the case and may require a detailed statement of the pertinent facts that pose the issue. Thus, "Whether the warrantless search of defendant's car after a routine traffic stop was 'reasonable' under the Fourth Amendment?" is better than "Whether the search violated the Fourth Amendment?" but better still is, "Whether a warrantless search of defendant's car was 'reasonable' under the Fourth Amendment, where the search was conducted without defendant's consent and without probable cause but pursuant to the authority of a state statute, and where police issued the defendant a citation for speeding but did not arrest him before conducting the search?"[7]

---

[6]We are less interested in the appellate court's "judgment" or "disposition" of the case—that is, in the court's decision to affirm, reverse, or vacate and remand the lower court's decision. Though there is no consistently observed distinction between these terms, it is helpful to understand the "decision," "judgment," or disposition as what the court decided to do with the case: the opinion is the discussion of the issues, holdings, and principles leading to the court's judgment. Precedents reside almost always in the opinions.

[7]See *Knowles v. Iowa,* 525 U.S. 113, 119 S.Ct. 484, 142 L.Ed.2d 492, http://laws.findlaw.com/us/525/113.html (1998).

another rule. If the argument is syllogistic or is an extended syllogism, the *ratio deci-dendi* is the major premise. If the argument reflects a process of weighing and bal-ancing different factors by the court, the *ratio decidendi* may be called a "test."

Most opinions identify the questions and issues that they address. You may ask, "Why not simply look for and follow the court's own statement of the issues, holdings, and *ratio decidendi?*" Because the court's statement of the issue or question is not always the most precise statement of the narrow point upon which the court's rea-soning ultimately focuses. You should use the court's own statements as a guide, but be ready to put into your own words the question, the holding, and the rule or princi-ple that your analysis leads you to infer to be the "real" key to the court's decision.

The brief should not—indeed, it cannot—include reference to everything men-tioned in the opinion, and sometimes the lasting significance of a case is not the issue holding and rationale of the majority opinion, but the dissent, as in *Abrams v. United States;* a concurrence, as in *Youngstown Sheet and Tube v. Sawyer;* or the steps the court takes in constructing a rule, as in *Baker v. Carr.*[8] If quizzed on such matters in class, only the familiarity with the case resulting from reading and rereading the opin-ion can bail the student out of the predicament. A brief is no substitute for a thor-ough review and analysis of the opinion.

Finally, a word about the facts of the case. It may seem ironic or, worse, heretical to put off until last the discussion of the role of the facts of the case in the common law legal system. The **doctrine of precedent** or **stare decisis** is grounded on the principle that factually similar issues should be resolved by the same legal rule or principle. Cases that are potential precedents are either **followed** on the grounds that their facts are essentially the same or **distinguished,** and thus not followed, because the facts are significantly different. This is evident in cases in which the issues concern the application of legal rules to the facts, such as the question of whether a detached garage is a "dwelling house" for the purpose of common law burglary.

But the facts of the case also determine the range of relevant rules on the first type of question—questions relating to *which* general rule should be applied. If the facts are that the defendant walked up to the victim one day in a parking lot, cursed her, and then punched her, there would be no question of applying rules of burglary or theft or fraud—crimes relating to property. The facts immediately limit the range of applicable rules to crimes against the person: for example, assault, battery, and aggravated assault. Some general rules, such as the Fourth Amendment, have spawned so many distinct lines of interpretation—for example, rules for warrantless searches of individuals, rules for warrantless automobile searches, and rules for war-rantless searches of residences—that the fact that the search in question is of a car

---

[8]*Abrams v. United States,* 250 U.S. 616, 624 (Mr. Justice Holmes, dissenting), 40 S. Ct. 17, 63 L.Ed. 1173, http://laws .findlaw.com/us/250/616.html (1919); *Youngstown Sheet and Tube v. Sawyer,* 343 U.S. 579, 634 (Mr Justice Jackson, concurring in the judgement and opinion of the Court), 72 S. Ct. 863, 96 L.Ed. 1153, http://laws.findlaw.com/us/343/579.html (1952); and *Baker v. Carr,* 369 U.S. 186, 82 S. Ct. 691, 7 L.Ed.2d 663, http://laws.findlaw.com/us/369/186.html (1962).

immediately focuses the lawyer's attention on the considerable body of cases that elaborate the detailed rules relating to automobile searches.[9]

The facts therefore play a role in determining which general legal rule applies in a given case, but the rule then determines which facts are relevant. New students of the law often get bound up in the facts of the cases and include fact after fascinating fact in their briefs of the cases regardless of the relevance of the fact to the legal issues under scrutiny. For this reason, despite the central importance of the facts of the case to the principle of stare decisis, it is a good practice to try to identify the legal issues, holdings, and rationales of the case first, and then to note only those facts that are essential to understanding these aspects of the opinions.

## SUGGESTED BRIEFING FORMAT

**Question(s)/Issue(s):** In constitutional law cases, the question very often asks whether a particular law violates a particular provision of the United States Constitution. Present the issues as precisely as possible.

**Holding:** The holdings are the answers to the questions stated above.

**Rationale for Holding:**

1. **Principle/Rule/Test/*Ratio Decidendi*/Major Premise:** A principle stated in general terms with no specific reference to the facts of the case being briefed.

2. **Minor Premise:** Applications of the general principle—or elements of the general principle—tied to particular facts of the case.

3. **Conclusion:** The conclusion of each rationale should be the same as the holding.

**Facts:** Once the basic argument of the court has been stated, select only those facts that are necessary for the argument—the material facts.

In cases in which the question concerns which general rule should apply, the rationale for the holding—which is the court's determination of which rule should apply—may be neither a syllogism nor a balancing test, but considerations of philosophy, history, policy, or precedent.

## SAMPLE BRIEF

### Allen v. Wright 468 U.S. 737 (1984)

**Question(s)/Issue(s):** Where plaintiffs are black parents of children attending public schools in districts undergoing school desegregation, do they have standing to sue the Commissioner of Internal Revenue and the Secretary of the Treasury to compel

---

[9]See, for example, Wayne LaFave's five volume treatise on Fourth Amendment law: *Search and Seizure: A Treatise on the Fourth Amendment*, 3d ed. (St. Paul: West Publishing Co., 1996).

enforcement of IRS regulations that deny tax-exempt status to private schools that practice racial discrimination?

**Holding:** The plaintiffs do not have standing (O'Connor for a five to three majority, Marshall not participating.)

**Rationale for Holding:**

**1. Principle/Rule/Test/*Ratio Decidendi*/Major Premise:** Standing to sue requires the allegation of a distinct and palpable, judicially cognizable, personal injury to the plaintiff that is fairly traceable to the defendants' action and that is likely to be redressed by the requested relief.

**2. Minor Premises:** (1) Here, plaintiffs' claim that they are harmed by the mere fact of government's failure to enforce the regulations is not, under current precedent, judicially cognizable (citing *Richardson* and *Valley Forge*).

(2) Here, plaintiffs' claim of stigmatic injury because of the government's generalized discrimination on the basis of race is too abstract and does not constitute a distinct and palpable personal injury suffered by the plaintiffs themselves (citing *Moose Lodge, O'Shea*, and *SCRAP*).

(3) Here, plaintiffs' claim that the government's actions caused their children to suffer the harm of a diminished ability to receive an education in a racially integrated school is not fairly traceable to the government actions challenged by plaintiffs in this case where there was no allegation that the number of discriminatory private schools in plaintiffs' communities would make withdrawal of the tax exemptions result in an appreciable difference in public school integration.

**3. Conclusion:** Therefore, here the plaintiffs' allegations do not establish a distinct and palpable, judicially cognizable injury that is fairly traceable to the defendant's action, and thus the plaintiffs do not meet the requirements for standing to use.

# Appendix C

# Theories of Judicial Decision-Making

## THE MODELS

The study of courts and case law has led to a vigorous debate about how judges go about deciding cases and why they make the decisions they do. Three basic theories, approaches, or models recur throughout the debate, and within each of these positions exists a number of variants and refinements. Those who argue from the **legal model** maintain that the decision of cases is fundamentally an attempt by judges to apply legal rules and precedents to the facts of new cases and thus to decide cases logically and dispassionately, keeping their own personal, nonlegal views out of the process. This approach closely fits the guide to analyzing and briefing cases in the preceding appendix because the model assumes that the rationale set forth in a court opinion accurately reflects the reasoning process of the judge(s) who authored the opinion.

Those who argue from the **attitudinal model** maintain that judges decide cases primarily according to their personal, nonlegal, policy preferences—political, economic, or social preferences, for example—and then seek to legitimize their decision by finding legal precedents and principles to support their decision. This theory of "result-oriented jurisprudence" discounts the *ratio decidendi* of the opinion as the authoritative source from which the decision flows; rather, the source of the decision is a nonlegal policy, and the *ratio* flows from the decision. It is not difficult today to find a judicial quotation to support just about any legal decision in our mature, centuries-old archive of legal rules and principles; thus, judges do not have far to seek in order to find legal rules or principles to support the policy they wish to pursue.

A third argument has been put forward by those who find both earlier approaches overly simplistic. Sometimes called the **institutional model,** and sometimes the "strategic" model, the theory maintains that judges do not make decisions in isolation; they are part of larger institutions that they must confront as they attempt to implement their preferred policy. Thus, a judge may be a trial judge, a part of a three-judge panel, a member of a larger *en banc* appellate court, a member of an intermediate appellate court, or a justice on a court of last resort: each of these judicial situations carries with it different institutional influences and obstacles that individual judges or a small bloc of judges must negotiate if they are to see a case decided according to their preference. Though the institutional model in principle might be applied to the actions of judges who personally adhere to either a legal or an attitudinal perspective, those who have applied it thus far have usually assumed that the attitudinal model most correctly describes judges' motivations.

The subject of judicial decision making is a large one. I would like to use whatever space this brief appendix will allow merely to describe in a bit more detail the foundations and some of the implications of these models and to offer a few comments concerning their usefulness to students of law.

## FOUNDATIONS AND IMPLICATIONS

Until the twentieth century, most of the descriptions by judges and legal scholars of how judges decide cases emphasized the disinterested, intellectual nature of judicial decision making. Judges "found" or "discovered" in case law and statutes the legal principles that they needed to resolve the disputes before them. In the words of Chief Justice John Marshall in *Osborn v. Bank of the United States*:

> Judicial power, as contradistinguished from the power of the laws, has no existence. Courts are the mere instruments of the law, and can will nothing. When they are said to exercise a discretion, it is a mere legal discretion, a discretion to be exercised in discerning the course prescribed by the law; and, when it is discerned, it is the duty of the court to follow it. Judicial power is never exercised for the purpose of giving effect to the will of the judge; always for the purpose of giving effect to the will of the legislature; or, in other words, to the will of the law.[1]

Taken to an extreme, this process of finding the appropriate legal principle may be made to appear relatively simple and the decision-making process a routine matter of syllogistic deduction. Critics have used the terms "mechanical jurisprudence" or "slot machine jurisprudence" to describe this account of decision making and have sometimes pointed to Justice Owen Roberts's statement in *United States v. Butler* as an example of this approach:

---

[1] 22 U.S. (9 Wheat.) 738, 866, 6 L.Ed. 204, http://laws.findlaw.com/us/22/738.html (1824). See also Alexander Hamilton's argument for judicial review in *Federalist* 78: "It can be of no weight to say that the courts, on the pretense of a repugnancy, may substitute their own pleasure to the constitutional intentions of the legislature. This might as well happen in the case of two contradictory statutes; or it might as well happen in every adjudication upon any single statute. The courts must declare the sense of the law; and if they should be disposed to exercise WILL instead of JUDGMENT, the consequence would equally be the substitution of their pleasure to that of the legislative body. The observation, if it prove any thing, would prove that there ought to be no judges distinct from that body."

There should be no misunderstanding as to the function of this court in such a case. It is sometimes said that the court assumes a power to overrule or control the action of the people's representatives. This is a misconception. The Constitution is the supreme law of the land ordained and established by the people. All legislation must conform to the principles it lays down. When an act of Congress is appropriately challenged in the courts as not conforming to the constitutional mandate the judicial branch of the Government has only one duty; to lay the article of the Constitution which is invoked beside the statute which is challenged and to decide whether the latter squares with the former. All the court does, or can do, is to announce its considered judgment upon the question. The only power it has, if such it may be called, is the power of judgment. This court neither approves nor condemns any legislative policy. Its delicate and difficult office is to ascertain and declare whether the legislation is in accordance with, or in contravention of, the provisions of the Constitution; and, having done that, its duty ends.[2]

Problems with the slot machine model were already discerned in the late nineteenth and early twentieth century, both by judges and other law-trained scholars and by students outside the profession.[3] Some legal scholars, called "legal realists," criticized the narrow, black-letter conception of "law" (called "legal positivism") assumed by the Marshall-Butler model and argued that law and legal discourse are something much broader. Later, with the development of behavioral social science, political scientists adopting the behavioral approach and seeking to approach decision making "scientifically" also rejected the slot machine model. These two bodies of scholars—legal realists and behavioral social scientists—contributed to the development of the attitudinal model.

One of the first representatives of the attitudinal model, C. Herman Pritchett, began his 1948 study of the Supreme Court by citing Lord Kelvin's statement that "when you cannot measure, your knowledge is meager and unsatisfactory."[4] Referring to Clemenceau's remark that "war is too important a matter to be left to the generals," Pritchett said, "I regard law as too important a matter to be left to the lawyers." He said that his approach was "that of a political scientist interested in the social and psychological origins of judicial attitudes and the influence of individual predelictions on the development of law." The book was the first study of the Supreme Court that attempted to characterize individual justices and "blocs" or coalitions of justices according to their "value systems," specifically *political* value systems. "It is my view

---

[2]297 U.S. 1, 62, 56 S.Ct. 312, 80 L.Ed. 477, http://laws.findlaw.com/us/297/1.html (1936).

[3]Charles Evans Hughes, who was then governor of New York, shortly thereafter an associate justice of the United States Supreme Court, and later still the chief justice of the United States, is noted for saying in extemporaneous remarks in 1907 to the Elmira, New York, Chamber of Commerce: "We are under a Constitution, but the Constitution is what the judges say it is, and the judiciary is the safeguard of our liberty and of our property under the Constitution." Half a century later, Justice Robert Jackson voiced a similar opinion about the authority of the Supreme Court in *Brown v. Allen*: "We are not final because we are infallible, but we are infallible only because we are final." 344 U.S. 443, 540; 73 S. Ct. 397, 97 L. Ed. 469, http://laws.findlaw.com/us/344/443.html (1953)(Jackson, J., concurring in the result).

[4]*The Roosevelt Court: A Study in Judicial Politics and Values, 1937-47* (1948), xi.

that the Supreme Court inevitably acts in a political context and that the greatest danger to the Court and from the Court comes when that fact is inadequately realized."[5]

Studying the nonunanimous decisions of the Court, and focusing on cases concerning (1) civil liberties, (2) the rights of criminal defendants, (3) economic regulation by the states, (4) economic regulation by the federal government, and (5) labor law, Pritchett was able to find blocs of "left-wing" or liberal justices and "right-wing" or conservative justices. Over the decade of opinions that he studied, the cohesion of the blocs varied, and there were always a couple of moderate or nonaffiliated justices, too. With tables and charts, Pritchett plotted the alignments of justices on these issues and also the incidence of agreement and disagreement between individual justices. His definition of "left-wing/liberal" was straightforward enough and reflected a common understanding of the American political fault lines of the time: liberals were pro–civil liberties, pro–defendants' rights, pro–economic regulation by the state and federal governments, and pro-labor; conservatives were "anti-" all of these.

The scholarly skepticism and criticism of the legal model that were evident in Pritchett's groundbreaking study were markedly intensified in the work of two of Pritchett's leading successors, Jeffrey Segal and Harold Spaeth. Describing their disagreement with the legal model, they remark at one point: "The legal model serves only to rationalize the Court's decision and to cloak the reality of the Court's decision-making process."[6]

> The justices . . . do not admit the validity of the [attitudinal model] as an explanation of their decisions. To do so would give the lie to their mythology that the justices, their lower court colleagues, and off-the-bench apologists have so insistently and persistently verbalized: that judges exercise little or no discretion; that they do not speak; rather, the Constitution and the laws speak through them.[7]

The attitudinal model, by contrast, "holds that the Supreme Court decides disputes in light of the facts of the case vis-à-vis the ideological attitudes and values of the justices." As with Pritchett's political "value systems," Segal and Spaeth identify the relevant ideologies and values by current American political standards and particularly according to justices' positions on the issues of civil rights and liberties: criminal procedure, civil rights, the First Amendment, due process, and privacy. In deciding these issues, the responses of the justices reflect significantly different, though recognizably political, positions. "Simply put, Rehnquist votes the way he does because he is extremely conservative; [Thurgood] Marshall voted the way he did because he is extremely liberal."[8]

---

[5]Pritchett's remarks remind one of the reports of Socrates' questioning of the poets in Plato's *Apology* and *Ion*.

[6]*The Supreme Court and the Attitudinal Model* (1993), 34. The statement is substantially repeated in the 2002 version of the work: *The Supreme Court and the Attitudinal Model Revisited*, 53.

[7]Ibid., 33.

[8]Ibid., 65. In contrast to the adjudication of civil liberties issues, where sharp divisions between justices occur, Segal and Spaeth conclude that on issues other than civil liberties "the voting . . . varies but little by comparison." *Ibid.*, 255.

Like Pritchett, Segal and Spaeth also emphasize that they wish to engage in a "scientific" study of law, one that, unlike the studies by the followers of the legal model, attempts to analyze and explain judicial decision making on the basis of theories that generate hypotheses and predictions that can be empirically verified. They find the legal model deficient—"meaningless"—on this count also.

If the line between the mechanical approach and the attitudinal approach seems clear, the line between these approaches and the institutional approach does not. The "institutional" label has been applied to several perspectives. Walter Murphy, writing not long after Herman Pritchett, extended the attitudinal approach to include consideration of the interaction and compromise that each Supreme Court justice experiences in working toward a majority opinion amidst eight other justices.[9] No two justices, not even justices in the same bloc, see each issue identically. Agreement on a final opinion requires trade-offs and maneuvering—it requires "strategy"—if an individual justice is to influence that opinion. After all, half a loaf (joining a majority opinion rationale that is marginally acceptable) is better than none (having to dissent). How, Murphy asked, can a policy-oriented justice "minimize, though he probably may never overcome, the major institutional checks on his power?" What range of choices is open to him? How can possible choices be expressed? Murphy's emphasis was on the individual judge as policy maker, though he noted that the American legal and political *institutions* limit judges to "peculiar kinds of authority and discretion." Each justice must take account of the other justices in the course of developing a particular public policy.

Murphy's approach has usually been identified as the "strategic" approach or model of judicial decision making. Some now include this approach within the "institutional" model.[10] On the other hand, Segal and Spaeth have recently labeled Murphy's book an example of "rational choice" analysis, an approach that attempts to "apply and adapt the theories and methods of economics to the entire range of human political and social interactions."[11] Rational choice theorists, according to Segal and Spaeth, assume that individual policy makers have not just one but a number of preferences that can be ranked hierarchically. In given situations, such as the institutional setting in which Supreme Court justices decide cases, judges must choose among available alternatives in order to achieve their highest possible priority.

Ronald Kahn divides the approaches differently. Both the attitudinal and the strategic approaches focus ultimately on the individual justices, and both assume that judges use legal symbols simply to justify their nonlegal policy preferences. Kahn calls these approaches "instrumental" because of the way judges use the law. Alternatively, he suggests that Supreme Court decision making can be approached "constitutively" to account for the "set of institutional norms and customs, *including legal principles and theories*," that "justices believe that they are required to act in

---

[9]*Elements of Judicial Strategy* (1964).

[10]See Forrest Maltzman, James F. Spriggs II, and Paul J. Wahlbeck, *Crafting Law on the Supreme Court: The Collegial Game* (2000), 13.

[11]*The Supreme Court and the Attitudinal Model Revisited* (2002), 97–100.

accordance with [in order to fulfill] particular institutional and legal expectations and responsibilities" (emphasis added).

A recent collection of essays entitled *Supreme Court Decision-Making: New Institutionalist Approaches* collects Kahn's essay and others that represent a range of approaches to judicial, and principally Supreme Court, decision making. The essays assume that courts not only limit judges' ability to act and make policy, but also provide goals, standards, and responsibilities that motivate and direct judges' purposes and intentions.[12] Segal and Spaeth reject most of these approaches, but they regard the rational choice approach more positively—even optimistically. This is probably due in part to the fact that rigorous rational choice theory meets Segal and Spaeth's criteria for an empirical science. When focused upon the institutional factors at work *within* a court, they say, the behavioral models generated by rational choice theorists have produced results "either consistent with the earlier attitudinal works, or, at least, not inconsistent with them." These "internal" rational choice theorists, while not yet producing results superior to the attitudinal approach, might well do so in the future.

> The rational choice model . . . holds greater promise. If the next decade provides us with verified equilibrium-based predictions, the model will have gone where the attitudinal model has not gone and cannot go.[13]

Whether we follow Segal and Spaeth in considering the rational choice and strategic models as further elaborations of the attitudinal model, or whether we follow Kahn, Clayton and Gillman, and others in considering them part of a new institutionalist approach by virtue of their recognition of the institutional influences on individual judges, it does appear that the analysis of judicial decision making is increasingly taking account of the particular institutional setting of the judicial decision maker: the court.

# A FEW COMMENTS AND CONSIDERATIONS

Before concluding this survey, I would like to suggest a couple of points that one might consider when evaluating these approaches to the study of judicial decision making. The first is pretty simple: when asking how judges decide cases, one should first note which court the judge or judges are on—trial courts, intermediate appellate courts, state courts of last resort, or the United States Supreme Court. Their respective institutional situations are significantly different. Trial judges in both the state and federal systems are accorded a great deal of discretion in managing trials, but these management decisions, though crucial in the development of the legal issues that

---

[12]Clayton and Gillman, *Supreme Court Decision-Making: New Institutionalist Approaches* (1999). Kahn's essay appears at 175.

[13]Segal and Spaeth, 434. Segal and Spaeth contrast "internal" rational choice theorists to "external" or "separation of powers" rational choice theorists. The externalists' focus is not limited to what takes place within the Court but extends to the policy makers of Congress and the executive branch.

eventually may come before the appellate courts, are hardly "political" and are understandably of little interest to political scientists.[14]

The main focus of students interested in the judging process has been on the process of deciding the merits of cases. Of course, judges on all courts must also judge the merits of the legal arguments before them, but the discretion that different judges have—the freedom to depart from precedent and pursue personal policy preferences—varies significantly because of appellate review.[15] Clearly, the judges on the courts of last resort have greater discretion to depart from precedent and to provide new interpretations to statutes and constitutions, and not surprisingly students who apply attitudinal and institutional models focus far more on these judges and courts than on the lower courts.

It is no accident that the major works of Pritchett, Murphy, Segal and Spaeth, and Clayton and Gillman that we have cited on the subject of judicial decision making all focus on the United States Supreme Court. All of them recognize in their work the unique nature of the Supreme Court and the unique opportunity it affords to those who apply these two models.[16] Thus, what we have been mainly talking about in this appendix thus far is not *judicial* decision making, but *Supreme Court* decision making, though in principle the models are applicable to other courts and are indeed being applied to them.[17] Nevertheless, there are good reasons for the focus on the Supreme Court, and this brings up a second point, or set of points, that should be considered.

The current debate over the nature of judicial decision making rests ultimately on definitions of "law," "policy," and "politics." The damning effect of the attitudinal, strategic, rational choice, and most institutional models on the legal model and on the commonly held notions of judicial decision making itself comes from the charge that judging is not the principled activity that it pretends to be. Instead of rationally applying only "laws" or legal norms to disputes, judges are using laws to justify—to "cloak," say Segal and Spaeth—their nonlegal determination of who should win the case. This does not mean the judging is arbitrary and capricious; on the contrary, the studies we have cited suggest that the justices attempt to rationally apply nonlegal policies—political, economic, and social—to the disputes and that these nonlegal policies are more fundamental in their decision-making process than legal principles.

This charge, and it is nothing less than an accusation, depends for its force upon how we define the concepts of "law" and "policy" and of "political," "economic," and

---

[14]See, for example, Judge Jerome Frank's *Courts on Trial* (1949) for recognition of the importance of the process of judicial fact-finding. The discretionary behavior of trial court judges is presently of interest to psychologists.

[15]Recall how strongly bound to precedent the lower courts are and how that discipline makes attorneys the "gatekeepers" of the legal system. *Supra*, 141–142.

[16]Pritchett says that the Supreme Court is the "obvious focus [f]or it is a court predominantly engaged in hearing public law controversies, and its judges have an opportunity to influence public policy which seems shocking to those familiar with the more limited scope for judicial discretion found in the legal systems of most other countries." Segal and Spaeth note the Supreme Court's "unique environment . . . that facilitates the operation of the attitudinal model."

[17]Advocates of legal models, on the other hand, tend not to focus on the Supreme Court. See, for example, Edward Levi, *An Introduction to Legal Reasoning* (1949).

"social" policy. It is presumed that policy is not law, and "political" is not "legal." If we define law very narrowly, as the legal positivists do when they say that law is limited to the rules or commands of a sovereign, and we build a legal model upon that narrow concept, then anytime that judges engage in reasoning or behavior that is not the syllogistic deduction of a holding from a black-letter legal rule, they are not engaged in legal reasoning. If they are not engaged in legal reasoning, they are engaged in policy reasoning or political (or economic or social) reasoning.[18] In the American frame of government, "policy making" or "politics" is not what judges are supposed to be doing, and it is not what the judges themselves say that they are doing. Hence, we have a conceptual problem, a constitutional problem, and perhaps even a legal problem of fraudulent misrepresentation on our hands.

The problem of deciding legal disputes that do not neatly fit under clearly defined legal rules—the problem of "hard cases"—is not a problem that was first discovered by attitudinalists. One of the leading legal philosophers of the past few decades, Ronald Dworkin, maintains that American jurisprudence since the nineteenth century has devoted itself largely to one question: "How do courts decide difficult or controversial lawsuits?"[19] When we focus on the Supreme Court, the situation is still very much as Wesley McCune described it half a century ago:

> Each case is a wheel within other wheels. The court accepts for decision mostly those cases that are not clear cut: it seldom gets a crack at a simple one. One principle seldom disposes of a case; others cut across it sharply, touch it at angles or impinge on it with a broad sweep.[20]

Compounding the complexity of Supreme Court decision making is the unique legal nature of our Constitution. Dworkin only echoes what many have noted when he says that "our constitution made legal issues out of problems that in England were political only." Thus, the "law" that the justices must apply to the facts in the constitutional law cases that they decide (or reject) each term is an amalgam of law and politics.

It should, then, be no further surprise that the strongest indications of attitudinal divisions among justices occur precisely in constitutional cases and especially in deciding those issues that, in the United States at least, are equally legal and political. What is the proper division of powers between the federal government and the states? What are the limits of governmental authority over the expression of ideas by individuals? What procedures are fair to society and to criminal suspects alike? To what degree should government regulate commercial activity? Are our ideas on these subjects essentially political, social, or economic policies that we bring to the law, or

---

[18]This distinction is implicit, for example, in this remark by Walter Murphy: "As long as law remains one of the most common means of formalizing public policy, the judicial office of the United States will involve *political, i.e. policymaking,* power" (emphasis added). *Elements of Judicial Strategy,* 1.

[19]*Taking Rights Seriously* (1978), 3. By "jurisprudence" and "legal philosophy," I mean the broad and general study of law, usually not from an attitudinal or institutional perspective, but also not exclusively from the perspective of the "legal model" as it has been described here.

[20]Wesley McCune, *The Nine Young Men* (New York: Harper, 1947), quoted in Pritchett, *The Roosevelt Court: A Study in Judicial Politics and Values, 1937-47,* 255.

are they constitutional (that is, legal) ideas that influence our politics, economics, and social perspectives? Some Americans, we should note, take the Constitution very seriously as a source and a standard of *political* policies.[21]

And then is logical or syllogistic reasoning the only truly legal or judicial approach to the Constitution? This answer, too, requires definitions of the terms "law," "legal," and "judicial." The narrow legal positivist conception of law is not the only conception. One of the early critics of legal positivism, Roscoe Pound, in unabashedly proposing the use of law as an instrument of "social engineering," said that law "is more than a body of rules":

> It has rules and principles and conceptions and standards for conduct and decision, but it also has doctrines and modes of professional thought and professional rules of art by which the precepts for conduct and decision are applied and developed and given effect.[22]

We might add to this list that law also has "policies," and that legal policies are factors that judges must consider in interpreting statutory and constitutional language for the first time or in applying statutory and constitutional rules to new cases of first impression. The policies, rules, principles, and conceptions—in short, all of the factors adduced by Roscoe Pound—may all be said to be part of the "professional" reasoning of lawyers and judges and the "mere legal discretion" that Chief Justice Marshall mentioned in the passage quoted earlier from *Osborn v. Bank of the United States*. Even Herman Pritchett, who may perhaps be considered the founder of the attitudinal approach, was later moved to say:

> There is room for much interpretation in the texts of constitutions, statutes, and ordinances, but the judicial function is still interpretation and not independent policy making. It is just as false to argue that judges freely exercise their discretion as to contend that they have no policy functions at all. Any accurate analysis of judicial behavior must have as a major purpose a full clarification of the unique conditions under which judicial policy making proceeds.[23]

This recognition by a social scientist of the complexity of judicial decision making is increasingly evident in the writings of many contributors to the institutional

---

[21]Though he clearly marked the United States Constitution as "law" in *Marbury v. Madison*, Chief Justice Marshall also recognized its unique legal nature in *McCulloch v. Maryland*: the nature of a constitution, he said, "requires, that only its great outlines should be marked, its important objects designated, and the minor ingredients which compose those objects be deduced from the nature of the objects themselves." He concluded the paragraph: "[W]e must never forget that it is *a constitution* we are expounding." *McCulloch v. Maryland*, 17 U.S. (4 Wheat.) 316, 401, 4 L.Ed. 579, http://laws.findlaw.com/us/17/316.html (1819).

[22]*Interpretations of Legal History* (1923), 156. See also Lief Carter, *Reason in Law* (1994), 3, 6: "Law is a language, not simply a collection of rules." "The law, then, is a language that lawyers and judges use when they try to prevent or resolve problems—human conflicts—using rules made by the state as their starting point."

[23]Pritchett's "retreat," as Segal and Spaeth call it, from his earlier position, originally appeared in *Frontiers of Judicial Research*, ed. Joel Grossman and Joseph Tanenbaum (New York: Wiley, 1969), 42, quoted in Segal and Spaeth, *The Supreme Court and the Attitudinal Model Revisited*, 52.

model. Although the language in which the recognition by these contributors of the complexity is expressed still suggests an interaction of judges' essentially nonlegal policy preferences confronting an institutional environment that demands articulation of those preferences in legal or judicial language, the line between nonlegal policy preferences and legal preferences is fading.[24] How can we determine whether the source of a judge's decision is the law or political policy in a constitutional case, given the nature of the Constitution and the nature of law? It is unrealistic to assume that judges, no matter how experienced, have preconceived positions or policy preferences on each or even on most of the legal issues that come before them. Is it possible that on such questions of first impression, judges inquire into legal rules, principles, doctrines, policies, and precedents for a reasonable *legal* response—that is, might judges "seek" and then, perhaps, "find" the law in such cases? It appears to this writer that it is psychologically and professionally plausible that such legal factors have a pull on a professionally trained lawyer and judge and that they do not simply provide the technical jargon in which to cloak nonlegal policy preferences.

A conception of law that is broader than the legal positivist definition will also force reconsideration of the legal model of judicial decision making. When the legal model is understood as the model of mechanical or slot machine jurisprudence, it is essentially a straw man argument that provides a large target for critics within and without the legal profession and provides no explanation of the process of professionally deciding hard cases. Certainly, the earlier-quoted account of constitutional decision making by Justice Roberts in the *Butler* case is disingenuous at worst, overly simplistic at best. The ease with which judges can "square" a statute with the Constitution must have been lost on Justices Harlan Stone, Louis Brandeis, and Benjamin Cardozo, because they dissented in the *Butler* case.

Rendered in the midst of the era of "substantive due process," Roberts's assertion that the Court "neither approves or condemns any legislative policy" is dubious, as is Chief Justice Marshall's statement in *Osborn* that "judicial power is never exercised for the purpose of giving effect to the will of the judge," given Marshall's nationalist approach to constitutional interpretation and the questionable and tendentious logic of *Marbury v. Madison*. Justice Oliver Wendell Holmes criticized the majority in the "yellow dog contract" case for intentionally advancing an economic theory under the guise of merely interpreting the law when he said, "The Fourteenth Amendment does not enact Mr. Herbert Spencer's Social Statics."[25] And Justice John Harlan accused the majority in the important Fourth Amendment case of *Mapp v. Ohio* of "reaching out" for an opportunity to overrule a prior case and selecting an inappropriate case to do just that.[26]

---

[24]See the quote from Ronald Kahn, *supra*.

[25]*Lochner v. New York*, 198 U.S. 45, 75, 25 S.Ct. 539, 49 L.Ed. 937, http://laws.findlaw.com/us/198/ 45.html (1905)(Holmes, J., dissenting). We might suggest to Justice Holmes that the First Amendment also does not enact Mr. John Stuart Mill's Essay on Liberty.

[26]367 U.S. 643, 672-73, 81 S.Ct. 1684, 6 L.Ed.2d 1081, http://laws.findlaw.com/us/367/643.html (1961)(Harlan, J., dissenting).

These four cases were decided during eras marked by commentators as periods of judicial activism. One of the aspects of the complex phenomenon referred to as "judicial activism" is judges willfully reaching out for legal vehicles to carry their policy preferences into effect: "Activism and restraint are functions of the extent to which judicial review can be fairly considered an enforcement of the will of the Constitution, without an infusion of the judge's own political beliefs and preferences."[27] That Supreme Court opinions are sometimes motivated by such willfulness is evident in the dissents of Justice Holmes and Justice Harlan in *Lochner* and *Mapp*. Self-justifying denials of the kind that Marshall offers in *Osborn* are sometimes simply not plausible.

The legal model implicit in Justice Roberts's *Butler* quote is also overly simplistic. We cannot ignore the common law heritage of our courts. With that heritage goes the *law-making* function of common law judges. New causes of action and new theories of liability are accepted by courts even though no legislature has enacted an appropriate statute. For example, the "right of privacy," a speculative principle that existed only as an argument in a law review article in 1890, became a cause of action recognized in a majority of American states without the benefit of statutory authority.[28] The judicial consideration and adoption of new causes of action can only be explained by the inquiry into and the consideration of the full inventory of judicial factors contained in Roscoe Pound's list.

The courts are obviously in a different position when they are interpreting statutory and constitutional language (as they were in the *Osborn, Lochner, Butler,* and *Mapp* cases) from when they are interpreting legal rules that authoritatively exist only in court opinions (as they do in cases that establish new causes of action). Perhaps that was what Justice Roberts in *Butler* was alluding to when he described the function of the Supreme Court "in such a case." But the difficulty of interpreting the words of a statute or constitution, even when we assume a good faith, dispassionate effort by judges who have no preconceived position on the issue before them, is also well-documented by the innumerable books and articles—as well as discussions in court opinions—that have been written and continue to be written on the subject.

If we desire an understanding of judicial decision making in all its varieties—not just Supreme Court constitutional interpretation, but also statutory interpretation and common law adjudication by appellate and trial courts—we need more than reductionist models such as the three that we have discussed. Perhaps Lawrence Baum has summed it up best: "We are a long way from achieving explanations of judicial behavior that are fully satisfactory. . . . The primary reason is not scholarly deficiencies . . . [but] the inherent difficulty of explaining human nature."[29]

---

[27]Christopher Wolfe, *Judicial Activism* (1986), 2.

[28]William Prosser, *Law of Torts* 3d ed. (St. Paul: West Publishing Co, 1964), 829–851.

[29]*The Puzzle of Judicial Behavior* (1997), xi.

# SELECTED BIBLIOGRAPHY AND RECOMMENDED READINGS

Baum, Lawrence. *The Puzzle of Judicial Behavior*. Ann Arbor: University of Michigan Press, 1997.

Carter, Lief H. *Reason in Law*. 4th ed. New York: HarperCollins, 1994.

Clayton, Cornell W., and Howard Gillman. *Supreme Court Decision-Making: New Institutionalist Approaches*. Chicago: University of Chicago Press, 1999.

Dworkin, Ronald. *Taking Rights Seriously*. Cambridge: Harvard University Press, 1978.

_____. *Law's Empire*. Cambridge: Harvard University Press, 1986.

_____. *A Matter of Principle*. Cambridge: Harvard University Press, 1985.

Frank, Jerome. *Courts on Trial*. Princeton, NJ: Princeton University Press, 1949.

Levi, Edward H. *An Introduction to Legal Reasoning*. Chicago: University of Chicago Press, 1949.

Maltzman, Forrest, James F. Spriggs II, and Paul J. Wahlbeck. *Crafting Law on the Supreme Court: The Collegial Game*. New York: Cambridge University Press, 2000.

Murphy, Walter F. *Elements of Judicial Strategy*. Chicago: University of Chicago Press, 1964.

Pound, Roscoe. *Ideal Element in Law*. Indianapolis: Liberty Fund, 2002.

_____. *Interpretations of Legal History*. Cambridge: Cambridge University Press, 1923; reprint, Gloucester, MA: Peter Smith, 1967.

Pritchett, C. Herman. *The Roosevelt Court: A Study in Judicial Politics and Values, 1937–47*. New York: Macmillan, 1948.

Segal, Jeffrey A., and Harold J. Spaeth. *The Supreme Court and the Attitudinal Model*. New York: Cambridge University Press, 1993.

_____. *The Supreme Court and the Attitudinal Model Revisited*. New York: Cambridge University Press, 2002.

Shapiro, Martin. *Law and Politics in the Supreme Court: New Approaches to Political Jurisprudence*. New York: Free Press, 1964.

Smith, Rogers M. "Political Jurisprudence, the 'New Institutionalism,' and the Future of Public Law." 82 *American Political Science Review* 89–108 (1988).

Sunstein, Cass, ed. *Behavioral Law and Economics*. New York: Cambridge University Press, 2000.

Tarr, G. Alan. *Judicial Process and Judicial Policymaking*. St. Paul, MN: West Publishing Company, 1994.

Wolfe, Christopher. *Judicial Activism*. Pacific Grove, CA: Brooks/Cole, 1986.

# Appendix D

# Additional Federal Courts

I. Constitutional Courts
   A. Original Jurisdiction—United States Court of International Trade
   B. Original (and Appellate) Jurisdiction—Foreign Intelligence Surveillance Court and Foreign Intelligence Surveillance Court of Review
   C. Appellate Jurisdiction—United States Court of Appeals for the Federal Circuit
II. Legislative Courts
   A. Original Jurisdiction—United States Tax Court
   B. Appellate Jurisdiction—United States Court of Appeals for Veterans Claims

## CONSTITUTIONAL COURTS

### Original Jurisdiction—United States Court of International Trade
### Web site: http://www.cit.uscourts.gov

Late in the nineteenth century, Congress established a Board of General Appraisers to determine the customs duties on imports to the United States. Until 1909, appeals from the decisions of the board could be taken to the United States circuit courts, but in that year Congress created the Court of Customs Appeals and gave it exclusive jurisdiction to review the board's determinations.

In 1926, the Board of General Appraisers was superseded by the Customs Court. In 1929, additional jurisdiction to review patent cases was given to the Court of Customs Appeals and its name was changed to the Court of Customs and Patent Appeals. In the 1980s, Congress created two new courts to assume the functions of the Customs Court and the Court of Customs and Patent Appeals—(1) the Court of International Trade, established in 1980 to replace the Customs Court,[1] and (2) the Court of Appeals for the Federal Circuit, established in 1982 to exercise the jurisdiction of the Court of Customs and Patent Appeals and additional jurisdiction.[2]

The present United States Court of International Trade is a court of nine judges located in New York City, although it is authorized to hold sessions in other ports of the United States.[3] Eight hundred ninety three cases were filed with the court in 2003. All of its jurisdiction is exclusive, and all of it addresses matters of trade, particularly tariffs and customs.[4] Original cases can be filed by the United States or other parties against the United States under certain sections of the Tariff Act of 1930, but the court also reviews determinations of the secretaries of labor, commerce, and the treasury, as well as of the International Trade Commission on tariff matters.

## Original (and Appellate) Jurisdiction—Foreign Intelligence Surveillance Court and Foreign Intelligence Surveillance Court of Review

At times the Congress creates distinct tribunals or courts within the existing Article III judiciary by authorizing the formation of special divisions of the United States District Courts or Courts of Appeals and the assignment of sitting Article III judges to these divisions. For example, the old "Independent Counsel" statute (the now-expired Ethics in Government Act of 1978) established a three-judge division of the United States Court of Appeals for the District of Columbia Circuit "for the purpose of appointing independent counsels."[5]

In 1978, Congress also created a pair of courts to hear and approve applications by the government to engage in electronic surveillance for the purpose of *foreign* intelligence.[6] The Foreign Intelligence Surveillance Court (FISC) was originally allotted 7 Article III judges, but the USA Patriot Act of 2001 increased that number to 11.[7] The 1978 Act also established a three-judge appellate Foreign Intelligence Surveillance Court of Review. The proceedings of these courts are secret, but in 2002 two memoranda from the court were made public and have been the subject of intense interest and discussion.[8]

---

[1] 28 U.S.C. § 251. The authorization statutes are found in 28 U.S.C. §§ 251–57.

[2] 28 U.S.C. § 41. P.L. 97-164, Title I, § 101, 96 Stat. 25 (1982).

[3] 28 U.S.C. § 256.

[4] 28 U.S.C. §§ 1581–1585.

[5] 28 U.S.C. § 49.

[6] 50 U.S.C. § 1803. *Domestic* wiretaps were authorized ten years earlier by the Omnibus Crime Control and Safe Streets Act, Pub. L. 90-351, Title III, 82 Stat. 197 (1968).

[7] Oct. 26, 2001, P.L. 107-56, Title II, § 208, 115 Stat. 283.

[8] See *In re All Matters Submitted to the Foreign Intelligence Surveillance Court*, 218 F. Supp. 2d 611 (F.I.S.C. 2002).

## Appellate Jurisdiction—United States Court of Appeals for the Federal Circuit
## Web site: www.fedcir.gov

The court is located in Washington, D.C., and currently has 12 authorized judge-ships.[9] As mentioned above, this court was created in 1982 to replace the old Court of Customs and Patent Appeals, which was an Article I court. Accordingly, the U.S. Court of Appeals for the Federal Circuit hears all appeals from the U.S. Court of International Trade, which superseded the Customs Court.[10] The Court of Appeals for the Federal Circuit has also been given exclusive jurisdiction over appeals (1) from the United States Court of Federal Claims (§1295(a)(3)); (2) from the United States district courts in cases dealing with trademarks, patents, and copyrights (§1295(a)(1)&(2)); (3) from the Merit Systems Protection Board (§1295(a)(9)); and (4) from boards of contract appeals in the federal agencies (§1295(a)(10)).

In the year ending September 30, 2003, just over 1,500 cases were filed in the United States Court of Appeals for the Federal Circuit.

# LEGISLATIVE COURTS

## Original Jurisdiction—United States Tax Court
## Web site: http://www.ustaxcourt.gov

The United States Tax Court, which succeeded the Tax Court of the United States in 1969, was first created in 1924 as the Board of Tax Appeals. The court is made up of 19 judges, each of which serves a 15-year term, and sits primarily in Washington, D.C.[11] The judges do, however, travel to more than 80 American cities to hear cases.

The volume of cases before the tax court has declined significantly in recent years. In 2004 a few more than 22,000 cases were pending before the tax court; in 1994, that number was more than 31,000, and in the 1980s more than 85,000 cases were pending. Changes in the tax law that accord taxpayers more opportunity to set-tle disputes with the Internal Revenue Service before having to go to court may account for the decline in litigation. The Office of the Clerk of the Court has esti-mated that about 80 percent of the cases filed with the court are settled by the par-ties. The court issues between 500 and 600 opinions each year.

The primary function of the tax court is to resolve disputes over the amount of taxes owed by taxpayers to the federal government; thus, the parties in each case are

---

[9]28 U.S.C. §§ 44 and 48(a).

[10]28 U.S.C. § 1295(a)(5).

[11]26 U.S.C. § 7441.

[12]26 U.S.C. §§ 6214, 7442.

the federal government and one or more taxpayers.[12] The jurisdiction of the court, however, is quite limited. Only taxpayers who have received a Notice of Deficiency or a Notice of Determination from the Internal Revenue Service may file a case in the tax court. Other courts, notably the United States district courts, may also determine federal tax liability, but for many taxpayers the tax court is more accessible and less expensive than the district courts. The United States courts of appeals have exclusive appellate jurisdiction over tax court decisions.[13]

## Appellate Jurisdiction—United States Court of Appeals for Veterans Claims
## Web site: www.vetapp.uscourts.gov

The United States Court of Veterans Appeals was created in 1989 to review appeals from the Board of Veterans Appeals. Congress changed its name in 1998.[14] The court presently consists of one chief judge and six associate judges, each serving 15-year terms.[15] The court is located in Washington, D.C.

All of the cases reviewed by the United States Court of Appeals for Veterans Claims concern the disposition of claims filed by individuals regarding benefits they may be due as veterans of the United States military. Such claims are initially filed with the regional offices of the Department of Veterans Affairs (VA). From the decisions of the regional offices, the veterans may appeal to the Board of Veterans Appeals, which hears the appeals in panels of three.[16] Those decisions can then be appealed to the United States Court of Appeals for Veterans Claims. Decisions of the United States Court of Appeals for Veterans Claims are reviewable in turn by the United States Court of Appeals for the Federal Circuit.[17] Thus, veterans with claims for VA benefits may get five bites at the judicial apple.

The appellate jurisdiction of the court is mandatory: the court must review the merits if the case is properly filed.[18] Over 2,500 appeals were filed with the court in 2003.

---

[13]26 U.S.C. § 7482.

[14]38 U.S.C. § 7251. The statutory framework for the Board of Veterans Appeals is found at 38 U.S.C. § 7101 *et seq.*

[15]The statute authorizes two to six associate judges. 38 U.S.C. § 7253.

[16]The Board of Veterans Appeals consists of a chairman, appointed to a six-year term by the president with the advice and consent of the Senate; a vice chairman; and additional members, who are appointed upon the recommendation of the chairman and with the approval of the president by the secretary of veterans affairs. The members sit in panels of three to decide appeals from the regional offices. See http://www.va.gov/vbs/bva.

[17]38 U.S.C. § 7292.

[18]38 U.S.C. § 7252.

# Appendix E

# The Funnel Effect

Few cases, civil or criminal, go through all of the applicable procedural steps that we have described. Cases filed in United States courts, state and federal, are subject to tremendous attrition during their presence in the legal system. This attrition, due to settlements between the parties and to voluntary and involuntary dismissals, is somewhat misleadingly referred to as the "funnel effect"—a lot of cases go into the system, but few proceed to trial and judgment.

For example, in 2003, over 323,000 cases, civil and criminal, were filed in U.S. district courts. The number of trials on the merits to decide civil liability or criminal guilt or innocence was only 7,933—2.5 percent of the number of cases filed. Even counting the number of "trials" in the broad sense—here meaning any sort of contested evidentiary hearings—only 15,894 were held in the district courts. Of course, due to the normal length of the litigation process, most of these trials were of cases that had been filed one or more years previously, and it would not be correct to say that only 2.5 percent of the actual cases filed in 2003 came to trial in 2003; however, the differential between the numbers of cases filed and the numbers of cases tried in a given year has been consistent enough to make the general observation that far less than 5 percent of the cases filed in the district courts come to "trial," in either the narrow or the broad sense of that term.

The distinction between civil cases and criminal cases here is significant. More criminal cases proceed from filing to trial than do civil cases. Again using 2003 federal court numbers (with the lag-time proviso in the paragraph above), we find that 252,962 civil cases were filed and 4,036 (1.6 percent) cases went to trial on the merits, while 70,642 criminal cases were filed and 3,897 (5.5 percent) cases went to trial on the merits. Less than 1 in 50 civil cases, but 1 in 19 criminal cases, went to trial.[1]

Once a case is filed, it can be removed from the litigation process either voluntarily or involuntarily. For example, of some 250,000 civil cases terminated in the

---

[1] Similar attrition is evident in state court proceedings, although significant differences in court systems among the several states make generalization difficult. According to data gathered by the National Center for State Courts, in 2002 only 3 percent of the felony cases that were filed and 8 percent of the civil cases that were filed were disposed of by trials on the merits. (Each of these categories reflects data from only 21 states.)

United States district courts in 2003, 16.3 percent were terminated without any court action. Presumably, most of these cases were withdrawn by the plaintiffs voluntarily after settling or coming to terms with the defendants. Another three-quarters of the cases (73.9 percent) were terminated before pretrial proceedings were begun. Again, many of these cases were settled by the parties, although some were involuntarily dismissed ("thrown out") by the court on motions by the defendant to dismiss. Another 8.1 percent were terminated during or after pretrial proceedings, again because they were settled or involuntarily dismissed on motions for summary judgment. Less than 2 percent of the cases terminated were terminated during or after trial on the merits.

Federal criminal cases are also subject to attrition. In 2003, 9.5 percent of the criminal defendants in federal courts had their charges dismissed by the United States attorneys prosecuting their cases. Almost 86 percent of the defendants pleaded guilty before trial, many as part of a plea bargain. Less than 5 percent went to trial, and of them 79 percent were found guilty and 21 percent were acquitted.[2]

The attrition continues along the whole path of litigation, for relatively few of the cases filed or even tried are then appealed.[3] In 2003, of the more than 320,000 cases, civil and criminal, that were filed in the United States district courts, only 46,358 cases were appealed from the district courts to the U.S. Courts of Appeals, *and most of them were filed by convicted criminals!*[4] In state courts, over 96 million cases were filed in the courts of original jurisdiction in 2001, but only 278,000 cases (0.3 percent) were appealed, and several thousand of those appealed were from state administrative agencies, not from state courts of original jurisdiction.

Indeed, attrition of a sort is present even before cases enter the judicial system. In both civil and criminal categories, the number of cases filed in courts reflects only a fraction of the potential amount of meritorious cases that might be filed and a fraction of even the amount of cases brought to the attention of lawyers or law enforcement officials. Two examples may illustrate this, one from criminal law and one from civil.

Consider for a moment: of all the crimes committed in a single day, how many are reported? Of those reported, how many are then investigated, and how many of the investigations lead to arrests? How many of those arrested are prosecuted?

No one goes to prison for crimes of which the authorities are not aware. Yet a substantial number of crimes go unreported each year, *including more than half of all*

---

[2]The statistics for criminal case terminations are measured here in terms of defendants, not cases.

[3]The number of appeals usually exceeds the number of trials in a system because a significant number of cases are involuntarily dismissed or disposed of by summary judgment before coming to trial, and the dismissals and dispository summary judgments, of course, are appealable. Thus, some appeals are from litigants dissatisfied with the results of trials and some are from litigants who have been "thrown out of court" and who want to be able to continue toward trial.

[4]In 2003 there were 11,968 appeals in criminal cases and 34,390 appeals in civil cases filed in the United States Courts of Appeals. These numbers reflect 16.9 percent of the number of criminal cases filed and 13.6 percent of the number of civil cases filed in 2003. Almost all of the criminal cases were filed by criminal defendants, and over half of the civil appeals were filed by state and federal prisoners. Habeas corpus and civil rights actions by prisoners are civil, not criminal, actions. The effect of these prisoner cases is discussed in more detail in the chapter on federal and state courts.

*violent crimes.* Even when a crime is reported to the police, it is not always possible to make an arrest. Homicides are [followed] by arrest in three of every four cases, but for other crimes the figure is much lower. Consequently, a large number of criminals—those whose crimes are never reported and those who escape detection—do not enter the Offender-Based Transaction System [of the United States Department of Justice.][5]

Even determining what happened to the arrestees is not easy, according to the Bureau of Justice Statistics (BJS). "What happens to a person after being arrested for a crime—from a statistical perspective—is often impossible to determine. . . . [T]o find out what happened to all offenders arrested for [a particular] crime throughout the United States during a specified period—say a particular year—is currently impossible."[6] That was written in 1983, but many of the problems of data collection cited by BJS still remain.

The second example comes from an old study recounted by Samuel Mermin. Some 86,100 instances of automobile accident injuries that occurred in Michigan in 1958 were tracked from injury to final legal action, if any was pursued.[7] Of the 86,100 victims, only 12,100 consulted lawyers, and only 4,000 then filed cases in court.

This is really not surprising since no doubt many of the injuries were not serious or did not require expensive medical attention. Then again, many of the victims had insurance that paid the medical as well as the property damage bills. The study reported that of these 74,000 victims, 24,700 victims settled their cases—probably their insurance companies negotiated most of these settlements—and 49,300 did not pursue any claims even by settlement.

Of the 12,100 victims who did consult legal counsel, about 4,100 dropped their cases after consulting an attorney; 4,000 settled their claims, presumably with the aid of counsel; and 4,000 filed cases in court. These figures reflect several important aspects of the attorney function in the United States.

In American courts, attorneys often take personal injury and other tort cases on a **contingent fee** basis. This means that the attorneys who take cases will be paid only if they win a financial award—referred to as a "judgment," "judgment of damages," or simply "damages"—for their clients. Typically, the fee is a percentage of the judgment, perhaps one-fourth if the case is settled before trial, one-third of the judgment if the case goes to trial, and 40 percent if the judgment is won or sustained on appeal. Since being paid requires satisfaction of the clients' claims in a manner that is to some degree acceptable to the clients, lawyers have traditionally exercised the function of gatekeeper to the courts. The lawyer is the first legal officer, in a sense, to evaluate the legal merit of a client's case and advise the potential litigant either to pursue the case or to drop it. If the lawyer takes the case under a contingent fee arrangement, the case probably has enough legal merit to justify the lawyer's risk of

---

[5]United States Department of Justice, Bureau of Justice Statistics, *Bureau of Justice Statistics Bulletin*, November 1983, 1 (emphasis added).

[6]Ibid.

[7]Cited in Samuel Mermin, *Law and the Legal System: An Introduction*, 2d ed. (Boston: Little, Brown, 1982), 70–72.

time and effort. If the case is too risky, the lawyer might still take it, but on a straight fee-for-services basis, and many potential plaintiffs decide not to pursue matters when they first learn of the amount the lawyer expects for a retainer and for the hourly rate.

Another aspect of the legal practice is reflected in the numbers of settled and filed cases. Although there are exceptions, lawyers generally prefer to settle cases rather than litigate them. It is much more cost efficient and much less stressful to negotiate a settlement by phone and in comfortable insurance company or law firm offices than to embark on the time-consuming, energy-draining, and always risky course of litigation. Filing suit is usually the course of last resort.

But attempts to settle do not always flow smoothly. Sometimes the other parties or their insurance companies or lawyers do not seem to want to listen or make reasonable responses to the claimant's requests. Sometimes they have more important things to do. To get their sincere attention, therefore, lawyers must sometimes hit them right between the eyes with a two-by-four—a *lawsuit*—and thus this course of last resort becomes the ultimate weapon.[8] Suing people for thousands of dollars almost always gets their attention and had better get their lawyers' attention, for now a failure to respond may result in the court awarding the plaintiff a default judgment for the full amount of the claim.

Thus, of the 4,000 cases that were filed in the Michigan study, doubtless many were filed simply to encourage settlement. The figures bear this out: of the 4,000 cases filed, 2,200 were settled before the pretrial discovery process was completed. Four hundred of the filed cases were dropped without settlement. Of the remaining 1,400 cases that were continued through pretrial discovery, another 800 were settled and 100 were dropped before trial. Even of the 500 that went to trial, 140 were terminated without payment before judgment and an undetermined number were settled before judgment. Eighty judgments were appealed. Compare these numbers to the 2002 federal court statistics recounted earlier in this section.

An important factor in considering the attrition from the initial occurrences of the accidents themselves to the final court judgments is the role played by legal rules and principles of the kinds studied in law courses. From the first hearing of a claimant and potential client's story to the final stages of settlement negotiation or litigation, the attorneys for all parties are assessing and gauging the strengths and weaknesses of their case against winning a satisfactory judgment in court. The advice they give their clients or potential clients and the moves they make after taking cases, especially common law tort actions such as personal injury cases, are guided by appellate court rulings and opinions. This reliance upon case law, of course, is also aided by a trial lawyer's experience as a litigator and by his familiarity with the people and practices associated with the local court before which the case will be tried. As we saw when we discussed the immediate and extended consequences of Supreme Court and other appellate court opinions, these few opinions, through their influence on judges and attorneys, indirectly affect untold millions of people every day.

---

[8] Perhaps Sun Tsu's adage applies: "To keep the peace, prepare for war." Or, better, "To get a piece, prepare for war."

# Index